U1021369

General Introduction to Natural and Cultural Geography of Chongqing

By Chongqing Local Chronicles Office

重庆大学出版社

图书在版编目（CIP）数据
重庆地情概览：英文 / 重庆市地方志办公室编著.
-- 重庆：重庆大学出版社，2021.9
ISBN 978-7-5689-2954-7
Ⅰ. ①重… Ⅱ. ①重… Ⅲ. ①重庆—概况—英文
Ⅳ. ①K927.19
中国版本图书馆CIP数据核字（2021）第179628号

General Introduction to Natural and
Cultural Geography of Chongqing
重庆地情概览
CHONGQING DIQING GAILAN

重庆市地方志办公室　编著
策划编辑：贾　曼
责任编辑：陈　曦　　版式设计：陈筱萌
责任校对：邹　忌　　责任印制：张　策
*
重庆大学出版社出版发行
出版人：饶帮华
社址：重庆市沙坪坝区大学城西路21号
邮编：401331
电话：（023）88617190　88617185（中小学）
传真：（023）88617186　88617166
网址：http://www.cqup.com.cn
邮箱：fxk@cqup.com.cn（营销中心）
全国新华书店经销
重庆升光电力印务有限公司印刷
*
开本：720mm × 1020mm　印张：20.25　字数：419千
2021年9月第1版　2021年9月第1次印刷
ISBN 978-7-5689-2954-7　定价：128.00元

Editorial Committee of Chongqing Local Chronicles

Chongqing Housing and Urban-Rural Development Committee（市住房城乡建委）
Chongqing Urban Management Bureau（市城市管理局）
Chongqing Transportation Bureau（市交通局）
Chongqing Water Conservancy Bureau（市水利局）
Chongqing Agriculture and Rural Affairs Committee (市农业农村委)
Chongqing Commission of Commerce（市商务委）
Chongqing Culture and Tourism Commission（市文化旅游委）
Chongqing Health Commission（市卫生健康委）
Chongqing Veterans Affairs Bureau（市退役军人事务局）
Chongqing Emergency Management Bureau（市应急局）
Chongqing Audit Bureau（市审计局）
Foreign Affairs Office of the People's Government of Chongqing (市政府外办)
Chongqing State-owned Assets Supervision and Administration Commission（市国资委）
Chongqing Market Supervision Bureau（市市场监管局）
Chongqing Bureau of Statistics（市统计局）
Chongqing High People's Court（市高法院）
People's Procuratorate of Chongqing（市检察院）
Chongqing Garrison Command of the Chinese People's Liberation Army（重庆警备区）
Chongqing Archives（市档案馆）
Chongqing Local Chronicles Office（市志办）

Editorial Office of *General Introduction to Natural and Cultural Geography of Chongqing*

Chief Editor	Liu Wenhai(刘文海)
Deputy Editor	Xia Xiaoping(夏小平)
Executive Chief Editor	Yin Zhi(殷智)
Editorial Staff	Yin Zhi(殷智)　Zeng Wei(曾伟)
	Dong Ningbo(董宁波)
	Xiong Shuqian(熊蜀黔)
	Hong Xia(洪霞)　Guo Yongbin(郭永彬)
Editors	Si Yiche(司逸澈)　Chen Xinru(陈欣如)
Translators	Wang Jie(王洁)
English-Version Proofreaders	Shi Yong(石勇)　Liang Jingjing(梁晶晶)

Foreword

Chongqing is a land of natural beauty.

Chongqing boasts a city with cultural appeal.

"Running far away are the waves of the Han River (汉水). Flying high are the clouds and rain of Wushan Mountain (巫山)". Surrounded by mountains and rivers and hugged by valleys and canyons, Chongqing has been a renowned historical and cultural city where men of letters gathered, merchants converged and a place of strategic importance since ancient times. "The State of Ba (巴国) witnessed rises and falls in its long history". Over 3,000 years ago, the Ba People (巴人) established their country and capital city here, which later became the birthplace of Bayu Culture (巴渝文化). As the Jialing River (嘉陵江) was called the "Yu River" (渝水) in ancient times, Chongqing was also called "Yu" (渝) in the abbreviated form. In the 1st year of Chongning (1102) of the Northern Song Dynasty (北宋崇宁), "Yu Zhou" (渝州) was renamed "Gong Zhou" (恭州). In the 16th year of Chunxi (1189) of the Southern Song Dynasty (南宋淳熙) , Zhao Dun(赵惇), Emperor Guangzong of Song, ascended to the throne, and "Gong Zhou" was ascended to "Chongqing Fu" (重庆府). This is the origin of the name "Chongqing". Since the Qin Dynasty (秦朝), this ancient city of Chongqing has been built four times before taking shape. In the year 1891, Chongqing became one of the earliest inland trading ports that was opened to the outside world. In the War of Resistance Against Japanese Aggression, the National Government (国民政府) moved to Yu, and Chongqing became the "War-time Capital" and the far east commanding center of the World Anti-Fascist War. It was also the location of the Southwest Bureau of the Central Committee of the Communist Party of China (中共中央西南局) represented by comrade Zhou Enlai. China Democratic League（民盟）, China National Democratic Construction Association (民建), Jiu San Society (九三学社), and Federation of Comrades of the Three People's Principles (三民主义同志联合会), as one of the predecessors of The Revolutionary Committee of Kuomintang (民革), were all established here. Since the founding of the People's Republic of China, it was the seat of the Southwest Bureau of the Central Committee of CPC and Southwest Military and Political Commission (西南军政委员会). Chongqing was also the political, economic and cultural center in southwest China, as well as the key area of "Strategic Area Construction in National Defence" (三线建设); meanwhile, it was the first pilot city that exercised the comprehensive reform of the economic system. Since Chongqing became a municipality directly under the central government in 1997, its economic and social developments have all been made around its national orientation as an important central city, an economic hub in the middle and upper reaches of the Yangtze River, a key base of modern manufacturing, an integrated transportation hub in southwest China as well as an inland open highland. As a result, tremendous progress has been made in all its causes.

Surrounded by great mountains and rivers and seated under the solemn and magnificent Baidicheng (白帝城), Kuimen (夔门), the most majestic mountain pass, has been the everlasting theme for men of letters; on the steep cliffs of Dazu (大足), the wisdom and artistry in the making of Dazu Stone Carvings made it a masterpiece that has drawn worldwide attention in the history of grotto art. The open and vast natural environment has bred loyalty, bravery, integrity, benevolence, openness and inclusiveness of the Chongqing people. The sons and daughters of Bayu have created a brilliant history and culture with their industriousness. In the critical moment of being defeated and losing the country, Ba Manzi (巴蔓子), a commander of the Ba State, cut his throat in order to save his country. Diaoyucheng (钓鱼城) was the specific place where the invincible Mongolian Khan Mongke Khan lost his life after failing to conquer this city. Qin Liangyu (秦良玉), a heroine, beat the drum to go out for a battle that recaptured Chongqing. For independence and freedom, Zou Rong (邹容) was willing to be the pioneer of the revolutionary army; revolutionary pioneers such as Yang Angong (杨闇公) and Zhao Shiyan (赵世炎) sacrificed their lives for the cause of the revolution; Liu Bocheng (刘伯承) and Nie Rongzhen (聂荣臻) commanded great armies and won several decisive battles. In the eventful years of war, the national spirit endured the ordeal test and stood proudly; the martyrs and heroes' blood and loyalty will be remembered forever. In the vicissitudes of years, the historical heritages of the Bayu Culture, the Anti-Japanese War Culture, the Hongyan (红岩) Culture, and the Three Gorges (三峡) Culture of Chongqing always shine vividly and brightly.

With seventy years of exploration and struggle, every effort has been made for the prosperity of Chongqing, which has witnessed brilliant and fruitful achievements of reform and development. Since the founding of the People's Republic of China, Chongqing has grasped historical opportunities such as Strategic Area Construction in National Defence, the construction of the municipality, the Three Gorges Project (三峡工程), the Western Region Development of China (西部大开发), the Belt and Road Initiative[1] (一带一路), the construction of the Yangtze River Economic Belt (长江经济带建设). Old industrial bases are rejuvenating with vigor and vitality, and strategic emerging industries are burgeoning and flourishing. The innovation-driven engine works so powerfully that it is pushing high-quality development in economy and society and creating high-quality life for the people. The construction of infrastructures is being accelerated. The "four-hour to Chongqing" (四小时重庆)[2] goal has been realized, and the "one hub and ten lines" (一枢纽十干线) railroad network is connecting cities with

[1] The Belt and Road refer to the Silk Road Economic Belt and the 21st-Century Maritime Silk Road.

[2] This refers to the construction of a large radial fast channel network with the main city of Chongqing as the axis, with expressways as the main framework, supplemented by ordinary highways, so as to enable people from all districts and counties in Chongqing to arrive in the main city within 4 hours by vehicles.

villages. The settlement of migrants has been done, and the outlook of urban and rural areas is renewing with each passing day. All social causes are progressing. Chongqing has gradually become a land of natural beauty and a city with cultural appeal and a sustainable growth of people's sense of gain, sense of happiness and sense of security. As an open highland in inland, Chongqing is rising at an accelerated speed. Based on the golden waterway of the Yangtze River and China-Europe Express (Chongqing), an open route has been formed fully-fledged, thus jointing the construction of the New International Land-Sea Trade Corridor in the framework of the Belt and Road Initiative, which has ascended to national strategy.

History always grants people with wisdom and power in a special way. This year marks the 70th anniversary of the founding of the People's Republic of China. In order to study and apply President Xi Jinping Thought on Socialism with Chinese Characteristics for a New Era and the spirit of the 19th National Congress of the Communist Party of China, to better meet the ever-growing cultural needs of the people, to enhance cultural confidence, to hold the roots of Chongqing as a mountain city, to help fulfill the goals of "two points" "two lands" and "two highs" , to give play to "three roles" and create sound political ecology, the Chongqing Local Chronicles Office organized the compilation of *General Introduction to Natural and Cultural Geography of Chongqing* (《重庆地情概览》) and *General Introduction to Urban and Rural Conditions of Chongqing* (《重庆市情概览》) earnestly. The former focuses on Chongqing in history and the latter emphasizes on present Chongqing. Based on historical local chronicles and new socialist local chronicles, *General Introduction to Natural and Cultural Geography of Chongqing* introduces Chongqing from comprehensive and three-dimensional perspectives with pictures and illustrations that display Chongqing in the aspects of its history, culture, social changes, reform and development since ancient times, exploring the tenacious, indomitable, upright and frank spirit of the Chongqing people, promoting the image of Chongqing and build the city brand. This book includes natural environment, population and nation, historical development, economic development, culture and tourism, social cause development, ecological civilization construction, Three Gorges Migrants, etc.

"A tour in Chongqing, a gain in vision." Although *General Introduction to Natural and Cultural Geography of Chongqing* could not include all the elements of Chongqing, and it is undoubtedly an encyclopedia that introduces you with its magnificent mountains and rivers, profound history and culture and elegance of city life. It is a card that displays the charm of Chongqing, a platform as well as a window to see Chongqing. History is the origin of reality, for it always rewinds us not to forget why we started and reminds us of our mission towards the "Chinese Dream" —the great rejuvenation of the Chinese nation. It is our dearest wish that this book could provide nutritious spiritual nourishment for the cadres and the people in Chongqing, and offer cultural assistance to embark on a new journey and contribution to the new era. We hope this book can help people from all walks of life understand Chongqing and get familiar with Chongqing and fall in love with Chongqing.

Editorial Team

August 2019

Contents

Chapter One　Natural Environment

Section One　Natural Geography

Chongqing is located in southwest China and in the upper reaches of the Yangtze River. It is located between 105°17' to 110°11'E and 28°10' to 32°13' N. The area under Chongqing jurisdiction is 82,400 square kilometres with a length of 470 kilometres from east to west and a width of 450 kilometres from north to south. It borders on Hubei Province (湖北省) and Hunan Province (湖南省) in the east, Guizhou Province (贵州省) in the south, Luzhou (泸州市), Ziyang (资阳市), Suining (遂宁市) of Sichuan Province (四川省) in the west, Shaanxi Province (陕西省) and Guang'an (广安市), Dazhou (达州市) of Sichuan Province (四川省) in the north. Numerous rivers run through the city (district) with the main stream of the Yangtze River running through from the west to the east at a length of 665 kilometres. With the main stream of the Yangtze River as the axis, the Jialing River (嘉陵江), the Wujiang River (乌江), the Qijiang River (綦江), the Daning River (大宁河) and hundreds of other branches gather here. These rivers run through mountains and form various gorges and canyons. The Yangtze River runs through Wushan Mountain (巫山) and forms the notable Three Gorges, namely, the Qutang Gorge (瞿塘峡), the Wuxia Gorge (巫峡) and the Xiling Gorge (西陵峡). The complex geomorphology is featured by the following characteristics. First, the terrain sees great ups and downs, with east, south and southeast higher than the west. The highest point in the east is the Yintiao Ridge(阴条岭) of the Daba Mountain(大巴山) , with an altitude of 2,796.8 meters; the lowest point is the Yangtze River surface in the Wushan Mountain, with an altitude of 73.1 meters before the Three Gorges reserve water. Second, there are various terrain types which are dominated by mountains. Third, the area difference in geomorphic configuration is obvious. Fourth, Karst topography is widespread. The unique characteristics of Karst valley landscape include stone forest, peak forest, depression, monadnock, karst cave, underground river and canyon, etc.

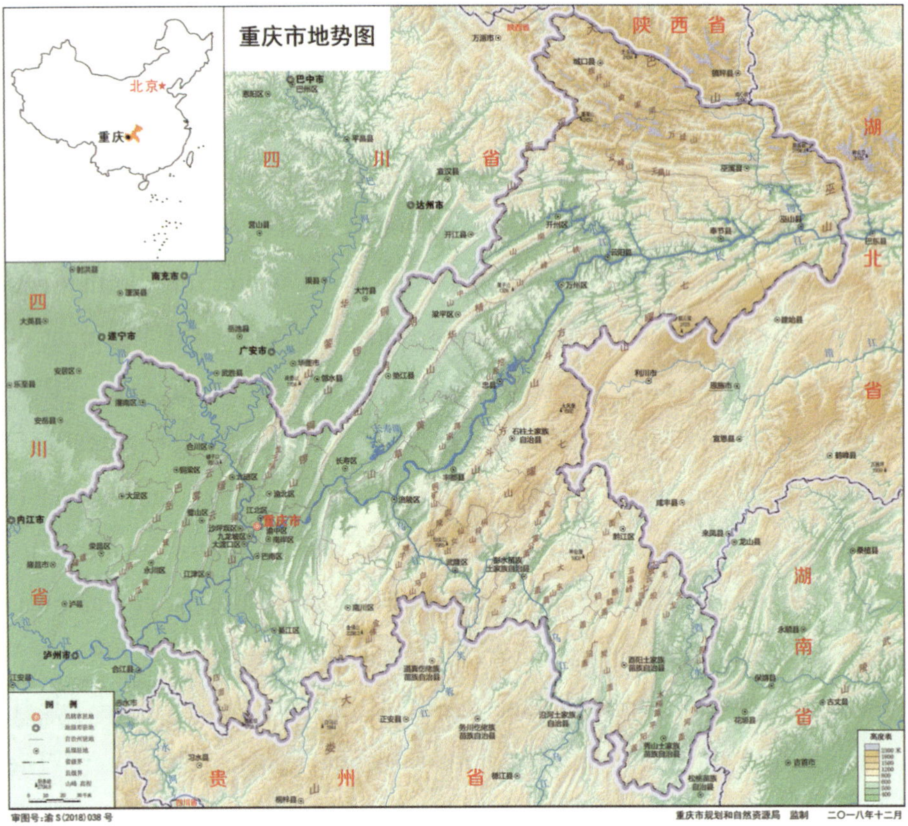

Picture 1-1 Chongqing Chorography

Ⅰ.Geology

Geology is composed of stratum and geologic structure. Stratum refers to the rock formation that is formed at a specific time and environment with unified characteristics and meanwhile shows distinct difference from the layer above and below. Stratum of all ages see full-fledged development in the city. There are various sedimentation types, so the fossils are preserved very well. Paleozoic strata include Sinian, Cambrian, Ordovician, Silurian, Devonian, Carboniferous, and Permian. Mesozoic strata include Triassic, Jurassic and Cretaceous. The Cenozoic strata are Quaternary.

The geologic structure of Chongqing area is composed of west Chongqing fold belt, east Chongqing fold belt, southeast Chongqing fold belt and arc-shaped fold belt in Daba mountain. It is featured by ancient and multi-phased characteristics. In pre-sinian period, Chongqing, the same with Sichuan Basin (四川盆地), was in the phase of geosyncline development.

In the end of Proterozoic era, the Jinning Movement turned fold reversion of geosyncline in pre-sinian period into the phase of Platform development. The early Paleozoic era provided carbonate deposition in neritic facies. After long-term denudation and de-planation in Caledonian and Mid-early Hercynian period, the powerful Yangxin transgression came to Chongqing city from southeast. In the early phase of transgression, Liangshan group was deposited with iron, aluminium and coal. Later, with increased transgression, Chongqing area was in a relatively stable neritic environment and deposited 300 to 400-meter-thick limestone (Qixia Formation and Maokou Formation). In the end of early Permian epoch, Chongqing area experienced transient rise due to Dongwu Movement. The crest of Maokou Formation was corroded. In the early period of the late Permian, the descendance of Chongqing area formed coastal-limnetic basin. The frequent shakes brought in continental-marine interaction, temperate climate, flourishing plants, and deposited 92 to 164-meter-thick Longtan Formation that is marine-terrigenous and contains abundant coal resources.

In Indo-sinian period, following late Permian, the sedimentation activity continued in early to middle Triassic and thus accumulated 1,000 to 1,400-meter-thick carbonatite and clastic rocks. In the later period of early Triassic before Indo-sinian movement, the climate was dry and hot; evaporation was intense; seawater concentrated and its salinity kept increasing, thus formed super-saline sea basin environment that contained abundant salt minerals.

In late Indo-sinian movement, the strong uplift of Jiangnan paleo-continent forced Chongqing area to elevate its east-leaning normalcy towards a northwest-leaning single slope. The relic sea in late Triassic epoch was pushed to northwest. The crustal movement in the end of the middle Triassic uplifted Chongqing area to land, thus ended marine sediment and transferred into the phase of continental facies. The climate in late Triassic was warm and wet. Flora flourished and deposited 284 to 782-meter-thick continental coal-bearing clasolite. Through Indo-sinian movement, the Huaying Mountain(华蓥山) paleo-uplift (Luzhou-Kaijiang paleo-uplift) was formed and the Chongqing area had not continued deposit for a long time before it transferred into a structure with denudation as its main feature.

Picture 1-2 Geologic Feature in Qijiang Baiyun Temple(綦江白云观)

In Mesozoic era, Jurassic succeeded generally the sedimentation activity in the Late Triassic, and the climate became dry and hot, thus deposited 2,455 to 3,741-meter-thick red mudstone. The Ningzhen orogeny at the end of the Late Jurassic elevated the Chongqing area, and the Late Jurassic suffered substantial erosion. Lacking sedimentation in early Cretaceous, Chongqing area only has a thousand-meter-thick deposit of Jiaguan formation red clasolite formed in Late Cretaceous that was parallel but not integrated on Late Jurassic strata. The crustal movement in Late Cretaceous created great folds and cracks that formed mountain ranges, which formed the basic framework of present structure. When Yanshan movement was completed, Chongqing area, under the influence of internal and external forces, entered into a brand-new phase of geological development—Himalayan tectonic period and formed the structural framework nowadays.

Ⅱ.Geomorphology

Chongqing is located in the east edge of the second step of China's terrain. It is one part of the paralleled ridge-valley of East Sichuan, and it is also the boundary between the hills and east edge of Sichuan Basin and the mountainous region in the south edge. The complex geomorphological composition provides respective natural basis for the breeding of diverse and abundant land resources, biological resources, hydropower resources, etc. The geomorphology of Chongqing bears the following characteristics.

1.Great Disparity in Topography, Obviously Stratified Geomorphology

Picture 1-3 Qianjiang Xiaonanhai (黔江小南海) Geopark of China

The topography in Chongqing sees great ups and downs. The highest place is Yintiao Ridge of the Daba Mountain in Wuxi County (巫溪县), and its altitude is 2,796.8 meters; the lowest point is Peishi Yuxikou (培石鱼溪口) in Wushan County (巫山县). Before impoundment of the Three Gorges Project, the altitude of the Yangtze River was only 73.1 meters, and the relative altitude difference was 2,723.7 meters. In general, the topography in the east, southeast and south is higher, which is featured mainly by mountainous regions with an altitude of 1,500 meters, whereas the topography in the west is lower, which is featured by hills with an altitude of 300 to 400 meters.

The geomorphologic evolution difference in different stages and the intermittent large-scale uplift of neotectonics result in obvious stratification in geomorphology and formed seven stages of stratified geomorphology in Chongqing area.Their heights are 300 meters, 500 to 600 meters, 700 to 900 meters, 1,000 to 1,100 meters, 1,500 meters, 1800 to 2000 meters, 2,200 to 2,400 meters respectively.

2.Complex and Diversified Geomorphology with Mountainous Regions as Main Feature

Chongqing geomorphology can be divided into 4 types: mountainous regions, hills, mesas and plains.

3.Widespread and Typically Developed Karst Landform

The wide exposure of carbonate rocks (limestone, dolomite, etc.) and their large-scale and concentrated distribution in the east and southeast contribute to the well-developed Karst landform underground and in the surface. Karst tough valley landscape that is specific in Chongqing is formed in anticline strip mountainous regions. Typical Karst landform, such as stone forest, fungling, depression pool, monadnock, ponor, karst cave, underground river and canyon, are distributed in the east and southeast Karst mountainous regions. Among them are much beautiful and miraculous sceneries.

Picture 1-4 Tiansheng Sanqiao in Wulong, Chongqing (武隆天生三桥)

4.Obvious Regional Difference in Geomorphic Configuration

Controlled by tectonic structure, the geomorphic configuration of Chongqing displays obvious regional difference. They are divided as follows. (1) Hill landscape distributes in northwest Huaying Mountain and west Bayue Mountain (巴岳山), with shallow and mid-depth hills as majority, deep and flat high hills as minority. It is one of the main agricultural areas which lacks forest resources. (2) The paralleled ridge-valley of East Sichuan, which is located between the Huaying Mountain and the Fangdou Mountain (方斗山), is composed of more than twenty north-east-orientation anticline and syncline structure within. Syncline shallow and middle-height hills, hills alongside the rivers and troughs are the majority, whereas low and middle height mountainous regions are the minority. It is the place where cities and towns, industries and mines most concentrate and it is the largest agricultural area in Chongqing. (3) The Daba Mountain region in the northwest, which is mainly featured by middle-height mountains, is the primary area with forest resources. With high mountains and steep slopes, most of the agricultural land in this area is infertile. (4) The east, the southeast and the south belong to Wushan and the Dalou Mountain region (大娄山区). Karst landform such as stone forest, underground river and karst caves developed very well. Middle-height and low mountains are the main features and it is also an important area with forest resources in Chongqing.

Picture 1-5 The Ayi River in Pengshui, Chongqing (彭水阿依河)

Ⅲ.Climate

The climate in Chongqing belongs to subtropical humid monsoon climate. Climate resources are rich in this area, and the stereoscopic climate is evident. With early spring, hot summer, rainy autumn and warm winter, Chongqing is featured by humid air, coincided rain and heat, frequent disasters, less sunshine, low wind speed, as well as much cloud and mist. The annual average temperature of Chongqing is 17.5℃, with an extreme maximum temperature of 44.5℃ (Qijiang) and an extreme minimum temperature of -13.2℃ (Chengkou) ; the annual average precipitation is 1,125.3 millimetres; the annual average sunshine duration is 1,154.4 hours, and it is one of the regions that receives the least sunshine in China; the annual average relative humidity is 79.9%; the average wind speed is 1.1 meter/second, the static wind frequency is as high as 45.5%. The five features are listed as follows.

1.Warm Winter and Early Spring, Abundant Heat

Chongqing is surrounded by mountains, which makes it insusceptible to the cold current from the north in winter and therefore enjoys warm winter. The average temperature in the coldest month is 5.0 ℃ to 8.2℃ , 3℃ to 4℃ higher than the middle and lower reaches of the Yangtze River at the same latitude.

2.Abundant Precipitation with Uneven Distribution of Time and Space, Much Night Rain, High Air Humidity

The citywide annual precipitation is abundant, with higher precipitation in southeast and lower in northwest, higher in mountainous regions and lower in hills and level grounds. The inter-annual variation of precipitation is large.

3.Weak Solar Radiation, Short Duration of Sunshine

Chongqing is one of those regions in China that receive the least solar radiation and sunshine. The annual solar radiation is only 3,390 megajoule per square meter or so, 31%, 28% and 60% lower than Wuhan, Nanjing and Lhasa respectively. The annual sunshine duration is 980 to 1,580 hours.

4.Monsoon Climate, Rain and Heat Coincide

The seasonal distribution of sunshine duration, heat and precipitation vary greatly in Chongqing, which enjoys monsoon climate and the same period of rain and heat.

5.Great Vertical Difference of Climate, Evident Stereoscopic Climate

The topography in Chongqing sees great ups and downs, especially in mountainous regions in the northeast, the east, the southeast and the south, where the interlace of mountain ranges and valleys form a complex topography fabric that is featured by coldness, warmth, dryness, humidity, exposure to the sun and hidden by foliage. The diversified and stereoscopic local climate ecological environment is greatly beneficial to the exploitation and development of the stereoscopic agricultural system with mountains and hills as its unique advantage.

Ⅳ.Hydrology

The water-collecting area in Chongqing is 82,300 square kilometres. There are 449 rivers whose water-collecting capacity was above 30 square kilometres. The average annual water resource volume is 56.78 billion cubic meters. The annual average inflow water volume for many years is 383.7 billion cubic meters. The outflow water volume is 438.6 billion cubic meters. The majority of rivers belong to precipitation replenishment type. Influenced by uneven distribution of precipitation, the runoff in summer is larger than that in late autumn, and spring as rainfall in summer is more abundant. The complex geologic structure and much fault bring about many hot waters and thermal springs as well as rich mineral water with high quality.

1.Rivers

Picture 1-6 Fengjie (奉节) Section of the Yangtze River

All the waters that run vertically and horizontally in Chongqing area belong to the Yangtze River System. These rivers form an asymmetric and centripetal network of water system. Statistics show that there are 374 rivers that cover an area of more than 50 square kilometres, 167 rivers that cover an 50 to 100 square kilometres area, 152 rivers that cover an 100 to 500 square kilometres area, 19 rivers that cover an 500 to 1,000 square kilometres area, 18 rivers that cover an 1,000 to 3,000 square kilometres area, 18 rivers that cover an area above 3,000 square kilometres.

The Yangtze River: the Yangtze River enters Chongqing at Shima Town (石蟆镇), Jiangjin District (江津区). It runs through 17 districts and counties with a length of 691 kilometres in Chongqing area and leaves Chongqing from Peishi Village (培石乡) in Wushan County. The average annual runoff of the entrance Zhutuo Station (朱沱站) is 269.2 billion cubic meters over the years; the average annual runoff of the exit Wushan station is 429.2 billion cubic meters over the years. Among the Three Gorges of the Yangtze River, there are the Qutang Gorge (瞿塘峡) and the Wuxia Gorge (巫峡) in Chongqing area. After the completion of the Three Gorges Project, the rise of water level improves the capacity of its channels. In wet seasons, 10,000-ton fleet can go directly from middle and lower reaches to the Chongqing port.

The Jialing River: the Jialing River flows into Chongqing from Gulou Town (古楼镇), Hechuan District (合川区), merges with two major tributaries—the Qujiang River (渠江) and the Fujiang River (涪江) in Hechuan City (合川) and it enters the Yangtze River at Chaotianmen (朝天门) in Yuzhong District (渝中区).

Its length in Chongqing area is 152 kilometres, and its width is 150 to 400 meters. The average annual runoff of Beibei Station (北碚站) is 65.9 billion cubic meters, and the average annual sediment concentration is 2,191 gram per cubic meter. It cuts the anticline mountainside of the Huaying Mountain horizontally and the "Small Three Gorges" (小三峡) of the Jialing River are formed in this way. The Small Three Gorges are the Libi Gorge(沥鼻峡), the Wentang Gorge (温塘峡)and the Guanyin Gorge (观音峡).

The Wujiang River: the Wujiang River enters Chongqing at Heitaba(黑獭坝) in Youyang County (酉阳县). It runs through Pengshui (彭水) and Wulong, and enters the Yangtze River at Fuling District (涪陵区). Its total length is 993 kilometres with 223 kilometres in Chongqing area. The average annual runoff of the Wujiang River is 50.9 billion cubic meters over the years, and the average annual sediment concentration is 653 gram per cubic meter.

Picture 1-7 The Wujiang River Gallery

The Qujiang River: the Qujiang River flows into Chongqing area at Xianglu Village (香炉乡) in Hechuan District (合川区). It enters into the Jialing River at Qujia Village (渠嘉乡). Its length in Chongqing section is 72.7 kilometres. The average annual discharge is 744 cubic meters per second over the years; the average annual runoff of the Qujiang river is 23.47 billion cubic meters over the years, and the average annual sediment concentration is 1,185 gram per cubic meter.

The Fujiang River: the Fujiang River enters into Chongqing Municipality at Mixin Town (米心镇) in Tongnan District (潼南区). It runs through Tongnan District, Tongliang District (铜梁区), Hechuan District and pours into the Jialing River near Heyang Town (合阳镇) in Hechuan District. Its total length is 661 kilometres with 123.2

kilometres in Chongqing. The Fujiang River's fall is 56 meters, along its riverbanks are terraces and small dams. According to Xiaoheba (小河坝) Hydrological Station, the average annual runoff of the Fujiang River is 572 cubic meters per second over the years. The largest runoff of the Fujiang River is 28.7 thousand cubic meters per second (July 15th, 1981), while the smallest runoff is 53 cubic meters per second (March 22nd, 1973).

The Qijiang River: the Qijiang River enters Chongqing at Yangjiao Town (羊角镇) in Qijiang District and pours into the Yangtze River at Shunjiang Town (顺江镇) in Jiangjin District. Its total length is 223 kilometres and its length in Chongqing section is 157.5 kilometres. The average annual runoff of the Fujiang River is 3.85 billion cubic meters. The riverway is restricted by mountains and runs with twists and turns. The channels under Ganshui Town (赶水镇) have a capacity for freighters with 30 tons of goods.

The Xiaojiang River (小江): the Xiaojiang River flows into the Yangtze River at Shuangjiang Town (双江镇) of Yunyang County (云阳县). Its total length is 117.5 kilometres. The average gradient of the riverway is 12.5‰. The average annual runoff of the Xiaojiang River is 116 cubic meters per second over the years. The fall of the river is concentrated in the upper reaches of the river. Theoretically, the storage of the hydropower resource is 303.9 thousand kilowatt, and the exploitable hydropower resource is 102 thousand kilowatt, and the hydropower resource that has been exploited is 37 thousand kilowatt.

The Renhe River (任河): the Renhe River is originated at the Feilong Cave (飞龙洞) in Wangxiang Village (望乡村), Le'an Country (乐安乡) in Chenkou County (城口县). It runs towards northwest through the Weihe River (渭河), Gaowang (高望), Xiuwen County (修文县), Gecheng County (葛城县), Huangxi Town (黄溪镇) and Bashan (巴山), and it enters Wanyuan City (万源) in Sichuan Province at Chaxikou (岔溪口). It further runs through the Dazhu River (大竹河), Tianba River (田坝河) and enters the Maobaguan (茅坝关) in Ziyang County

(紫阳县), Shaanxi Province. It turns towards northeast through Gaotan Town (高滩镇), Wafangdian (瓦房店) City and enters into the Hanjing River (汉江) in Ziyang County. The drainage basin is located in the Daba Mountain area and belongs to middle and high mountain geomorphology. Therefore the mountains are high and vigorous with a large number of long mountain ridges, steep slopes and narrow canyons. The carbonate rock formation and karst are well-developed. The length of the mainstream is 163 kilometres and the average gradient of the riverway is 3.9 ‰. The average annual runoff in its estuary is 221 cubic meters per second over the years. The length in Chengkou County (城口县) is 128 kilometres and the drainage area is 2,358 square kilometres. The average gradient of the riverway is 9.6 ‰. The average annual runoff in its exit is 66.7 cubic meters per second over the years. Theoretically, the storage of the hydropower resource is 303.8 thousand kilowatts, and the exploitable storage of hydropower resource is 210 thousand kilowatt. The hydropower resource that has been exploited is 4 thousand kilowatt.

The Daning River (大宁河): the Daning River is originated at Dasheng Temple (大圣庙) in Wuxi County and enters into the Yangtze River in Wuxi County. The length of the river is 142.7 kilometres. The average annual runoff in its estuary is 98 cubic meters per second over the years. This river cuts from north to south and forms famous natural landscape such as the Small Three Gorges and Mini Three Gorges (小小三峡) in the Daning River.

Picture 1-8 The Daning River

The Longxi River (龙溪河): the Longxi River is originated at Mingda Town (明达镇) in Liangping District (梁平区). It runs through Dianjiang County (垫江县) and enters east into the Yangtze River in Changshou District (长寿区). Its total length is 218 kilometres and its average annual runoff is 54 cubic meters per second over the years. This river falls sharply from the upper reaches to the lower reaches. While it is detrimental to sailing, it is beneficial for the building of the hydropower station. In the early 1950s, the building of a great dam in Shizitan (狮子滩) helped the formation of the Changshou Lake (长寿湖). 5 hydropower stations were built step by step and the installed capacity was nearly 100 thousand kilowatts.

The Yulin River (御临河): the Yulin River belongs to Level 1 tributary in the north shore of the Yangtze River. It is originated at Linshan (邻山) in Linshui County (邻水县), Sichuan Province. It is called Yuxi (玉溪) in Linshui County and Meixi (梅溪) when it runs into Changshou District. It enters into the Yangtze River in Taihonggang (太洪岗) of Luoqi Town (洛碛镇) in Yubei District (渝北区). Its length is 218 kilometres and its average annual runoff is 50.72 cubic meters per second over the years. Its length in Chongqing area is 58.4 kilometres and it covers an area of 908 square kilometres. The fall between the high flow and the low flow is sharp and its riverbed is prone to silt up. Every year, there are two months of silting so that sailing is unavailable. The building of the Dahong River Hydropower Station (大洪河水电站) resulted in the formation of the Dahong Lake (大洪湖). The capacity of the reservoir is 323 million cubic meters and the installed capacity is 35 thousand kilowatts.

The Modao Stream (磨刀溪): the Modao Stream belongs to the Level 1 tributary in the south shore of the Yangtze River. It is originated at Shanshuping (杉树坪) in the piedmont of the Wuling Mountain (武陵山), Shizhu County (石柱县). It runs through Lichuan City (利川市) in Hubei Province and Wanzhou District (万州区) in Chongqing and enters into the Yangtze River in Xinjinkou (新津口), Yunyang County. The upper reaches of the river belong to the Qiyao Mountain (七曜山) and the Wulong Mountain's middle-height ridge and valley geomorphology; the lower reaches of the river belong to parallel valley's low mountain and hill geomorphology. It leaps from southeast to northwest and sees great ups and downs. Its total length is 170 kilometres. The average gradient of the riverway is 5 ‰. The average annual runoff in its estuary is 60.3 cubic meters per second over the years. It covers an area of 2,790 square kilometres in Chongqing area. The fall of the river is concentrated in the middle reaches. Theoretically, the storage of the hydropower resource is 242.3 thousand kilowatts, and the exploitable hydropower resource is 159.5 thousand kilowatts, and the hydropower resource that has been exploited is 72.5 thousand kilowatts.

The Furong River (芙蓉江): the Furong River is originated at Shiwengzi (石瓮子), Suiyang County (绥阳县) in Guizhou Province. It enters into the Wujiang River (乌江) in Jiangkou Town (江口镇) of Wulong District in Chongqing. Its length in Chongqing area is 35 kilometres. According to the measurement in Changba (长坝) hydropower station, the largest runoff is 5,650 cubic meters per second (June 16th, 1964) and the smallest runoff is 7.8 cubic meters per second (September 30th, 1960).

The Qiongjiang River (琼江): the Qiongjiang River is also named the Anju River (安居河). It enters into Chongqing at Guanghui Town (光辉镇) in Tongnan District. It runs through Tongnan District, Tongliang Distrit and enters into the Fujiang River in Anju Town (安居镇). Its length in Chongqing area is 95.4 kilometres, and the average annual runoff in its estuary is 37.8 cubic meters per second over the years; the average annual runoff is 1.191 billion cubic meters over the years. The flat riverway is beneficial for sailing.

Picture 1-9 The Furong River (芙蓉江)

The Laixi River (濑溪河): the Laixi River is originated at Gaoping Town (高坪镇) in Dazu District (大足区). It runs through Dazu District, Rongchang District (荣昌区) and flows out of Chongqing at Qingjiang Town (清江镇) and into Luxian County (泸县) in Sichuan Province, and it enters into the Tuojiang River (沱江) in Hushi Town (胡市镇) of Luxian County. Its length in Chongqing is 133 kilometres and the average annual runoff out of Chongqing is 20.1 cubic meters per second over the years; the average annual runoff is 633 million cubic meters over the years.

2. Underground Rivers

Picture 1-10 The Puhua Underground River in Qianjiang(黔江蒲花暗河)

The underground river is also called subterranean stream. Karstification results in the formation of karst caves and underground passages in areas mainly covered by carbonate rocks. When the surface rivers flow through ponors, they flow into the underground and form underground rivers. The Chongqing Municipality is rich in carbonate rocks and the karst topography is well-developed. Therefore, underground waters are very common. The exposure of carbonate rocks in Chongqing takes two forms. First, the large and extensive exposure locates in the Daba Mountain area (大巴山区), the Wushan Mountain area (巫山山区) and the Dalou Mountain area (大娄山区) in east and southeast Chongqing. In these mountainous areas, the carbonate rock stratum is thick; the lithology is pure; the tectonic fissure is developed; the karst topography is well-developed. Depressions, ponors and underground waters can be seen here and there, especially in Qianjiang (黔江), Youyang (酉阳) and Pengshui (彭水) areas, and underground rivers with a length of several thousand metres are very common. Second, strip distribution in anticline mountains, and aulacogen and depressions are formed under karstification. Restricted by topography and the distribution of carbonate rocks, underground waters along strip anticline mountains are under-developed and short, but the section of these waters is relatively high. For example, in Chongqing, there are 31 underground waters found in 10 anticline hilly areas. Among them, the Laolongdong (老龙洞) underground river in South Hot Spring (南温泉) anticline is very distinctive. The four-thousand long underground river develops along underground gallery and its water never dries up throughout the year.

3.Hot Spring

Hot spring refers to those springs with a water temperature above 20 ℃ or those whose temperature is higher than local annual average temperature. No volcanic activity appears in Chongqing in modern times and hot springs are far from igneous rock areas. The formation of hot springs has nothing to do with magmatic activity or volcanic activity, whereas it is related to geologic structure, lithology and geomorphic characteristics. The thermal water in hot springs is generally buried in areas that are 1,000 to 2,000 meters deep under syncline structure ground. Its heat source is mainly from terrestrial heat. The geologic structure in Chongqing is characterized by high and steep anticline as well as wide and flat syncline. Fracture development is seen in anticline, and major dislocation in deep underground is connected to the surface so that hot water in deep underground could well up. In carbonate karst trough valley area of anticline mountains, atmospheric precipitation and surface water replenishment permeate downward and merge with hot water,

Picture 1-11 South Hot Spring

so the temperature of hot water is lowered, and the underground hot water follows the deep cracks cut by rivers and emerge as a hot spring. Therefore, the water temperature of hot springs in Chongqing is not high, generally 25℃ to 47℃ , and belongs to medium and low temperature hot water. The highest temperature of Xiquan (西泉) in Tongliang District could reach 83.4℃ . Because of geologic structure and the deep cut of surface waters, hot springs are found in many places in Chongqing. There are more than 20 large-scale hot springs in Chongqing. According to water quality, bicarbonate water is found in Bishan(璧山) hot spring; chloride water is found in Jiangjin Maoerxia (江津猫儿峡) hot spring; sulphate water is found in Beibei (北碚) North Hot Spring. The famous hot springs in Chongqing are South Hot Spring, North Hot Spring, East Hot Spring and Tongjing (统景) Hot Spring. All of them have been developed into famous parks or leisure resorts in Chongqing suburbs.

4.Waterfall

Picture 1-12　Simian Mountain Waterfalls (四面山瀑布)

Waterfall refers to the current that pours from river valley which is horizontally cut. It is mainly formed by differential erosion of the soft and hard rocks in riverbed by running water. Chongqing Municipality boasts humid climate, rugged topography and numerous rivers, therefore waterfall landscape is very common. Waterfalls in Chongqing Municipality are mainly distributed in the upper reaches of those rivers in mountainous regions. Their formation is always related to the retrogressive erosion of rivers caused by intermittent uplift in neotectonics. The waterfalls' dynamic stance, grand and magnificent momentum, together with the colourful scenes they reflect, make them the most valuable tourism resources that deserve appreciation and add to the beauty of the scenic spots. Within the area of 82.4 thousand square kilometres in Chongqing, more than 10 waterfalls deserve appreciation from the perspective of tourism. Among them, the most famous are the Wangxiangtai Waterfall (望乡台瀑布) in the Simian Mountain Scenic Spot (四面山风景区), the Bailongguojiang Waterfall (白龙过江瀑布) in the Daning River Scenic Spot (大宁河风景区), the Jinfo Mountain Waterfalls (金佛山瀑布) in the Jinfo Mountain Scenic Spot (金佛山风景区), and the Heishan Waterfalls (黑山瀑布群) in Wansheng (万盛) tourist area.

5.Soil

The Chongqing Municipality is located in the warm and humid monsoon climate zone in a mid-subtropical area. Under such climate conditions, soil with zonal characteristics such as yellow soil and red soil is formed. However, the natural condition that forms the soil is very complex. First, the geomorphic condition is very complex. Large areas of middle and low mountains and deep-cut valleys, wide hills, flat grounds, high mountains and deep gorges coexist, and the topography witnesses great ups and downs. To a large extent, it redistributed the water and heat conditions in Chongqing area. Soil-forming factors, such as climate and biology, also witness marked vertical variation and regional difference. Second, the strata exposed ranges from Sinian strata to quaternary strata, thus lithology is complex and the parent material is diverse. Moreover, differences in hydrogeological condition and human production and utilization forms add to the complexity of soil-forming conditions and lead to the diversity of soil types in Chongqing. According to statistics, there are 5 soil orders, 9 great groups, 17 subgroups, over 40 soil genus and over 100 soil types in Chongqing, and there are also more soil varieties.

Section Two Natural Resources

Ⅰ.Land Resource

The complex and diverse natural conditions in Chongqing contribute to the diversified types of land resource. According to geomorphic composition, mountainous regions account for 75.8% of the land area in Chongqing municipality; hills (including flat hills, shallow hills and deep hills) account for 18.2%; mesas and plains are few and only account for 3.6% and 2.4% respectively. Thus, the main types of Chongqing land resources are mountainous regions and hills. Mountainous regions bring about disadvantageous effects on farming and transportation. Meanwhile, they also open up bright prospects for forestry, husbandry and diversified economy.

The total land area in Chongqing Municipality is 8.2403 million hectares, which accounts for 0.86% of the total land area in China; agricultural land area accounts for 1.74% of the total agricultural land area; forest land area accounts for 1.15% of the total forest land area; grassland area accounts for 0.06% of the total grassland area. Chongqing has a large population, but its per capita land resources of all types is lower than the national average level, especially the farming land, and the per capita farmland in Chongqing is only 71.8% of the national average level.

Ⅱ.Water Resource

Water resource is composed of surface water, underground water and transit surface water. The average annual precipitation of Chongqing Municipality was 1,184.1 millimetres (1956-2000 series, similarly hereinafter), namely, the average total annual precipitation was 97.575 billion cubic meters. The precipitation is mainly concentrated from May to September, accounting for 70% of the total precipitation.

Picture 1-13 Changshou Lake

The average annual runoff depth is 620.7 millimetres, in other words, the amount of surface water resource is 51.14 billion cubic meters. The ground water storage is 13.166 billion cubic meters, and the exploitable amount is 4.5 billion cubic meters.

In terms of geographical distribution, the precipitation sees a gradual declining tendency from the east to the west. The precipitation in Wuxi County in the east is the highest, with an average annual precipitation of 1,401.9 millimetres; the precipitation in Tongnan District in the west is the lowest, with an average annual precipitation of 975.6 millimetres.

The average annual amount of local total water resources is 56.776 billion cubic meters, and in a moderate dry year (P=75%, similarly hereinafter), the local total water resources is 46.067 billion cubic meters.

In terms of geographical distribution, the amount of water resource sees a gradual declining tendency from the east to the west. In terms of time distribution, the amount of water resource in flood season accounts for 70% of the total amount of water resource throughout the year.

The local water resource in Chongqing is insufficient, whereas the transit water is rather abundant. There are 36 transit rivers that enter Chongqing. The main river that exits Chongqing is the Yangtze River, and the average annual amount of transit water is 383.737 billion cubic meters.

Table 1-1 The Distribution of Surface Water Resource of River Systems in Chongqing

River systems	Precipitation		Local surface runoff (100 million m^3)				Per capita water rsource (m^3)
	Depth of precipitation (mm)	Total amount (100 million m^3)	Average amount	P=50%	P=75%	P=95%	
The main stream of the Yangtze River	1,203	579.56	292.08	280.90	222.16	155.56	1,604
The Jialing River System	1,101	103.67	42.28	38.97	26.94	14.82	650
The Mintuo River System	1,036	20.78	6.93	6.03	3.74	1.59	507
The Wujiang River System	1,248	199.70	109.44	106.98	88.68	66.32	4,329
The Hanjiang River System	1,256	29.65	20.93	20.08	15.70	10.67	12,465
The Yuanjiang River System	1,395	65.33	39.78	38.84	31.18	24.17	14,823

There are three main features of the water resource in Chongqing. First is uneven distribution of time and space, such as more in the east, less in the west, 70% in flood season, 30% in non-flood season. Second is insufficient supply in Chongqing. The per capita local water resource is 1,700 cubic meters, accounting 4/5 of the per capita water resource in China and 1/5 of the per capita water resource of the world. According to the internationally recognized standard of water shortage, Chongqing belongs to moderately water-deficient area with per capita amount of water ranging from 1,000 to 2,000 cubic meters. The 11 districts and counties in west Chongqing belong to severely water-deficient area, with per capita amount of water ranging from 500 to 1,000 cubic meters. Third, the transit water is abundant, but it is very difficult to develop and utilize. With mountains and hills as the main feature of Chongqing geomorphology, "Man walks upwards, and water flows downwards" is the typical feature.

Ⅲ.Fauna and Flora Resources

1.Fauna Resources

There are more than 600 fauna resources in Chongqing, with nearly 100 kinds of beasts, over 300 kinds of birds, over 50 kinds of reptiles, over 30 kinds of amphibians and over 100 kinds of fishes. Among these wildlife resources, 50 kinds are listed as rare land wildlife under special state protection, and nearly 100 rare species are listed as national first to third class protected species.

Picture 1-14 Francois's Leaf Monkey

10 species are listed as national first-class protected species. They are Francois's Leaf Monkey, Golden Snub-nosed Monkey, Gray Sub-nosed Monkey, Clouded Leopard, leopard, python, Black Stork, golden eagle, jade belt eagle and Slow Loris.

40 species are listed as national second-class protected species, including Macaca mulatta, Macaca thibetana, Manis pentadactyla, Cuon alpinus, Ursus thibetanus, Martes flavigula, Viverra zibetha, Viverricula indica, Catopuma temminckii, Moschus berezovskii, Procapra picticaudata, Goral, Chrysolophus pictus, Tragopan temminckii, Lophura nycthemera, Syrmaticus reevesii, Pucrasia macrolopha, Milvus korschun, Accipiter gentilis, Accipiter soloensis, Accipiter nisus, Accipiter virgatus, Buteo magnirostris, Buteo, Falco peregrinus, Falco amurensis, Otus bakkamoena, Bubo blakistoni, Glaucidium, Glaucidium cuculoides, Ninox scutulata, Asio otus, Asio flammeus, Aviceda subcristata, Pernis

ptilorhynchus, Platalea leucorodia, Cygnus columbianus, Aix galericulata, Tyto longimembris.

There are over 70 kinds of domesticated animals, among which the domestication of pig, sheep, cow and rabbit has certain advantages in China. The renowned "Rongchang Pig" (荣昌猪) is listed as top three of pig breeds in China. Shizhu County (石柱县) is the largest production base for Angora rabbit in China.

2.Flora Resources

Picture 1-15 Alsophila Spinulosa

Picture 1-16 Davidia Involucrate

There are 153 families, 640 genus and over 6,000 species of vascular plants in Chongqing. The richness of flora resource ranks the third in China, only second to Yunnan Province and Sichuan Province. There are more than 5,000 economic plants. According to their economic use, they can be divided as medicinal plant, oil plant, aromatic plant, tanning plant, dye plant, starch and sugar plant, textile plant, wild ornamental plant, wild edible fungi, etc. 9 wild plants in Chongqing are listed as first-class plants under special state protection. They are Davidia involucrate, Cathaya argyrophylla, Taxus chinensis, Taxus wallichiana, Bretschneidera sinensis, Metasequoia glyptostroboides, etc. 40 wild plants in Chongqing are listed as second-class plants under special state protection. They are represented by Phoebe zhennan, Cinnamomum camphora, Liriodendron chinense, Cercidiphyllum japonicim, Cibotium barometa, etc. 46 wild plants are under special protection in Chongqing. They are represented by Adiantum reniforme, Abies fargesii, Thuja sutchuenensis, Scutellaria tsinyunensis, Tangtsinia nanchuanica, etc.

Ⅳ.Mineral Resource

As the geologic structure in Chongqing is diversified, the formation of strata is full-fledged, with frequent magmation and perfect minerogenetic condition. Chongqing holds in store ferrous metal, nonferrous metal, noble metal, rare metal, metallurgical auxiliary material, chemical material, energy source, building material, and other non-metallic materials. By the end of 2015, 68 kinds of minerals (sub-minerals included) have been found in Chongqing, accounting for 39.7% among the 171 kinds of minerals (sub-minerals included) that has been found in China. The 49 ascertained resource reserves (including 3 energy mineral resources, 12 metallic ores, 34 non-metallic ores) account for 29.5% of the 159 (sub-minerals included) ascertained resource reserves in China. Chongqing has 17 ascertained resource reserves that listed as top 10 in China. They are witherite, konilite, ceramic sandstone, laterite, cement mudstone, salt mine, mercury, cast sandstone, strontium, aluminium, manganese, magnesia dolomite, natural gas, glass sandstone, talcum, barite, masonry sandstone.

1.Coal

The abundant coal resource in Chongqing is characterized by complete types and wide distribution. There are 251 ascertained resource reserves, including 1 large mineral deposit, 1 medium-sized mincral deposit, 88 small-sized mineral deposits and 161 mineral spots with 1.834 billion tons of reserves.

2.Natural Resources

Chongqing has abundant natural gas resources that are distributed widely. There are 36 identified gas fields, including 1 oil field, 31 oil (gas) -bearing structures and 130 gas pools with a basic reserve of 121.95 billion cubic meters.

3.The Iron Ore

There are 194 iron ore producing areas in Chongqing, including 4 medium-sized ones, 23 small-sized deposits, 167 mineralized spots. The identified iron ore reserves are 482.4477 million tons. However, the quality of the ores is poor, most of them could not be put into furnace for smelting.

4.The Manganese Ore

There are 8 manganese ore fields in Chongqing, including 3 medium-sized deposits, 1 small-sized deposit and 4 mineral spots with an explored reserve of 37.4738 million tons, which ranks as the third in China.

5.The Vanadium Ore

The Vanadium Ore is distributed in Wuxi, Yunyang, Fengjie, Chengkou, etc. It belongs to coexisting mineral and it is formed in Permian series and lower Cambrain series. This resource has great potential. The estimated reserve in two diggings in Tianba, Wuxi (巫溪田坝) and Jianping, Wushan (巫山建平) are 1.4422 million tons and 691.9 thousand tons respectively.

6.Bauxite

Bauxite is one of the advantageous minerals in Chongqing. There are 24 Bauxite fields in the city, including 1 large deposit, 7 medium-sized deposits, 4 small-sized deposits and 12 mineralized spots. The explored reserve is 68.97 million tons.

7.The Lead-Zinc Ore

There are 22 lead-zinc ore fields in Chongqing, including 1 medium-sized deposit, 3 small-sized deposits, 18 mineralized spots. The explored reserve of lead is 31.4 thousand tons and that of zinc is 309.9 thousand tons.

8.The Mercury Ore

There are 27 mercury ore fields in Chongqing, including 3 large-sized deposits, 2 medium-sized deposits, 3 small-sized deposits and 21 mineralized spots. The explored reserve is 14 thousand tons that ranks the third in China. Since ancient times, Chongqing area has been famous for its exploration of "cinnabar" (mercuric chloride). As early as Shang and Zhou Dynasties (商周), there is a legend that in the Three Gorges Area of the Yangtze River, people explored "cinnabar" as "panacea". In the Spring and Autumn Period and the Warring States Period (春秋战国时期), the exploration of "cinnabar" in the Ba State has a relatively large scale. When it came to the Qin Dynasty (秦代), cinnabar was used as a tribute to serve on the court. Qin Shi Huang (the first Emperor of Qin) (秦始皇) even established "Huaiqingtai" (怀清台)[1]. For thousands of years, Qianjiang, Youyang (酉阳) and Xiushan (秀山), have been rare and large mercury ore fields in China.

9.The Strontium Ore

The strontium ore in Chongqing is richly endowed by nature. The 3 ore fields that have been found are all large deposits. The accumulated explored reserve is 6.7141 million tons, which account for more than half of the explored reserve in China. Both the reserves and quality of ore fields rank the first in China and it is one of the world's super-large deposits.

[1] It is a place to memorize a widow called Huaiqing whose family was dedicated to exploring "cinnabar" in the Ba County.

10.The Barium Ore

The reserves of barium ore in Chongqing is 38.87 million tons, which ranks the second in China. Both the quality and grade are good. The value of industrial exploitation is high. The average content of barium carbonate is 49.92% and the average content of barium sulfate is 11.97%. The barium ore is intensively distributed in Chengkou County.

Chapter Two　Population

Section One　Demographic Situation

Ⅰ.Demographic Changes

In 316 B.C., the Qin State (秦国) defeated the Ba State (巴国). In 314 B.C., Ba Jun (巴郡) was established with Jiangzhou (江州) (urban area of Chongqing nowadays) under its jurisdiction, and a feudal system with household as production unit was established. To facilitate taxation and corvee, the Qin State started the compiling of household books to conduct a census. The Han Dynasty (汉代) succeeded the Qin system by maintaining the Ba Jun. In the 2nd year of Yuanshi of the Western Han Dynasty (西汉元始) (2), there were more than 700 thousand people in Ba Jun. In the 5th year of Yonghe of the Eastern Han Dynasty (东汉永和) (140), the population increased to 1.08 million. According to *Huayang Local Chronicles—the Local Chronicle of the Ba State* (《华阳国志·巴志》), the population reached 1.87 million in the 2nd year of Yongxing (永兴) (154).

After the chaos caused by war in late Eastern Han Dynasty (东汉) and the Three Kingdoms Period (三国), the Ba Jun became dilapidated and depressed, and the population witnessed a sharp decrease. When it came to the first year of Taikang (280) of the Jin Dynasty (晋太康), the Ba Jun covered an area of the Ba Jun in Eastern Han Dynasty (东汉巴郡), West Ba Jun (巴西郡), East Ba Jun (巴东郡) and Fuling Jun (涪陵郡). The population was only 130 thousand, less than 1/10 of that in the 2nd year of Yongxing (154). When Sichuan was ruled by Chenghan State (成汉), the Ba Jun and Jiangzhou were war-torn, and a large number of people fled to Jingxiang (荆湘), which led to a sharp decrease of population and depression of villages. Jiangzhou became a deserted county with only hundreds of households.

The Song Dynasty (宋代) witnessed the fastest development of Bayu's economy and a great increase of population. In the 3rd year of Yuanfeng (1080) (元丰), over 130 thousand households held a population of 670 thousand, an increase of 3 times than the Tang Dynasty (唐代).

In the early years of the Yuan Dynasty (元代), the prolonged war destruction led to the death and escape of numerous people. In the 27th year of the Yuan Dynasty (1290), the population was only 90 thousand, together with the same number of the homeless. The population was only 20% to 25% of that in the Southern Song Dynasty (南宋). After several generations of rehabilitation, Chongqing's economy gradually recovered. In the Ming Dynasty (明代), the population in Chongqing was already 1/3 of that in Sichuan.

In the end of the Ming Dynasty and the early Qing Dynasty (清代), the long-term chaos caused by war led to a sharp decrease of population. In the 24th year of Kangxi (康熙) (1685) in the Qing Dynasty (清朝), Chongqing was a city "Where high officials did business, and the homeless gathered, with no more than hundreds of households. Besides, in the prefectures and counties, there were dozens of, or a dozen of, or even one or two households." After years of rehabilitation and immigration, the population gradually recovered. In the 61st year of Kangxi (1722), there were already 560 thousand people in Chongqing. In the 17th year of Jiaqing (嘉庆) (1812) in the Qing Dynasty, the population was estimated as 2.36 million. In the 2nd year of Xuantong (宣统) in late Qing Dynasty, the population reached 6.92 million, a two-fold increase compared with that in the mid-Jiaqing period.

When Chongqing was established as a city in the year 1929, its jurisdiction only covered the urban area of the original Ba County (巴县) with a population of 230 thousand. On July 7th 1937, the War of Resistance Against Japanese Aggression broke out in full swing. In the next year, the national government moved westward to Chongqing. A lot of parties, militaries and government organs, scientific, technological, cultural and educational institutions, industrial and mining enterprises and people in the enemy-occupied area immigrated to Chongqing, and Chongqing population witnessed a sharp increase. Meanwhile, with the expansion of Chongqing jurisdiction, the population reached 520 thousand in 1938. In 1945, the population reached 1.25 million, a peak in the Republic of China (1912-1949). After the War of Resistance Against Japanese Aggression, the national government moved back to Nanjing, and the population in Chongqing witnessed a fall. In the end of 1948, the year before Chongqing won its liberation, the population was about 1 million.

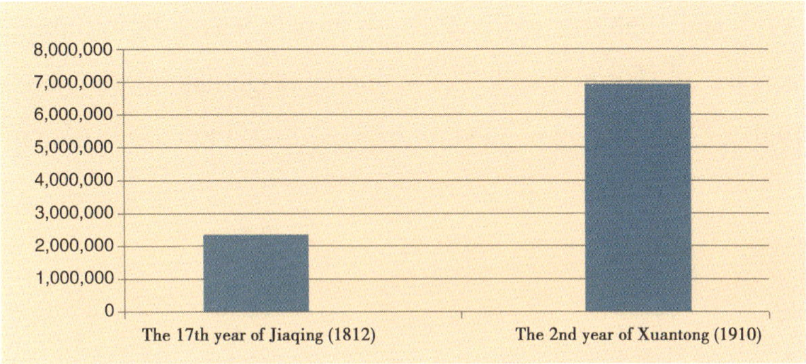

Picture 2-1 The Population of Chongqing Fu in 1812 and 1910

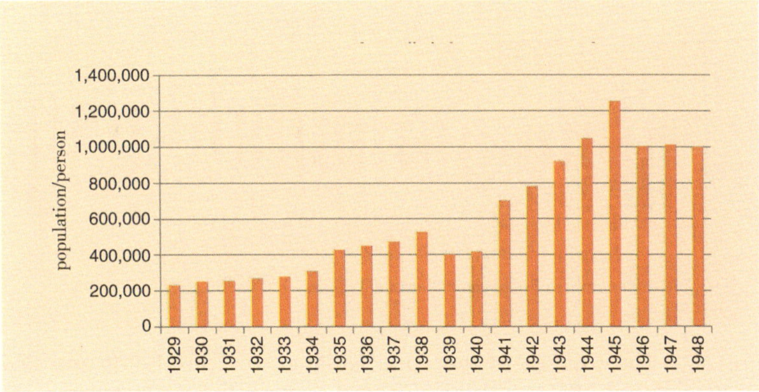

Picture 2-2 The Overall Demographic Change of Chongqing Between 1929 and 1948

After the founding of the People's Republic of China (PRC), Chongqing's economy developed at a fast speed. People's livelihood and medical conditions were improved significantly. The population increased. As the jurisdiction of Chongqing expands in every adjustment, the population size expands, too.

From 1954, the population in Chongqing witnessed the first baby boom. Between 1953 and 1958, the cumulative number of babies born was 3.574 million. Meanwhile, medical and health services were improved greatly, and malignant infectious disease and endemic were under effective control, and the state of health saw continuous improvement, and the mortality, especially infant mortality saw gradual declination. With the birth rate staying at a high level and the death rate declining step by step, natural population growth rate increased significantly. Between 1953 and 1958, natural population growth was 2.28 million, an annual average increase of 380 thousand. The annual average natural population growth rate was 19.91‰. The overall population increased from 8.9369 million to 10.0522 million.

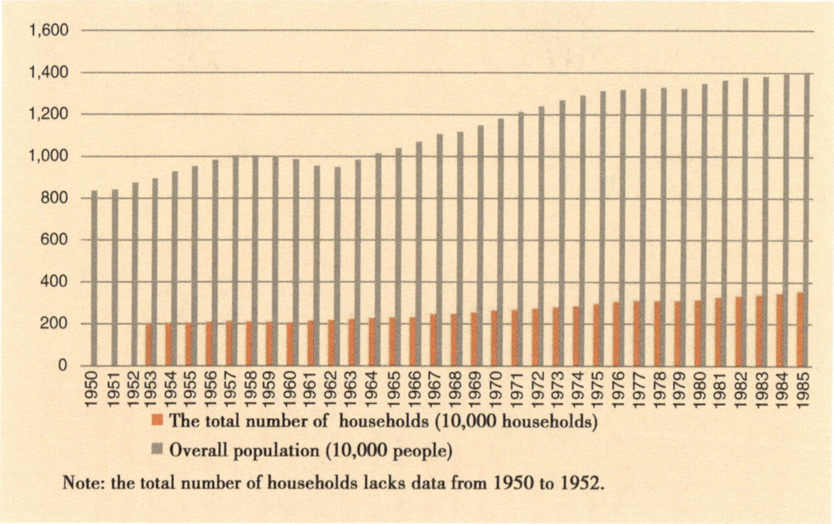

Picture 2-3 The Change of the Total Number of Households and Overall Population Between 1950 and 1985 (Original Yongchuan Area Included)

In the three difficult years of natural disasters from 1959 to 1961, the birth rate decreased from 23.16‰ in 1958 to 10.99‰ in 1961. The birth rate was overwhelmed by the sharp rise of the death rate, and the population witnessed a negative growth.

In the middle of the 1970s, the Family Planning Policy kept the growth rate under control. The natural rapid growth gave way to planned moderate growth. The birth rate declined gradually with a tendency of accelerated declination, from 28.06‰ in 1975 to 9.91‰ in 1978. From the middle 1980s to 2010, the birth rate fluctuated around 12‰, with 19.54‰ in 1986 and 19.10‰ in 2010 as the peaks, and 8.48‰ in 2001 as the bottom. The birth rate in 2017 was 12.12‰. The overall death rate shows a tendency of declination till 2005, except fluctuation in a few years. The death rate in 2005 was 4.40 ‰. After a slight fluctuation, the death rate in 2017 was 13.21‰. From 1975 to 2017, the natural growth of the population was 7.9723 million, and the annual average growth is 189.8 thousand. In the end of 1975, registered population in Chongqing was 13.1256 million; by the end of 2017, registered population in Chongqing reached 33.8982 million.

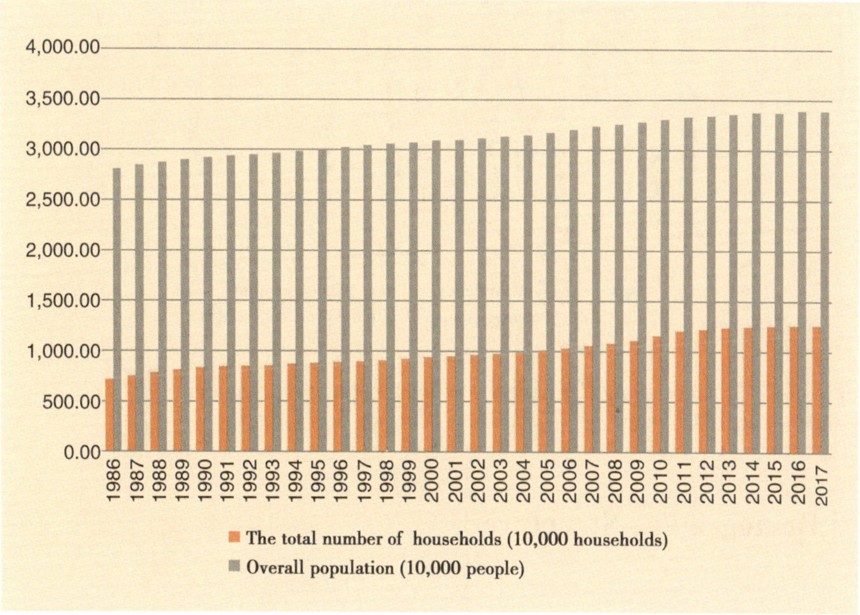

Picture 2-4 The Change of the Total Number of Households and Overall Population Between 1986 and 2017 (Wanxian, Fuling and Qianjiang Area Included)

From the perspective of permanent resident population, the number of permanent resident population is 28.73 million, after Chongqing became a municipality directly under the central government in 1997. Later it witnessed an annual gradual declination to 27.93 million in 2004 with a total decrease of 800 thousand, and an annual decrease of 114 thousand. After that, permanent resident population saw an annual gradual increase till 2017, and the number reached 30.75 million. The overall increase was 28.2 million from 2005 to 2017, an annual average increase of 217 thousand. This demonstrated that after Chongqing became a municipality directly under the central government, and its position as a central city in Western Region Development of China and the upper reaches of the Yangtze River added its attraction.

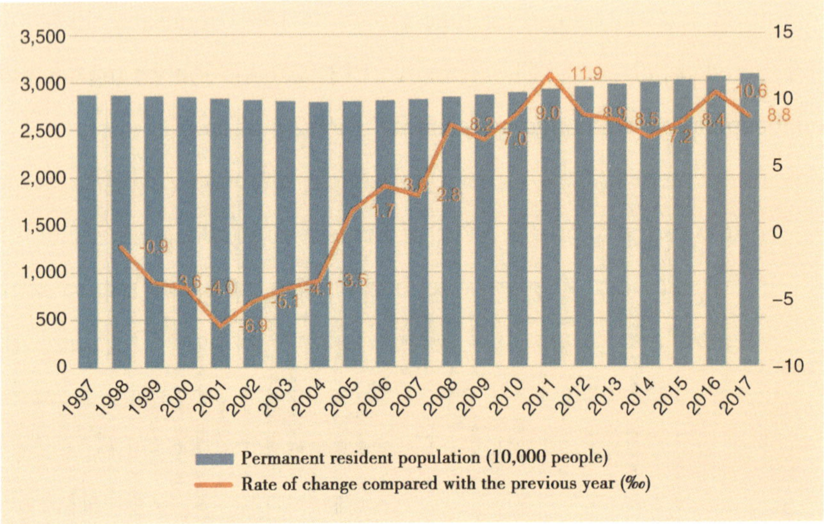

Picture 2-5 Chongqing Permanent Resident Population Between 1997 and 2017 and Its Rate of Change

Ⅱ.Demographic Structure

1.Gender Structure

In ancient Chongqing, social productivity was low, so the economic development was unstable, and people's livelihood could not be guaranteed. For thousands of years, females were under great depression and lived a tough life, and females were dominated by the thought that valued sons and belittled daughters. What's worse, the evil practice to desert and drown baby girls in ancient times led to higher female mortality, thus the disproportion of gender ratio was obvious.

In modern Chongqing, the gender ratio was still high. For example, in 1936, the gender ratio within Chongqing jurisdiction was 127. From the outbreak of the War of Resistance Against Japanese Aggression to the victory of this war, the gender ratio witnessed a sharp rise, with the lowest in 1938—136.94; and the highest in 1942—166.79. The reason behind this was that as a wartime capital, lots of parties and government offices as well as industrial and mining enterprises immigrated to Chongqing. In these offices and enterprises, an overwhelming majority were males.

After the founding of the People's Republic of China, the disproportion of gender ratio lasted but saw a slight declination. In 1952, gender ratio was as high as 109; in 1962, it declined to 104.18. After that, it witnessed almost annual rise.

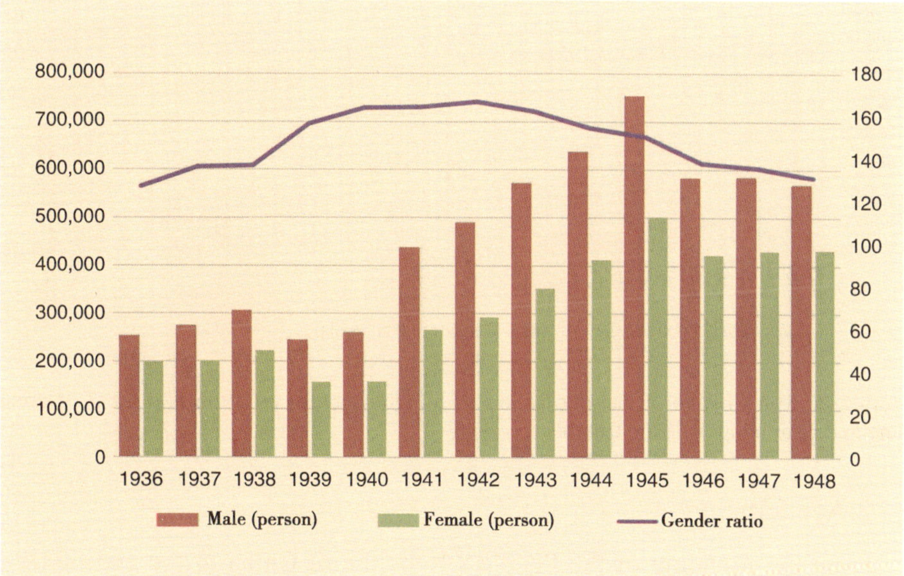

Picture 2-6 The Change of Gender Ratio in Chongqing Between 1936 and 1948

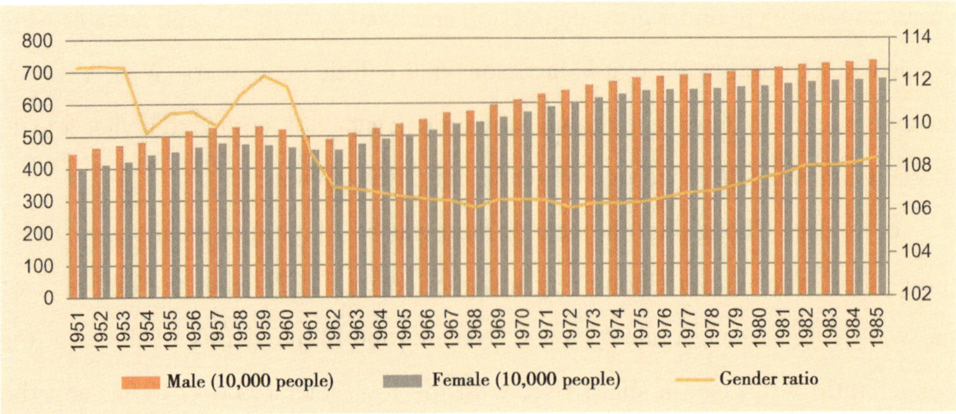

Picture 2-7 The Change of Gender Ratio in Chongqing Between 1951 and 1984 (The original Yongchuan Area included)

In the early 1990s, the gender ratio came back to that of early 1950s, namely, 109 or so. In 2005, the number of the male population was 1.2936 million more than that of the female population. Later, the gender ratio experienced a gradual declination. By the end of 2017, the gender ratio was 105.6 (registered population).

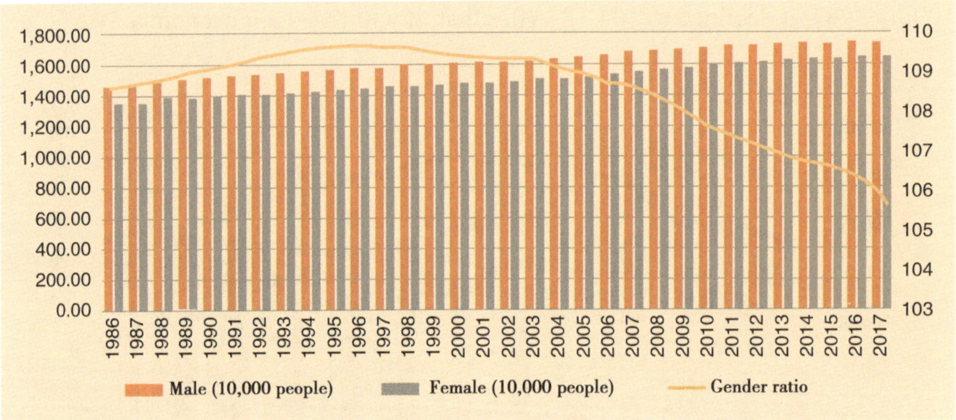

Picture 2-8 The Change of Gender Ratio in Chongqing Between 1986 and 2017 (Wanxian, Fuling and Qianjiang Area Included)

2.Age Structure

From the founding of the People's Republic of China to the end of 1960s, the age structure in Chongqing belonged to the youth type. During the 11 years between the first demographic census in 1953 and the second one in 1964, the coefficient of juvenile and children rose from 37.64% to 42.64%; the coefficient of the old fell from 3.83% to 2.8%. There are two main reasons. First is the high fertility level. Influenced by traditional concept of fertility and the error in population policy, people had a strong wish to give birth to children. The birth rate was very high except in a few years. The birth rate was 40‰ or so in most of the years, and in 1963, it was 47.84‰. The high birth rate contributed to the increase of young people, and the proportion of juveniles and children was enhanced. Second is the high mortality level. The development of the medical and health services took a long time. In the initial years after liberation, the death rate was above 10‰ in most years. The high fertility rate, together with the high mortality rate, influenced the ratio of the old and the young as well as the median aged, and thus alleviated aging trend of the population.

Table 2-1 Comparison Table of Chongqing Age Structure in Part of the Years

Year	Coefficient of children (%)	Coefficient of the aged (%)	The ratio between the aged and child (%)	Type of population
1982	29.43	5.15	17.50	Transformation between the Youth Type to the Adult Type
1990	21.70	5.80	26.70	The Adult Type
2000	21.83	8.84	36.35	The Aged Type
2005	20.60	11.00	57.70	The Aged Type
2010	16.98	11.56	68.08	The Aged Type
2017	16.87	13.22	78.36	The Aged Type

From 1970s to the end of 1980s, the age structure of Chongqing belonged to the adult type. In the 3rd census in 1982, the proportion of 0 to 14-year-old was 32.82%, and that of 65-year-old and above is 5.10%. The ratio of the old and the young was 15.56%, meeting the standard of the adult type. In the 4th census in 1990, the proportion of 0 to 14-year-old was 21.70%, already belonged to the aged type. But the proportion of 65-year-old and above is 5.83%. The ratio of the old and the young (26.87%) and the median age (26.73) still belonged to the adult type. The main reasons are follows. First, influenced by the family planning, the birth rate saw a sharp drop, from 41.84‰ in 1964 to 11.69‰ in 1982, and it kept this level till 1990. Second, the improvement of medical care led to a drop death rate, from 12.71‰ in 1964 to 6.84‰ in 1982. With the sharp drop of the birth rate and the corresponding drop of the death rate, the increase of the aged and child ratio and the median age fostered the age structure into the adult type and gradually towards the aged type.

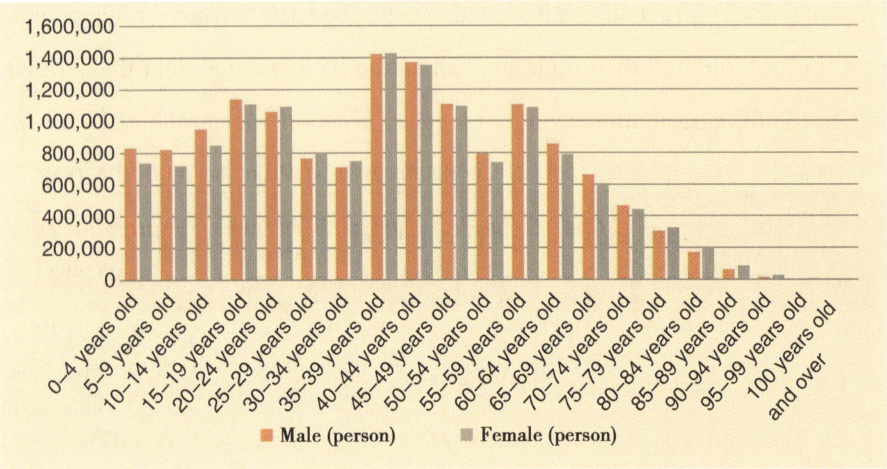

Picture 2-9 The Age Structure of Chongqing Permanent Resident Population in 2010

From early 1990s to 2000, the age structure in Chongqing entered into the aged type and showed a tendency of rapid development. In the 5th census in 2000, the proportion of 0 to 14-year-old was 21.84%, that of 65 and above was 8.01%, and the ratio of the old and the young was 36.70%, and the median age was 30.65, and the age structure in Chongqing entered into the period of the aged type completely. Later, the aging of the population became faster. In 2017, the ratio of the aged population increased 4.38% compared with that in 2000. The ratio of the aged and the young increased by 41.71%. From the perspective of population growth and from the 4th census to the 5th census, Chongqing gross population increased by 5.7%. In the corresponding period, the aged population increased by 45.3%. From the 5th census to 2017, Chongqing gross population increased by 8%. In the corresponding period, the aged population increased by 61.4%, much higher than gross population increase. In the end of 2017, the population of the 0 to 14-year-old was 5.1878 million, accounting for 16.87% of the gross population; the population of 15 to 64-year-old was 21.4984 million, accounting for 69.91% of the gross population; the population of 65-year-old and above was 4.0654 million, accounting for 13.22% of the gross population.

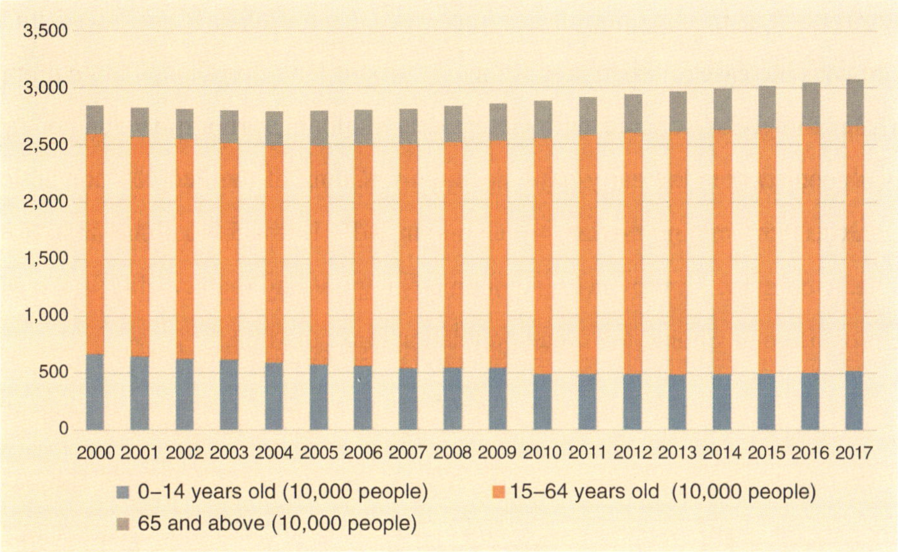

Picture 2-10 The Age Structure of Chongqing Permanent Resident Population Between 2000 and 2017

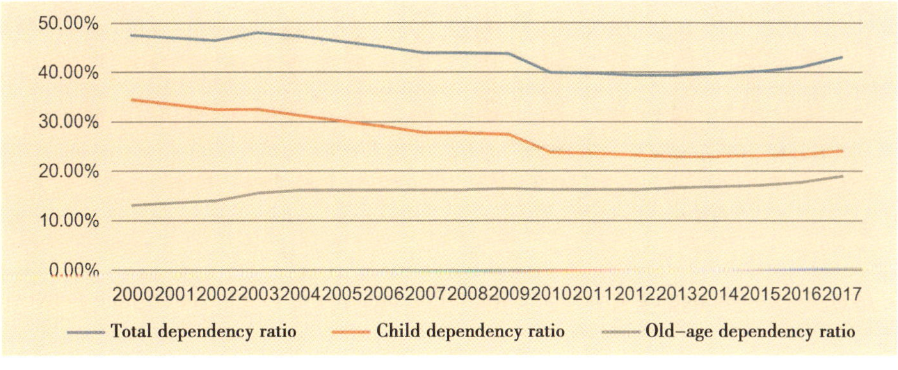

Picture 2-11 The Change of Chongqing Social Dependency Ratio Between 2000 and 2017

3.Urban and Rural Structure

Before the founding of the People's Republic of China, Chongqing urban economy already had a certain scale, but the rural economy was backward. The level of urbanization was low, and about 90% of the population lived in the rural area. After the founding of the People's Republic of China, in the wake of urbanization, great changes took place in the urban and rural structure. The urban population increased from 2.31 million in 1952 to 19.7 million in 2017, a net increase of 17.39 million, and an annual average increase of 267.5 thousand. The proportion in total population increased from 13.0% to 64.1%. With the continuous increase of urban proportion, the proportion of rural population dropped correspondingly. Compared with China as a whole, the proportion of Chongqing urban population in the early days since the founding of the People's Republic of China was 0.5%, higher than that of China. In 2017, it was 5.6% higher than that of China. Among the 12 provinces, autonomous regions and municipality in the west, the proportion of Chongqing urban population ranks the first.

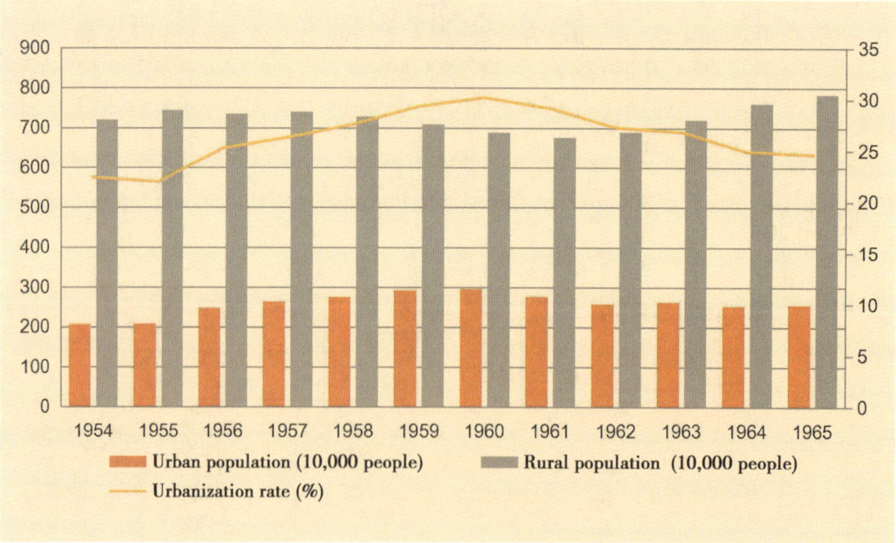

Picture 2-12 Chongqing Urban and Rural Population and Urbanization Rate Between 1954 and 1965

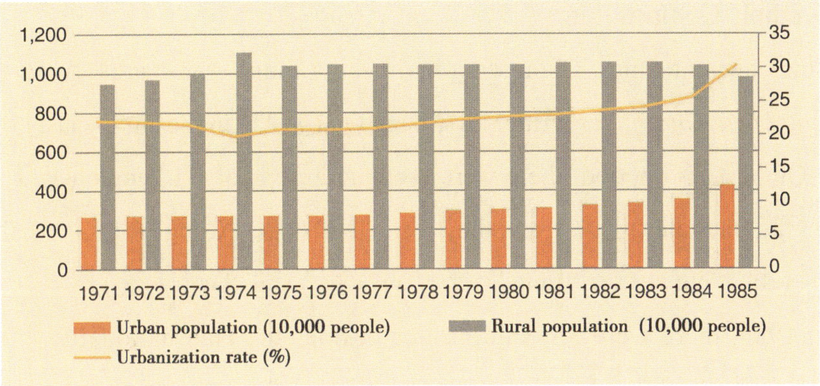

Picture 2-13 Chongqing Urban and Rural Population and Urbanization Rate Change Between 1971 and 1985

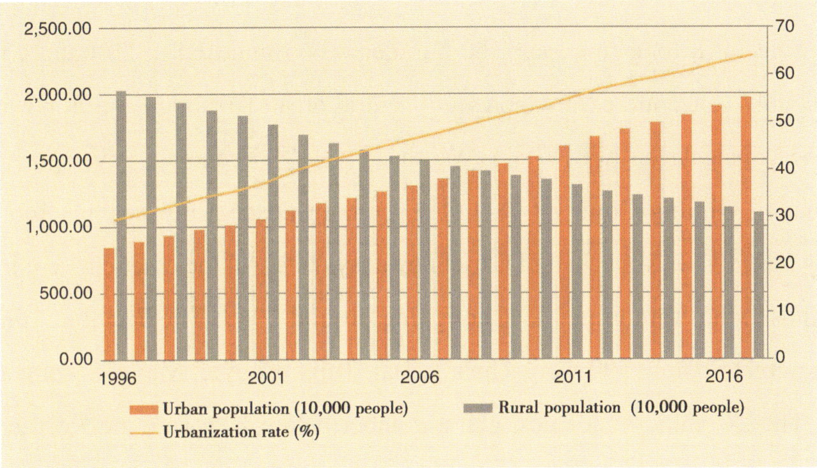

Picture 2-14 Chongqing Urban and Rural Permanent Residents and Urbanization Rate Change Between 1996 and 2017

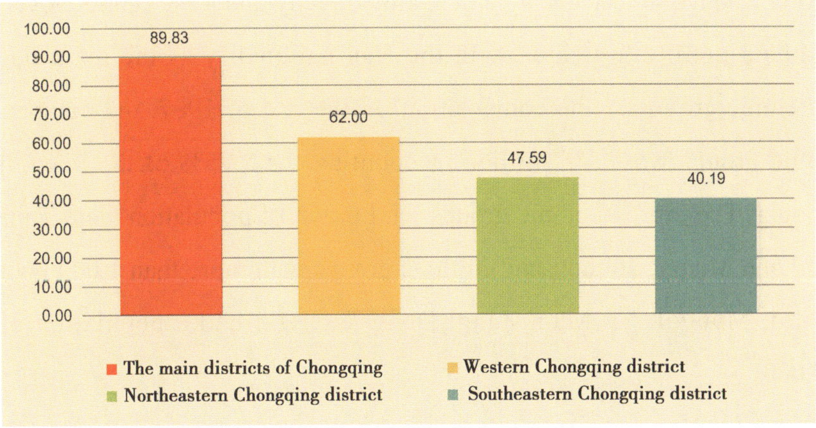

Picture 2-15 Chongqing Urbanization Rate of Each District in 2017

4.Ethnic Composition

Since ancient times, Chongqing had been a multi-ethnic area. According to *Huayang Local Chronicles* written by Chang Qu (常璩) in the Jin Dynasty (晋代), in Pre-Qin (先秦) period, there were 8 ethnic groups of Ba People (巴人) who lived in the Ba State (巴国), and they were "Pu" (濮) "Cong" (賨) "Cha" (苴) "Gong" (共) "Nu" (奴) "Rang" (獽) "Yi" (夷) and "Dan" (蜑) respectively.

In 1986, there were 35 ethic groups besides the Han nationality (汉族) in Chongqing, Sichuan Province. The number of the ethnic population was 15 thousand, accounting for 0.01% of the total population in Chongqing. Four ethnic groups, Hui (回), Miao (苗), Manchu (满) and Yi (彝) had been living in Chongqing for a long time, and the number was 5 hundred to 70 hundred. They were mainly concentrated in Chongqing central area (Yuzhong District nowadays), Nantong Mining Area (南桐矿区) (Wansheng (万盛) Economic Development Zone nowadays), Qijiang County (綦江县) (Qijiang District nowadays), Rongchang County (荣昌县) (Rongchang District nowadays) etc. All the other ethnic minorities were those who immigrated to Chongqing around 1949. The 7 ethnic minorities with a number below 500 were Zhuang, Bai, Tujia, Bouyei, Mongol, Zang and the Dong. The 24 ethnic minorities with a number below 100 were the Korean ethnic group, Uyghur, Yao, Hani, Kazak, Dai, Li, Va, She, Gaoshan, Lahu, Shui, Naxi, Tu, Daur, Mulam, Qiang, Jing, Blang, Saha, Gelao, Xibe, Russian ethnic and Hezhen.

After Chongqing became a municipality directly under the central government, it became a multi-ethnic area with the Han nationality as the main body and the 49 ethnic groups as the composition. In the end of 1997, the number of the 49 ethnic groups was 1.75 million, accounting for 5.75% of the population in Chongqing. The top two ethnic groups with the most population were Tujia (1.13 million) and Miao (520 thousand). Ethnic groups with more than 1,000 population were Hui, Mongol, Yi, Man, Zang, Dong, etc. Hui had a population of more than 8,000.

In 2010, according to the 6th census, all 55 ethnic groups can be found in Chongqing. The population of permanent ethnic groups were 1.937 million, accounting for 6.7% of the total population in Chongqing. Among them, Tujia had a population of 1.399 million, accounting for 72.2% of the total ethnic group population. Miao had a population of 482 thousand, accounting for 24.9% of the total ethnic group population. Other ethic groups with a large population were Hui, Mongol, Manchu, Korean and Zang, etc.

Picture 2-16 The Miao Nationality

Picture 2-17 The Tujia Nationality

Table 2-2 Chongqing Ethnic Demographics of Each Gender in 2010

Nationality	Permanent resident population		
	Total population	Male	Female
Total Population	28,846,170	14,608,870	14,237,300
The Han Nationality	26,909,061	13,617,247	13,291,814
Tujia Ethnic Group	1,398,707	717,687	681,020
Miao Ethnic Group Nationality	482,714	248,537	234,177
Hui Ethnic Group	9,056	4,658	4,398
Yi Ethnic Group	6,336	2,598	3,738
Mongol Ethnic Group	5,688	2,890	2,798
Zhuang Ethnic Group	4,634	2,066	2,568
Manchu Ethnic Group	4,571	2,431	2,140
Bouyei Ethnic Group	3,383	1,310	2,073

Continued

Nationality	Permanent resident population		
	Total population	Male	Female
Dong Ethnic Group	3,271	1,724	1,547
Zang Ethnic Group	3,086	1,250	1,836
Gelao Ethnic Group	2,808	1,298	1,510
Bai Ethnic Group	1,569	712	857
Hani Ethnic Group	1,398	365	1,033
Uygur Ethnic Group	1,162	605	557
Yao Ethnic Group	1,045	455	590
Dai Ethnic Group	881	239	642
Tu Ethnic Group	715	351	364
Qiang Ethnic Group	675	317	358
Korean Ethnic Group	637	331	306
Li Ethnic Group	587	277	310
Wa Ethnic Group	577	112	465
Lahu Ethnic Group	479	82	397
Naxi Ethnic Group	421	171	250
Lisu Ethnic Group	328	117	211
Blang Ethnic Group	288	45	243
Kazak Ethnic Group	259	104	155
She Ethnic Group	252	146	106
Other Ethnic Groups	209	119	90
Mulao Ethnic Group	208	80	128
Shui Ethnic Group	197	93	104
Sibo Ethnic Group	143	70	73
Daur Ethnic Group	118	47	71
Dongxiang Ethnic Group	102	56	46

Continued

Nationality	Permanent resident population		
	Total population	Male	Female
Jingpo Ethnic Group	82	21	61
Salar Ethnic Group	71	40	31
Maonan Ethnic Group	63	33	30
Pumi Ethnic Group	51	28	23
Gaoshan Ethnic Group	45	24	21
Russian Ethnic Group	40	15	25
Kirgiz Ethnic Group	28	11	17
Nu Ethnic Group	28	11	17
Yugur Ethnic Group	27	14	13
Jino Ethnic Group	27	9	18
Ewenki Ethnic Group	25	12	13
Jing Ethnic Group	25	14	11
Achang Ethnic Group	19	6	13
Monba Ethnic Group	16	8	8
Hezhe Ethnic Group	12	6	6
The Naturalized	11	6	5
Bonan Ethnic Group	9	8	1
Derung Ethnic Group	9	5	4
De'ang Ethnic Group	5	1	4
Uzbek Ethnic Group	4	2	2
Oroqen Ethnic Group	3	3	
Tajik Ethnic Group	2	1	1
Lhoba Ethnic Group	2	2	
Tatar Ethnic Group	1		1

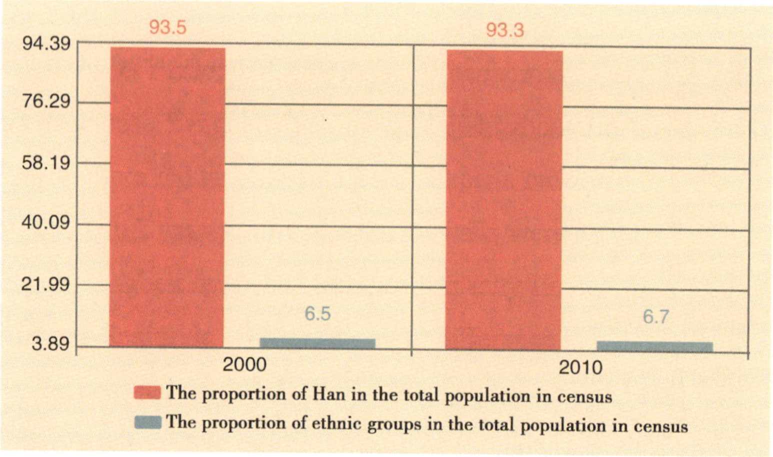

Picture 2-18 Chongqing Han and Ethnic Groups Proportion (data from the 5th and the 6th demographic census)

Ⅲ.Population Distribution

1.Population Density

Chongqing is one of the areas that are most densely populated. From the 17th year of Jiaqing (嘉庆) (1812) in the mid-Qing Dynasty, the population density of Chongqing Fu (重庆府) was 78 people per square kilometre. In the 2nd year of Xuantong (宣统) in the end of the Qing Dynasty, the population density increased to about 229 people per square kilometre.

In 1937, as a war-time capital, the large immigration of national government agencies, cultural units, universities and factories resulted in the explosive growth of population in Chongqing, and population density also reached a peak. According to statistics in 1944, the Chongqing population density reached about 3,566 people per square kilometre. After the victory of the War of Resistance Against Jappanese Aggeression, the national government moved back to Nanjing. With the emigration of several universities and factories, population density saw a drop.

After the founding of the People's Republic of China, as the Chongqing jurisdiction experienced continuous adjustment, its population density also witnessed fluctuation. In 1985, the population density was about 608 people per square kilometre. After it became a municipality directly under the central government in 1997, Chongqing area was expanded to 82.4 thousand square kilometre, and its population density dropped to 349 people per square kilometre. Hereafter, with the increase of migrant workers, its population density dropped slightly year by year. In 2004, it reached its bottom with 339 people per square kilometre. Afterwards, its population density increased year by year. In 2017, it was 373 people per square kilometre.

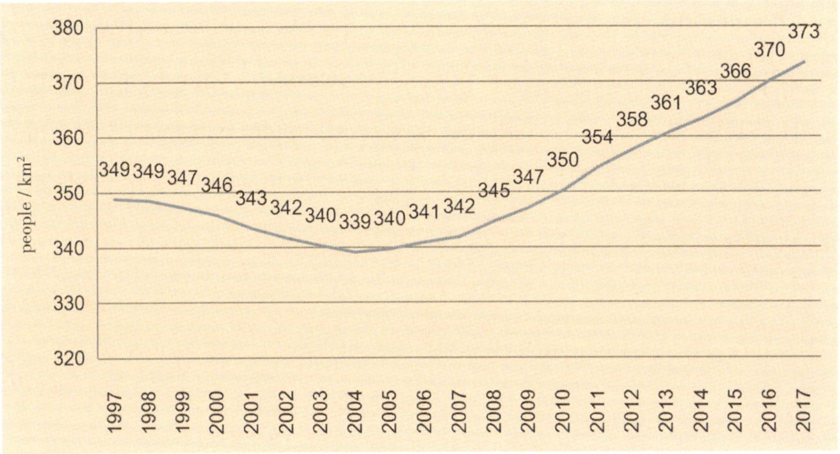

Picture 2-19 The Change of Chongqing Population Density Between 1997 and 2017

2.Characteristics of Distribution

The distribution of Chongqing population is extremely unbalanced. According to statistics in 2017, among those 38 districts and counties (including autonomous counties), there were 8 districts whose population density was above 1,000 people per square kilometre. They covered a total area of 3,644 square kilometres, and the gross population was 7.3996 million, and the average population density was 2,031 people per square kilometre. The most densely populated area was Yuzhong District, and the population density was as high as 28,239 people per square kilomctre. The least densely populated area was Beibei District (北碚区), and the population density was as high as 1,047 people per square kilometre. There were 8 areas whose population density was 500 to 1,000 people per square kilometre. They covered a total area of 11,933 square kilometres. The gross population was 7.1641 million, and the average population density was 600 people per square kilometre. There were 13 areas whose population density was 200 to 500 people per square kilometre. They covered a total area of 35,075 square kilometres, and the gross population was 12.1285 million, and the average population density was 346 people per square kilometres. There were 9 areas whose population density was above 0-200 people per square kilometre. They covered a total area of 31,718 square kilometres, and the gross population was 4.1187 million, and the average population density was 130 people per square kilometre. The population density in Chengkou County (城口县) was the lowest, only 57 people per square kilometre. Compared with the most densely populated Yuzhong District, the latter was 475 times of the former (2017).

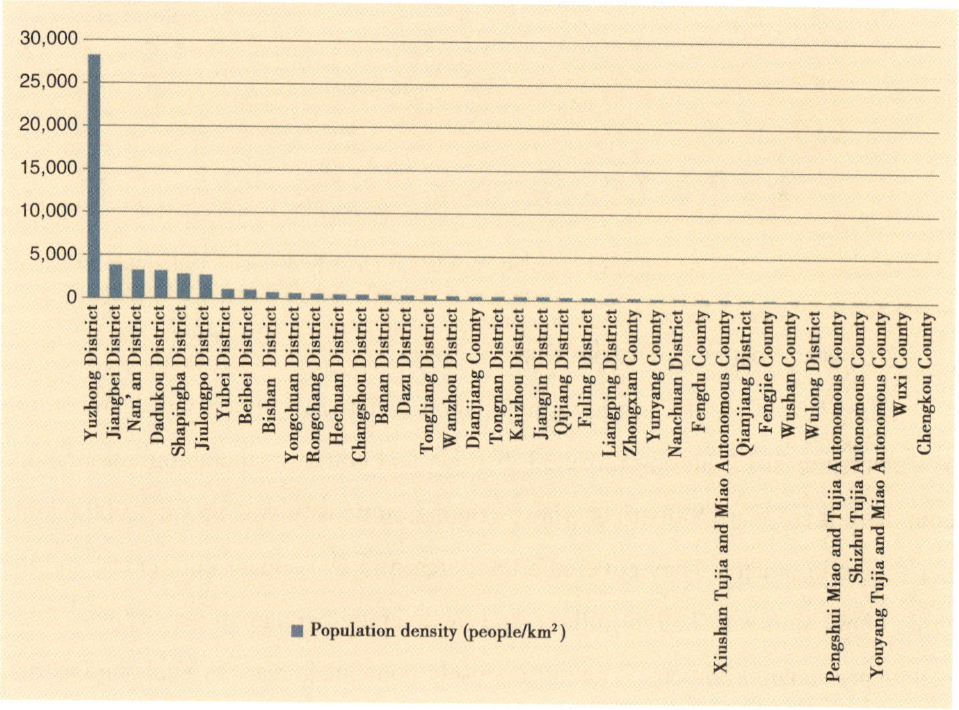

Picture 2-20 Population Density in Each District and County in Chongqing

Topography and economy are the most important factors that influence Chongqing population distribution. The city can be divided into two parts—the east and the west if a straight line is drawn from Chengkou-Fengdu-Baima Town of Wulong (城口 — 丰都 — 武隆白马镇). The west of this line covers 45% area of Chongqing, but the population was 70% of the city. The east of this line covers 55% area of Chongqing, but the population was 30% of the city. The terrain in the west of the Chengkou-Fengdu-Baima Town of Wulong line is mainly characterized by hills and is relatively low. It is also the most developed area of Chongqing. In the east of this line, the north, east and south are surrounded by low mountains such as the Daba Mountain, the Wushan Mountain, the Qiyao Mountain and the Wuling Mountain. The rugged terrain is characterized mainly by mountainous regions. It is also the underdeveloped area.

3.The Distribution of Nationalities

In the long process of historical development, the Hans and ethnic minorities live together over vast areas while some minorities live in concentrated communities in small areas.

Qianjiang District, Shizhu Tujia Autonomous County, Pengshui Miao and Tujia Autonomous County, Youyang Tujia and Miao Autonomous County, and Xiushan Tujia and Miao Autonomous County are main areas where ethnic minorities concentrate. They are called by a joint name—southeast Chongqing ethnic area. This area is located in the west of Wuling Mountain, and it borders western Hunan Xiangxi Tujia and Miao Autonomous Prefecture (湖南湘西土家族苗族自治州) and Hubei Enshi Tujia and Miao Autonomous Prefecture (湖北恩施土家族苗族自治州) in the east, Tongren City (铜仁市) of Guizhou Province in the south, and this area is the junction of Chongqing, Guizhou, Hunan and Hubei Provinces. It is not only the concentrated community of ethnic minorities, but also the old revolutionary area. Meanwhile, it is also the national poverty stricken area. It covers an area of 16.9 thousand kilometre, accounting for 20.5% of the total area of Chongqing. The overall population is 2.485 million (permanent residents) with 1.769 million ethnic minority population, accounting for 91.3% of the total ethnic minority population in

Chongqing. Besides, the number of the ethnic minority population who lives scattered is 144 thousand, accounting for 8.7% of the total ethnic minority population in the city. There are 14 ethnic townships. Among them, 10 are Tujia ethnic townships, and they are Henghe (恒合) in Wanzhou District (万州区), Dibao (地宝) in Wanzhou District, Mozi (磨子) in Zhongxian County (忠县), Qingshui (清水) in Yunyang County (云阳县), Yunwu (云雾), Longqiao (龙桥), Changan (长安), Taihe (太和) in Fengjie County (奉节县), Hongchun (红椿) and Dengjia (邓家) in Wushan County. Three towns are Miao and Tujia ethnic towns, and they are Houping, Wenfu and Houping (后坪), Wenfu (文复), Shiqiao (石桥) in Wulong District. One town is Miao and Kelao ethnic town, and it is Haokou in Wulong District. Ethnic minorities can also be found in other districts and counties.

4.The Quality of Population

The average education years in Chongqing witnesses an increase, and the proportion of highly educated population rises. After it became a municipality directly under the central government in 1997, Chongqing has consistently put education causes on its top priority and unswervingly implemented the strategy of rejuvenating Chongqing through science and education. Through increasing investment in education, expanding the scope of education, enhancing education level and exploring education resources, Chongqing has been trying to achieve the overall promotion of the cultural quality of its people. Among the population over 6 years old, the proportion of people with college degree or above increased from 3.4% in 2000 to 15.4% in 2016, an increase of 12.0%. The proportion of people with high school education increased from 9.6% to 18.9%, an increase of 9.3%. The proportion of people with junior high school education increased from 29.5% to 31.2%, an increase of 1.7%. The proportion of people with primary school education or lower dropped from 57.5% in 2000 to 34.5% in 2016, a decrease of 23.0%. On the whole, the proportion of the population with higher education increased, while that of the population with lower education decreased. With the promotion of the degree of education, the average education years of people above 15 years old witnessed an increase year by year. In 2016, the average length of education in Chongqing population was 9.76 years, an increase of 2.51 years compared with 7.25 years in 2000. The average education level of the whole city's population has transformed from junior high school to senior high school.

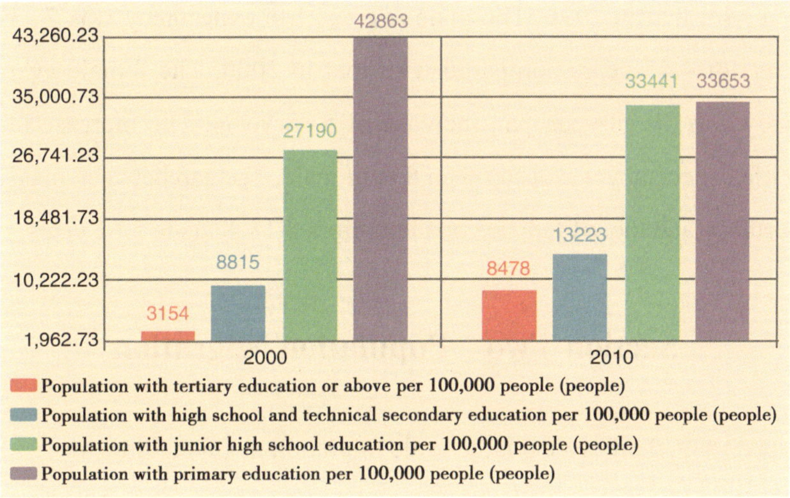

Picture 2-21 Education Structure of Registered Residence in Chongqing (data from the 5th census and the 6th census)

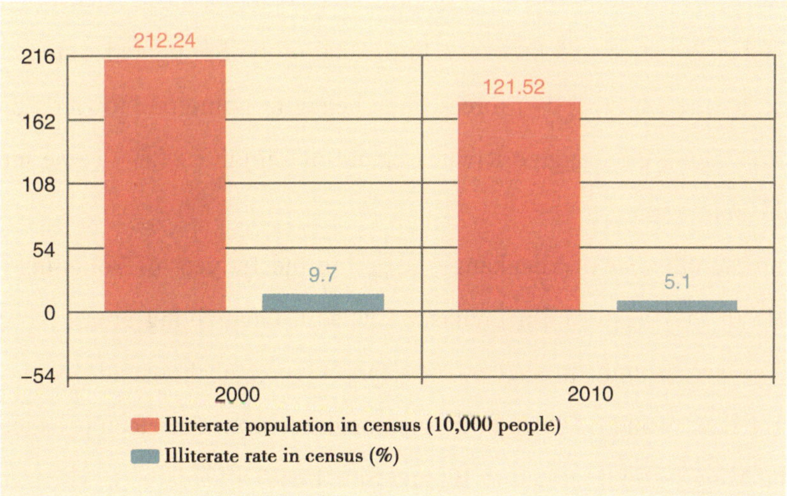

Picture 2-22 Chongqing Illiterate Population and Illiterate Rate (data from the 5th census and the 6th census)

The improvement of living conditions contributes to the increase of the average life expectancy. With the fast development of social economy, people's livelihood sees continuous improvement. Medical and health care system improves gradually, and Chongqing infant mortality rate drops sharply, and public health improves gradually, and the average life expectancy increases continuously. In 2016, Chongqing average life expectancy was 77 years, an increase of 6.59 years compared with that in 1996. The male average life expectancy was 74.37 years, an increase of 4.45 years compared with that in 2000. The female average life expectancy was 79.98 years, an increase of 5.88 years. The increase of female average life expectancy was faster than that of male. The gap between male average life expectancy and that of female expanded from 4.18 years to 5.61 years.

Section Two　Population Migration

Before 1949, there were 6 large-scale migration in Chongqing area.

According to experts, in the Spring and Autumn Period (春秋时期), besides the Ba State, which was enfeoffed by Zhou Dynasty (周朝) with "Ji" (姬) as the family name, Ba tribes in the form of primitive society concentrated in Qingjiang area of Hubei Province (湖北清江). In the end of the Spring and Autumn Period, oppressed by the Chu (楚国) forces, they began to immigrate towards the Three Gorges area along the Yangtze River. Legend of Linjun (廪君) came into being during this migration.

From the 6th year of Yuankang (元康) to the 1st year of Yongning (永宁) (296-301) in the Western Jin Dynasty (西晋), Guanzhong area (关中地区) suffered severe drought in successive years. Over 100 thousand people of Han (汉), Di (氐), Qiang (羌) and other nationalities from 6 prefectures such as Qin (秦) and Yong (雍) migrated to Ba and Shu areas (巴蜀地区), which triggered "Refugees Uprising" (流民起义) led by Li Te (李特) and Li Xiong (李雄).

In the 1st year of Yongjia (永嘉) in the Western Jin Dynasty, influenced by the "Upheaval of the Eight Princes" (八王之乱) and the "Refugees Uprising", Chongqing area suffered chaos caused by war and famines. Large numbers of residents migrated to Jingxiang (荆湘), and the population dropped sharply, and cities and towns became empty, and villages became stagnant. The once prosperous Jiangzhou City (Chongqing nowadays) became a deserted city with only hundreds of households.

In the 4th year of Xiankang (咸康) (338) in the Eastern Jin Dynasty (东晋), the Liao People (僚人) who once lived in the alpine regions in the borders of Guizhou Province and Sichuan Province migrated to the hills of central Sichuan and plains of western Sichuan. At first, the migration scale was over 100 thousand households, and later it increased to over 3 million households. The Ba-Yu area was also the migration destination where the Liao People concentrated. The number of Liao People was so large in Hechuan District and Tongliang District nowadays that the Southern Qi Dynasty (南齐) (479-502) changed it to Dongdangqu Liao County (东宕渠僚郡). Qijiang, historically called Yelangxi (夜郎溪), got this name from the Liao People's residence. Tongnan, Dazu and Rongchang areas were also the residence of the Liao People.

In the end of the Ming Dynasty and the early Qing Dynasty, peasant uprisings brought great social upheavals. For example, peasant rebels led by Zhang Xianzhong (张献忠) once broke into Chongqing City through Tongyuan Gate (通远门). Frequent wars resulted in a great loss of population in Sichuan and Chongqing area. In the 10th year of Kangxi in the Qing Dynasty (清康熙), in order to resume production, the government adopted a policy to grant citizenship for poor peasants who were willing to bring their family to Sichuan and reclaim land there. As a result, immigrants came in flocks, with the largest number of people from Hunan and Hubei. In the 17th year of Jiaqing (1812), the population in Chongqing Fu was already 2.34 million, and 85% of the population were immigrants from outside.

During the War of Resistance Against Japanese Aggression, as the national government moved to Chongqing, government agencies and organizations, enterprises and public institutions and people in occupied areas also moved to Chongqing. The population in Chongqing saw a sharp increase. According to incomplete statistics, after the outbreak of this war, about 1 million people from coastal regions and areas along the Yangtze River immigrated to Chongqing and its adjacent areas along the Yangtze River. The population in Chongqing then increased 1.23 times. Migrant population accounted for more than one half of Chongqing total population. After the victory of the War of Resistance Against Japanese Aggression, most of the migrant population came back to their native areas. The population in Chongqing downtown decreased from 1.2551 million in 1945 to 1.0057 million in 1946.

To summarize the internal reasons behind the above 6 population migrations were either wars or natural disasters, once these factors disappeared, the population showed a tendency of reverse flow or consequent flow, namely, immigrants went back to their native areas and emigrants came back to Chongqing.

According to the administrative division then (similarly hereinafter), from 1950 to 1978 (excluding 1954, 1967 and 1968 without data), the number of population migration was 9.972 million, and the number of annual average migration was 384 thousand, and the migration rate was 7.19%. The accumulative number of immigrants was 5.112 million, and that of emigrants was 4.8605 million, a mechanical increase of 251.5 thousand. The change of population migration is restricted by social, economic and political factors, the scale and speed differed from time to time. There were 3 climaxes of population migration.

The first population migration climax occurred at the beginning of the founding of the People's Republic of China. After Chongqing was liberated on November 30th, 1949, it became the station of Southwest Military and Political

Commission. In March 1953, it became a municipality directly under the central government. In order to strengthen the new people's regime, a large batch of cadres who came to the south and their family members became the main body of immigrant population. During the 4 years between 1950 and 1953, the total number of migrations was 1.013 million, and the number of annual average migration was 253.9 thousand. Among them, the number of immigrants was 581 thousand, and that of emigrants was 432 thousand, and the mechanical increase rate was 4.65%. It much higher than the natural growth rate (1.9%) in the corresponding period. In 1954, the Southwest Military and Political Commission was repealed. Chongqing changed from a municipality directly under the central government to a city in Sichuan province, and a large number of people emigrated. In 1955, 565 thousand people emigrated from Chongqing, and they outnumbered the people who immigrated to Chongqing by 39 thousand. The net emigration rate was 31.3%.

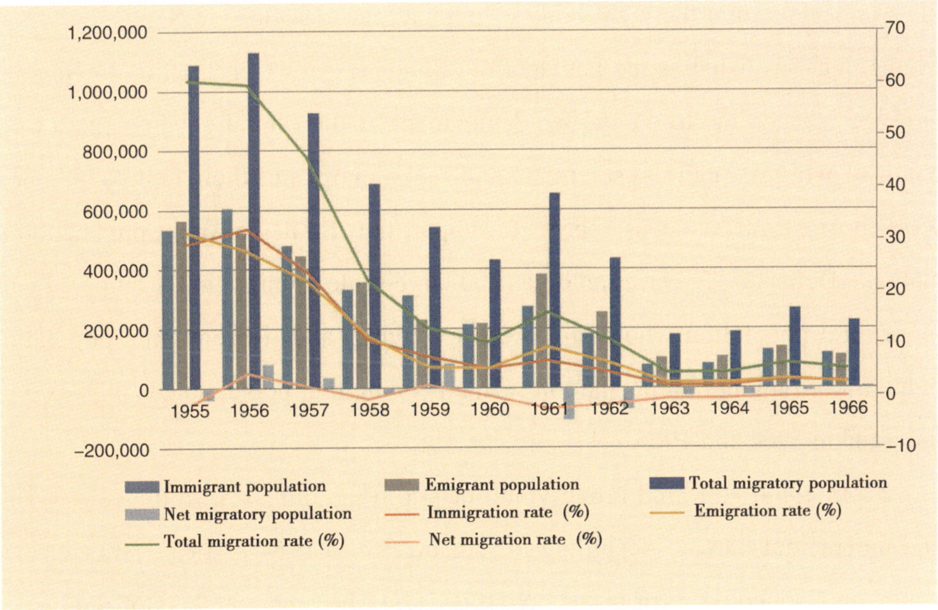

Picture 2-23 Chongqing Population Migration Status from 1955 to 1966

The second climax of population migration occurred in late 1950s and early 1960s. In the three difficult years between 1959 and 1961, rural population migrated outside. From the second half of 1961 to the end of May in 1963, in order to curtail urban population, 19.6 thousand staff were cut down from the labour force, and 250 thousand workers recruited from the rural areas were sent back to rural areas. From 1960 to 1963, 955 thousand people emigrated from Chongqing and outnumbered the people who immigrated to Chongqing by 208 thousand. The net emigration rate was 1.26%. The year of 1961 witnessed the most obvious imbalance of population migration. The emigrant population outnumbered immigrant population by 109 thousand, and the net emigration rate was as high as 2.63%. A migration climax with emigrant population outnumbering immigrant population was formed.

The third climax of population migration occurred from mid-1960s to before reform and opening-up. During this period, people who supported the "Strategic Area Construction in National Defence" immigrated to Chongqing, together with educated youths who went to the countryside and emigrants who went to support the frontier, became the main body of population migration. In September 1964, Chongqing was listed as the key area of "Strategic Area Construction in National Defence". According to the unified deployment by the central government, a large batch of workers, cadres, scientists and technicians and their family members were chosen from east coastal areas to support the "Strategic Area Construction in National Defence". This was an organized large-scale immigration. Compared with more rural population who emigrated for a living, and the emigrant population outnumbered immigrant population with a net emigrant population as high as 32.5 thousand in 1964 and 1965.

From 1964, educated urban youth began to go and work in the countryside and mountainous areas. According to statistics, from 1964 to 1977, 380 educated youths in Chongqing went to the countryside and became members of production teams, and over 21 thousand educated youths went to Yunnan to support frontier construction. During this period, the number of net migration population was 86 thousand. In 1977, educated youths stopped going to the countryside and began to go back to cities which reached a peak in 1979. The immigrant population was offset by the emigrant population. The mechanical increase was 67 thousand and the net migration rate was 1.07%.

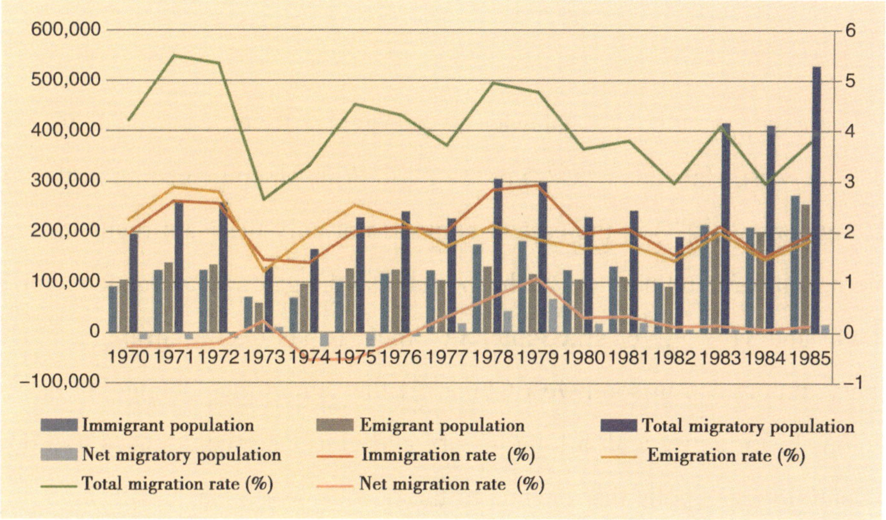

Picture 2-24 Chongqing Population Migration Status from 1970 to 1985

Since reform and opening-up, the nature of Chongqing migration was not only different from forced migration caused by wars or disasters before liberation, but also different from planned and organized migration under the planned economy before 1978. It became spontaneous population flow under the market economy. Inter-provincial labour export and import became the main factors behind population migration. Among the army of migrant labours, construction crew, individual peddlers, domestic labours and handicraftsmen were the main body.

Chapter Three Historical Development

Chongqing, as a golden gateway of the Yangtze River, connects Sanshu (三蜀) in the west, Hanmian (汉沔) in the north, Yunnan and Guizhou in the south, and Jingxiang (荆襄) in the east. It controls not only the main roads in eastern, western, southern and northern Sichuan, but also the gateway to Yunnan, Guizhou, Sichuan and Tibet. Ever since ancient times, it has been a strategic place of military importance in southwest China. At the same time, Chongqing has been a famous historic city with a long history and glorious revolutionary tradition. It is a central megalopolis that opened to the outside world early, with high degree of modernization and fast development of economy, culture and education. The dynamic integration of natural conditions with history and culture contributes to the increasing importance of Chongqing. In the history of the Chinese nation, Chongqing has contributed a series of important and amazing events that evoked both praises and tears. Numerous heroic figures with eternal fames emerged.

Section One Ancient Times

Ⅰ.Human Activities in Prehistoric Times

The history of Chongqing can be traced back to remote prehistoric era. The oldest primitive men was "Wushan Man" (巫山人) which found in Longgupo Site, Miaoyu Town of Wushan County (巫山县庙宇镇龙骨坡) and can be dated back to more than 2 million years ago. Judging from the Neolithic culture—"Daxi Culture"

(大溪文化) found in Daxi Town of Wushan County (巫山县大溪镇), the convenience brought about by the Yangtze River and the Jialing River enabled the pre-historic humans whose living was dependent on water to form dense primitive villages 6,000 or 5,000 thousand years ago along both sides of the Yangtze River.

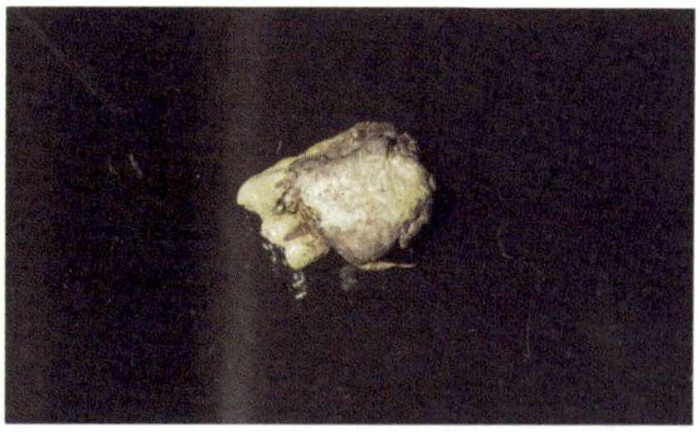

Picture 3-1 The Left Mandible of the "Wushan Man" Found in Longgupo Site, Miaoyu Town of Wushan County

Ⅱ.The State of Ba (巴国) in Slavery System

In the 11th century B.C., King Wu of Zhou (周武王) granted Ba area to the member of the royal clan with the family name Ji (姬). In its heyday, its territory reached Yufu (鱼复) (Fengjie in Chongqing nowadays) in the east, Bodao (僰道) [Yibin (宜宾) in Sichuan Province nowadays] in the west, Hanzhong (汉中) [Nanzheng (南郑) in Shaanxi Province nowadays] in the north, and Qianfu (黔涪) (from Pengshui and Qianjiang to northeast Guizhou Province and northwest Hunan Province) in the west. Its territory included south Shaanxi Province, west Hubei Province, northwest Hunan Province, north Guizhou Province and east Chongqing. The Ba people (巴人) were sincere and loyal to friends. They were also arduous and industrious, shrewd and brave, and good at singing and dancing. They were mainly engaged in farming, hunting, fishing, copper smelting, paint producing, wine brewing, salt trading, etc. In their long-term production activities, they created the unique Ba culture. The loyal and brave story of general Ba Manzi (巴蔓子) passed down till today and is still touching those who hear it.

Legend has it that over 2,000 years ago, civil strife occurred in the declining Ba State. Manzi, the senior general of Ba, acted under orders and asked the King of Chu (楚王) for rescue. He promised the King of Chu that after quelling the civil

Picture 3-2 The Statue of General Ba Manzi

strife, the Ba State would cede 3 cities to the Chu State. Before long, Chu State helped Ba State quell the civil strife and sent an envoy to Ba State for the promised 3 cities. In order to preserve the Ba State, Manzi admitted his promise but refused to cede 3 cities to the Chu State (楚国). He thanked Chu for its help in quelling the civil strife by chopping off his own head. The envoy of Chu brought Manzi's head back to Chu as a gratitude to the King who was touched by Manzi and ordered an elaborate funeral for Manzi's head. In praise of his loyal act, the King of Ba also ordered a ritualized funeral for Manzi's body. The General's Tomb in the main district of Qixinggang (七星岗) Chongqing was regarded by legend as the tomb of general Manzi.

Ⅲ.Ba Jun (巴郡) During the Qin and Han (秦汉) Dynasties

In 316 B.C., the Hui emperor of Qin (秦惠王) ordered Zhang Yi (张仪) and Sima Cuo (司马错) to annihilate the Shu State (蜀国) and the Ba State. In 314 B.C., Qin established Ba Jun [1] in previous Ba State. From the Han Dynasty to the Western Jin Dynasty (西晋), eastern Chongqing and northern Sichuan area with Chongqing as its centre followed the Qin System by establishing

Picture 3-3 Sculptures on the Siege of the City on Tongyuan Gate

[1] Jun is an ancient administrative area, which was larger than county in the Qin Dynasty.

the Ba Jun. Although changes were seen in its jurisdiction, all set Jiangzhou (江州) as the seat of local government.

The local government of Ba Jun under Qin was first established in Langzhong (阆中) of Sichuan Province, which also governed the 9 counties in Hanzhong. Four years later, Qin established Hanzhong Jun (汉中郡), the local government moved to Dianjiang (垫江) (Hechuan in Chongqing nowadays). As the salt in Bashu (巴蜀) and Hanzhong area is dependent on the supply of Badong (巴东) salt spring, Zhi (枳) (Fuling nowadays) and other areas in the lower reaches were occupied by the State of Chu. Badong salt spring was controlled by Chu. In order to get the salt spring, Zhang Yi chose to build Jiangzhou City in the water transportation hub—the confluence of the Yangtze River and the Jialing River as the new local government of Ba and logistic base for future attack against Chu. This was the beginning of Chongqing and the beginning of Chongqing as the regional political and economic centre of eastern Sichuan.

According to *Huayang Local Chronicles*, in the Han Dynasty, the local government of Ba Jun was in Beifu City (北府城) in the north of the Ba River (巴水) (the Jialing River nowadays), that is the old city of Jiangbei (江北) in Jiangbeizui (江北嘴). According to the ancient Chinese geography classic *Commentaries on the Waterway* (《水经注》), the east of Jiangzhou City was the Yangtze River and the west of Jiangzhou was the Jialing River. Therefore, it can be confirmed that Jiangzhou City was in the site of Jiangbeizui. In early November 2005, a large number of city wall ruins and eave tile pieces in the Qin and Han Dynasties were found in the construction site of the Central Business District (CBD) of Jiangbeicheng (江北城). This archaeologically confirmed that Jiangzhou in the Qin and Han Dynasties was located in Beifu City (北府城) north of the Jialing River. In recent years, through archaeological excavation of the Han Dynasty tombs in Yuzhong Peninsula (渝中半岛), experts reckoned that in the Qin and Han Dynasties, with the development of Jiangzhou's economy, a pattern called "Government in the North and City in the South" ("北府南城") with Jiangbeicheng as its political centre and Yuzhong Peninsula as its economic centre was formed. Why did Zhang Yi choose Jiangbei when he built Jiangzhou City instead of Yuzhong Peninsula with more military advantages？ Experts reckoned that the first reason is that in early Qin Dynasty, all Chinese city walls were earthen walls, and it was the same with Jiangbeicheng. The technical capacity limited the construction of a city in Yuzhong Peninsula with great height difference and complex topographic condition. Second, judging from the political and economic environment of the Qin and Han Dynasties, the political centre of China was in Guanzhong (关中), and little development was made in the middle and lower reaches of the Yangtze River. At this time, the Yangtze River was more like a boundary of civilization and along the Jialing River and against the current was closer to the centre of civilization. Sichuan was always regarded as the auxiliary of Guanzhong, and it was relatively stable without chaos caused by wars. As a result, Beifu City which was to the benefit of the transportation of the Jialing River was more preferable to Yuzhong Peninsula with more military advantages as a suitable site for Jiangzhou City.

After the State of Qin annexed Bashu, it took advantage of the wealth such as rice and silk in Bayu area as well as the bravery of the Ba people to enrich its political, economic and military power, and it successively annihilated the other six states. In 221 B.C., the State of Qin established the first unified feudal dynasty in Chinese history, the Qin Dynasty.

In the end of the peasant uprisings in late Qin Dynasty, Chu and Han became rivals. Liu Bang (刘邦), trapped in Hanzhong, took advantage of the abundance and human resources of the Bashu area and fought into Guanzhong and annihilated Xiang Yu (项羽), and he established a powerful dynasty called the Western Han Dynasty (西汉王朝).

In the 1st year of the Eastern Han Dynasty (东汉王朝) (25-36), Gongsun

Shu (公孙述), a general of Wang Mang (王莽), set up a separatist regime in the Bashu area and claimed himself to be king. In the strategic highlands at the mouth of the Qutang Gorge (瞿塘峡), he built a city called Ziyang City (子阳城) and stationed troops. As the white gas emitted in this city was like a white dragon, he proclaimed himself as the "Baidi" (白帝), and this city was thus called "Baidicheng" (白帝城).

In the Three Kingdoms period of late Eastern Han Dynasty, the military regime of Liu Bei (刘备) and Shuhan (蜀汉) area attached great importance to the management of the Yangtze River waterway in Jiangzhou and Bayu area. From the 1st year of Zhangwu (章武) to the 2nd year of Zhangwu (221-222), the State of Shu (蜀国) was defeated in the Battle of Yiling (夷陵之战) [also called the Battle of Xiaoting (猇亭之战)]. Liu Bei stationed in Baidicheng until his death. The allusion "Entrusting Orphan in Baidicheng" (白帝城托孤) was left behind.[1] In the 4th year of Jianxing (蜀建兴) (226), Duxianghou (都乡侯)[2] Li Yan (李严) became a general and moved to Jiangzhou City as Jiangzhou Duhu (都护)[3]. It was here that Li Yan organized the second construction of Jiangzhou City. The old city of Jiangzhou was in the north shore of the Yangtze River and the Jialing River confluence, in the Jiangbeizui area. It was built by Sima Cuo and Zhang Yi after the State of Ba was annihilated. From a military perspective, it is hard to guard the city here. After

Picture 3-4 Baidicheng in Fengjie

[1] Before death, the emperor of Shu, Liu Bei entrusted his adolescent son Liu Chan to his prime minister Zhuge Liang. Liu Bei urged Zhuge Liang that if Liu Chan was capable of being a good emperor, Zhuge liang should assist him; if his son was incapable, Zhuge Liang should replace him and claim himself to be emperor.

[2] an official rank in ancient China

[3] an official rank in ancient China

inspecting the surrounding environment of Jiangzhou City, Li Yan chose Yuzhong Peninsula as the new site for construction. Yuzhong Peninsula was also located in the confluence of the Yangtze River and the Jialing River, but it was between these two rivers. Its mountainous topography was surrounded by water on three sides which was easy to guard and hard to attack. It can be said that the insight of Li Yan was very shrewd, and it demonstrated the strategic choice of a military expert. According to experts, the scale of this construction was rather large. The south line along the river started from Chaotianmen (朝天门) to Nanjimen (南纪门), and the north line went along Daliangzi (大梁子), People's Park, and Jiaochangkou (较场口) (this is the ridge line of Yuzhong Peninsula). It covered an area of 2 square kilometres, and its scale was as large as the size of Chongqing City in Ming and Qing Dynasties. Except Tongyuan Gate which was not included in the city, the scale almost overlapped the construction by Dai Ding (戴鼎) in the Ming Dynasty. Therefore, this city was also called "the Big City of Li Yan". Different from the stone city walls we see now, these city walls were rammed by earth with two city gates called Qinglong Gate (青龙门) and Baihu Gate (白虎门). Qinglong Gate was near Chaotianmen nowadays. It was the starting point of the waterway. Baihu Gate was near Tongyuan Gate nowadays, it was the starting point of the land route. Li Yan also built Cangcheng (仓城) as a specific place to store army provisions inside this city. It was near Qiansimen (千厮门) nowadays. Fotuguan (佛图关) in west Chongqing was the only land route to Chengdu. It was surrounded by water on two sides and cliffs on three sides. Its precipitous terrain made it the most dangerous one among the four frontier fortresses and also a historic fort of strategic and military importance. Li Yan built Weicheng City (卫城) here

Picture 3-5　Baoding Gate (保定门)

to guard Chongqing city behind it. Besides, Li Yan also projected to cut through mountains to connect the Yangtze River and the Jialing River, thus Jiangzhou City would be an island city surrounded by water on four sides.

Ⅳ.Change of Organizational System in the Three Kingdoms Period, the Jin Dynasties (两晋) and the Southern and Northern Dynasties (南北朝)

In the Jin Dynasties and the Southern and Northern Dynasties afterwards, national secessions and frequent wars resulted in changes in Chongqing jurisdiction for many times. Jingzhou (荆州) (311), Bazhou (巴州) (553) and Chuzhou (楚州) (557) were established successively. After the establishment of the Sui Dynasty (隋朝) in 581, the state and county systems were carried out at the local level. In the 3rd year of Kaihuang (开皇) (583), "Chuzhou" (楚州) was renamed "Yuzhou" (渝州) (as the Jialing River was also called the Yushui River) in the Sui Dynasty. Its jurisdiction included three counties—Ba County, Jiangyang (江阳) (Jiangjin nowadays) and Hanping (汉平) (Fuling nowadays). When it came to the Tang Dynasty (唐朝), the Former and Later Shu (前后蜀) and the Northern Song Dynasty (北宋), although its jurisdiction and subjection experienced changes, Chongqing area had been called "Yuzhou" for over 500 years until the end of the Northern Song Dynasty. Nowadays, the abbreviation of Chongqing—"Yu" was originated from here.

Ⅴ.Gongzhou Fu (恭州府) and Chongqing Fu (重庆府) in the Northen Song and Southern Song Dynasties

In late Northern Song Dynasty, Zhao Shen (赵谂), a rebel from Yuzhou was killed. Taking the meaning of "exercising penalty in the name of God" (恭行天罚),

the ruler of the Northern Song Dynasty changed the name Yuzhou to "Gongzhou" (恭州) in the first year of Chongning (崇宁) (1102) and this name was used until the Southern Song Dynasty (南宋). In the first year of Longxing (隆兴) of the Southern Song Dynasty, Zhao Shen (赵昚), emperor Xiaozong of Song (宋孝宗) conferred the title "King Gong in Gongzhou" (恭州恭王) to his second son Zhao Dun. In February of the 16th year of Chunxi (淳熙) (1189), emperor Xiaozong of Song passed the throne to Zhao Dun, who became emperor Guangzong (光宗) of the Southern Song Dynasty. When the emperor of Guangzong ascended to the throne, according to the observance in the Song Dynasty, the area under the administration of "Fan"(藩) was to ascend to "Fu"(府) when he ascended to the throne one day. Thus, Gongzhou was renamed "Chongqing Fu" (重庆府) in that August. Later, the name of Chongqing has been used for over 800 years and is still in use today.

Picture 3-6 Protector Gate of Diaoyucheng

The Southern Song Dynasty enhanced Chongqing's status in Chinese history, and Chongqing also made indelible and remarkable contribution to the preservation of this dynasty. This was the epoch-making event "the Battle in Diaoyucheng" (钓鱼城之战) that almost rewrote world history.

In the 2nd year of Duanping (端平) (1235) in the Southern Song Dynasty, the Mongolian Army attacked the Southern Song Dynasty in two battalions. The eastern battalion attacked Xiangyang (襄阳) and the western battalion targeted at Sichuan. In the following year, the Mongolian Army initiated massive attack towards Shu and swept the whole Sichuan. "All 54 prefectures were captured, only several ones such as Kuizhou (夔州), Lu (泸), Guo (果) and He (合) existed." In the next years, the Mongolian Army went southwards several times and harassed

Sichuan and other areas. In order to reverse the dangerous situation and consolidate the power, from 1239, the Southern Song government dispatched several batches of officials to build defence lines in the upper reaches of the Yangtze River in Sichuan. Chongqing, located in the confluence of two rivers that could lock the throat of Sichuan and emerged with strategic importance in the war against the Yuan (元) armies. If Chongqing was lost, the Mongolian Army could march along the river and attack the Southern Song Dynasty from two sides. The Southern Song government dispatched Peng Daya (彭大雅) as Deputy emissary of Sichuan and magistrate of Chongqing to station in Chongqing and manage the comprehensive defence matters in eastern Sichuan. When Peng Daya assumed office, regarding the strategic position of Chongqing, he decided to strengthen its defence at all costs by building city walls around Chongqing.

Peng Daya expanded Chongqing City to the riverbanks along the Jialing River, which was characterized by cliffs. As an old Chinese saying goes, "Cliff walls are impregnable". With the help of this geographic advantage, human and material resources required were greatly reduced, and the defence capability was greatly enhanced. Peng Daya also included large areas with relatively even topography in the north of Daliangzi (大梁子) ［Xinhua Road (新华路) nowadays］ in the city, adding difficulty for attack. In 2015, in the Jialing River side, near Chaotianmen and Xishuimen (西水门), relics of Peng Daya's city walls were excavated, which proved that what he built was a stone city. This excavated city wall was 10-meter wide. It was rammed inside with earth and outside covered by huge stones on which fine chisel marks could be detected easily. Although this city was built in the chaos caused by wars, it was not built in haste. Every rectangular slab of stone was orderly arranged. After the completion of this construction, Peng Daya established 4 big stones on the city wall, on which "For the benefit of Shu, Peng Daya built Chongqing City in the Gengzi (庚子) year of Jiaxi (嘉熙) in the Song Dynasty" was inscribed.

Picture 3-7 Tongyuan Gate Wall

Meanwhile, Peng Daya sent lieutenant general Gan Run (甘闰) to stay in Hezhou (合州) (Hechuan nowadays) as the outpost for Chongqing to resist the Mongolian Army. Hezhou was the confluence of the Jialing River and its two branches—the Fujiang River (涪江) and the Qujiang River (渠江). The Jialing River ran from south to the north, and it converged with the Qujiang River first. Blocked by the Diaoyu Mountain (钓鱼山), it turned to the west to converge with the Fujiang River. Bypassing this mountain, it ran towards the north and met the Diaoyu Mountain again and then it turned southward. Thus, Diaoyu Mountain was surrounded by water on three sides. Gan Run found this mountain lofty and precipitous, and its geographic position was so perfect that it could restrict the Qujiang River in the northwest, Jialing River in the north, and Fujiang River in the east. Hence, he built Diaoyucheng (钓鱼城) here as mutual horns with Chongqing.

In 1242, the Southern Song government assigned Yu Jie (余玠) as Minister of War, emissary of Sichuan and magistrate of Chongqing. Yu Jie moved Sichuan military commission to Chongqing to manage the comprehensive defence matters in Sichuan. Chongqing thus became the political and military centre of Sichuan area for the first time. While in office, Yu Jie took the advice of the Ran brothers (冉氏兄弟) by moving Hezhou government to Diaoyu Mountain and built over 20 towns on this mountain so as to connect it with the 11 towns around. Therefore, a natural defence system with Diaoyucheng in Hezhou as a centre was formed.

Table 3-1 Eastern Sichuan Fortified Mountain Villages that Have Been Preserved to Date

Name of the village	Location	Name of the village	Location
Qingju Town	Now southeast of Nanchong City, Sichuan Province	Yunding Town	Now Jintang County, Sichuan Province
Tieniu Town	Now southeast of Peng'an County, Sichuan Province	Ziyun Town	Now Southeast of Qianwei County, Sichuan Province
Pingliang Town	Now south of Bazhong City, Sichuan Province	Xiaoning Town	Now east of Bazhong City, Sichuan Province
Dehan Town	Now east of Tongjiang County, Sichuan Province	Daliang Town	Now northeast of Guang'an City, Sichuan Province
Dahuo Town	Now south of Cangxi County, Sichuan Province	Dengaoshan Town	Now southeast of Yibin City, Sichuan Province
Shenbi Town	Now northwest of Hejiang County, Sichuan Province	Diaoyucheng	Now southeast of Nanchuan District, Chongqing
Santai Town	Now west of Fuling District, Chongqing	Longyan Town	Now southeast of Nanchuan District, Chongqing
Duogong Town	Now Yubei District, Chongqing	Panshi Town	Now the new county of Yunyang County, Chongqing
Tianci Town	Now northwest of Wushan County, Chongqing	Huanghua Town	Now east of Zhongxian Couty, in the middle of the Yangtze River, Chongqing
White Emperor Town	Now east of Fengjie County, Chongqing	Tiansheng Town	Now north of Wanzhou District, Chongqing
Chiniu Town	Now west of Liangping district, Chongqing		

In 1251, when Mongke (蒙哥) ascended to the throne as the Khan of Mongol, he actively prepared a war to annihilate the Song Dynasty. In 1258, his army was divided into 3 battalions to attack the Song Dynasty. He led main force with 40,000 armies into Sichuan with irresistible force until he was blocked by Diaoyucheng. Mongke the Khan supervised the military operations by himself in July 1259 and was injured by the huge cannon fired from inside the city. Leaving last words to massacre all inhabitants once this city was captured, he died in the following month in Wentang Gorge (温汤峡). Once Mongke the Khan died, many leaders and generals who were engaged in wars all over the world went back to the army to battle for the throne. An internal strife that would last for several years among the Mongolian nobles was ignited. The situation of the Eurasian war was thus reversed and the whole world history was rewritten. Afterwards, until the Southern Song Dynasty perished in 1279, the Mongolian army never managed to capture Diaoyucheng.

Ⅵ.The Founding of Capital by Xia (大夏) State

After the establishment of the Yuan Dynasty in 1271, Zhongshusheng (中书省)[1] was established, under it were Lu (路)[2], Fu[3], prefectures (州) and counties (县). Chongqing was once the capital of Sichuan Province. When the capital of Sichuan moved to Chengdu, Chongqing Lu (重庆路) was changed to Zongguan Fu (总管府) in 1279, as the residence of Sichuan South Xuanwei Si (宣慰司)[4], with one Si [Lushi Si (录事司)] , 3 counties (Ba County, Jiangjing and Nanchuan) and 4 prefectures (Hezhou, Fuzhou, Zhongzhou and Luzhou) under its jurisdiction. In late Yuan Dynasty, the leader of peasant uprising, Ming Yuzhen (明玉珍) led his army to attack Sichuan from Hubei in 1357. He occupied Chongqing and Sichuan and claimed to be king in Chongqing in 1363. The national

[1] a governmental agency

[2] a governmental agency under Zhongshusheng

[3] a governmental agency under Lu

[4] Si was a local governmental agency between province and prefecture.

title of this regime was set as "Xia" (夏), and the title of his reign was changed as "Tiantong" (天统). Chongqing was established as the capital. This was the second time for Chongqing to be established as a capital city. The territory of Xia reached Yichang (宜昌) in Hubei Province in the east, Chengdu and Leshan (乐山) in Sichuan Province in the west, Zunyi (遵义) and Tongzi (桐梓) in Guizhou Province in the south, and Hanzhong in Shaanxi Province and Wudu (武都) in Gansu Province in the north. Xia perished in the year 1371 and its territory was annexed into the Ming Dynasty.

Ⅶ.Chongqing in the Ming and Qing Dynasties

The Ming Dynasty established Chongqing Fu (重庆府) in Chongqing area, with its capital in the Ba County. Its jurisdiction included 3 prefectures, Hezhou, Zhongzhou and Fuzhou, 15 counties, Ba County, Jiangjin, Yongchuan, Rongchang, Dazu, Qijiang, Nanchuan, Changshou, Qianjiang, Tongliang, Dingyuan (定远) [Wusheng (武胜) nowadays], Fengdu, Dianjiang, Wulong and Pengshui. The Ming Dynasty also established Chongqing Wei (重庆卫), its jurisdiction included Shizhu and Youyang (酉阳) Xuanfu Si (宣抚司). In the years of Chenghua (成化), Bishan and Anju (安居) (Tongliang nowadays) were also included. The area of Chongqing Fu was almost the same with Chongqing today. To strengthen its rule in eastern Sichuan and Guizhou, the Ming Dynasty also sent officials rectifying armed forces to administer Chongqing Fu, Wei, each prefecture and county as well as national minority hereditary headmen in Guizhou and Youyang, etc. This demonstrated that in the Ming Dynasty, Chongqing had become a strategic city with military importance in Sichuan and Guizhou area. It was also a nationwide commercial port of importance.

In the end of the Yuan Dynasty, frequent wars greatly destroyed walls and moats of the city. Wrecked city walls and moats were not only detrimental to military defence but also brought inconvenience to people's living and hindered economic development. When the State of Xia died out, commander of Chongqing Wei, Dai Ding, rebuilt Chongqing city. According to *Chronicles of Ba County* (《巴县志》) in Qianlong (乾隆) period, "In early Hongwu (洪武) period of the Ming Dynasty, commander Dai Ding built a stone city here." Chongqing was handed over from Ming Sheng (明升)[1]. Chongqing, as the capital of the State of Xia, already had a certain scale and foundation. Therefore, Dai Ding's construction on Chongqing was a renovation on the basis of the capital of Xia. He laid stones for the city according to the mountain shapes and basically recovered Chongqing City form in the Song Dynasty.

The city built by Dai Ding was a stone city. All the city walls were built by rectangular stones. Compared with traditional earthen walls, they were firmer. The city walls were as high as 10 Zhangs (丈)[2]; the perimeter was 2,660 Zhangs and 7 Chis; the moat was along the river. According to the standard for weights and measures in the Ming Dynasty and Qing Dynasty, if converted into meters, the city walls were as high as 30 to 32 meters, and the perimeter was 8,000 to 8,500 meters. Its scale was as large as or larger than "the Big City of Li Yan" in the Shu and Han periods. Nowadays, people could still see 17 remnant city walls with a total length of 3,167.6 meters. 600 meters were sealed in the foundations and fort hills. Creation was made in the design of the city. Among the 17 gates, 9 could be opened and 8 could not be opened. This was Dai Ding's intention. Those 9 gates that could be opened stood for "nine palaces" (九宫), and those 8 gates that could not be opened stood for "eight diagrams" (八卦). With 9 opened and 8 closed, these gates stood for "nine palaces and eight diagrams", a theory of Yi-ology in ancient China. The "nine palaces and eight trigrams array" (九宫八卦阵) was derived from it and gradually became mainstream marching array in the Spring and Autumn Period and the Warring States Period. This design embodied Dai Ding's wish to

[1] the last king of Xia
[2] a unit of length, 1 Zhang≈3.3 meters

keep Chongqing stable forever.

In 1657, Chongqing was under the rule of the Qing government. Qing succeeded the Ming system by setting Chongqing area as Chongqing Fu. Its jurisdiction included 1 Ting (厅) —Jiangbei Ting (江北厅) and 2 Zhou (州) —He Zhou and Fu Zhou; its jurisdiction included 10 counties, Ba, Jiangjin, Changshou, Yongchuan, Rongchang, Jingjiang (景江), Nanchuan, Tongliang, Dazu, Dingyuan (Wusheng nowadays), and it established a town in Chongqing. The military headquarter was also set here, together with its east Sichuan branch, as the political and military agency in Chongqing area. After certain rehabilitation in early Qing Dynasty, Chongqing commodity economy burgeoned and saw primary development. Chongqing gradually developed from a strategic city of military importance in the Yuan and Ming periods to the most important commercial city in Sichuan and southwest China, and it laid foundation for Chongqing's modernization and formation of commercial hub in the days to come.

Section Two From Opening as a Commercial Port to the Eve of the War of Resistance Against Japanese Aggression

Ⅰ.From Opening as a Commercial Port to the Opium War

1.Chongqing Opened as a Commercial Port

After the Opium War (鸦片战争) in 1840, western colonial power penetrated towards Chinese interior. Chongqing, located in southwest China, suffered all-round aggression from foreign capitalism with religion as its vanguard, military as its backup, politics as its means and economic profit as its objective. Merchants, missionaries and tourists from the United Kingdom and the United States came to Chongqing in succession, making preparation for the establishment of consulates in Chongqing port as well as further economic and cultural penetration. In the 2nd year of Guangxu (光绪) (1876) in the Qing Dynasty, on the excuse of Incident of A.R. Margary (马嘉里事件), the United Kingdom forced the Qing government to sign *Sino-British Yantai Treaty* (《中英烟台条约》), which guaranteed the right to send staff to reside in Chongqing, thus foreshadowed the opening of Chongqing as a commercial port in the days to come. On March 31st 1890, China and the United Kingdom signed *Sino-British Yantai Treaty Amendment* (《烟台条约续增专约》) in Beijing. There are two most important clauses. First, Chongqing is opened as a commercial port at once the same as other ports. Second, it is of the United Kingdom merchants' will whether to freight from Yichang to Chongqing, or hire Chinese cargos, or prepare their own cargos. The United Kingdom formally acquired the right to open Chongqing as a commercial port.

On March 1st 1891, the establishment of Chongqing customs symbolized not only the formal opening of the Chongqing port, but also the penetration of imperialist powers led by the United Kingdom into the vast interior areas of west China. Following the United Kingdom, France, Japan, America, Germany came in succession and established consulates in Chongqing. While conducting political, economic, military and cultural aggression, they also took Chongqing as a springboard and bridgehead to start their total aggression in Sichuan and southwest China. The Japanese imperialists took advantage of its remining prestige in the Sino-Japanese War and forced the decayed Qing government to sign *Writ Between China and Japan* (《中日公立文凭》) on October 19th 1896, and they took it as legal basis for it to claim foreign concessions. After negotiating for several times, the Japanese consulate in Chongqing Yamasaki Katsura and eastern Sichuan Daoyin (川东道尹)[1] Bao Fen (宝

Picture 3-8 Wangjiatuo Japanese Concession

[1] an official title

菜) signed *Agreement on Japanese Merchants' Special Settlement in Chongqing* (《重庆日本商民专界约书》) on September 24th 1901, which guaranteed Japanese the privilege to establish foreign concession in Wangjiatuo (王家沱) of Nan'an District in Chongqing. The Japanese imperialists established "state within a state" in the city of Chongqing. The invasion of foreign capitals destroyed the natural economy in Chongqing area, but it fostered the opening up of Chongqing area and the primary development of national capitalism. Although this opening up was forced, humiliated, painful and disgraceful, its influence on Chongqing was tremendous and profound. Since then, as Chongqing fell into semi-colonial and semi-feudal society, it also started modern industrialization and urbanization course with difficulty. Chongqing capitalist industry and commerce were initiated and developed to some extent, paralleling with its opening up as a commercial port. In 1891, Sichuan merchant Lu Ganchen (卢干臣) and others built the first privately operated new factory Senchangtai (森昌泰) and Senchangzheng (森昌正) Match Factory. In 1908, Shumei (蜀眉) Silk Factory was built in Chongqing, and it was the first factory to use steam engines among Sichuan satin silk industry. In the same year, Chongqing Zhuchuan (烛川) Light Company was established, which enabled Chongqing to be one of the first cities in west China to use electric lamps. Until the Revolution in 1911, there had been 53 modern industries of various types in Chongqing. This number was almost the same with the 51 foreign firms, companies and business establishments. Besides, commerce, financial and transportation industry in Chongqing all witnessed

Picture 3-9 The Stone Inscription of "Chongqing Customs and Taxation Department" in No. 60 Haishi Road (海狮路), Xuantan Temple (玄坛庙) in Nan'an District. It has already been cut and collected by Chongqing Customs.

development and progress after its opening as a commercial port. Chongqing embarked on the road toward an industrial, commercial, financial and transportation centre in southwest China.

2.Chongqing People's Anti-imperialist Struggle

Picture 3-10 *Revolutionary Army* by Zou Rong (邹容)

After Chongqing's opening as a commercial port, imperialists started all-round aggression in political, economic, military, cultural and educational aspects. They colluded with decayed Qing Government and reactionary feudal warlords and took advantage of those privileges guaranteed by signing unequal treaties, building churches, factories and foreign firms all over Chongqing. Foreigners went on rampage. They bullied and exploited common people and committed all sorts of crimes. Those atrocities committed by imperialist aggressors, corrupt government and reactionary warlords provoked determined resistance among Chongqing people who inherited the glorious tradition of revolution. The struggle against western religion flared up in different regions contributed to Yu Dongchen Uprisng (余栋臣起义) in Dazu between 1890 and 1898. The number of insurrectionary armies soon developed to more than 6,000. They occupied Dazu, Tongliang, Bishan, Rongchang, and Hechuan; they put forward a slogan of "Swearing to avenge national humiliation" and dealt a heavy blow to the foreign forces of aggression. After the failure of Boxer Rebellion (义和团运动) in the north, Chongqing Boxers issued posters and raised a slogan of "Eliminating the Qing Dynasty, exterminating the foreigners and rejuvenating the Han Nationality". They were the first who held the banners of anti-imperialism and anti-feudalism.

Picture 3-11 Chaotianmen in 1910, Wooden Boat Docked by the River

In the economic struggle, Chongqing gentries established "Jianghe (江合) Mining Corporation, LTD." to contend with British merchants' Huaying (华英) Company that "monopoly our mining rights and despoil our economic rights". With the support of Chongqing people and after repeated struggles, Jianghe Mining Corporation, LTD. took back the "mining rights in Jiangbei" usurped by the British merchants at a cost of 220 thousand liang (两)[1] silver, which dealt a heavy blow to the British imperialists' economic aggression.

When Yu Dongchen Uprising and Boxer Rebellion failed, Chongqing people did not surrender. A large batch of men and women with lofty ideals continued to explore the truth of anti-imperialism and national salvation. In 1897, reformist Song Yuren (宋育仁) founded the first journal with a tendency of bourgeois reformism—*Yu Bao* (《渝报》), to publicize reform ideas extensively. Zou Rong, as a vanguard of revolution army, created *Revolutionary Army* (《革命军》) which played an important role in the spread of bourgeois democratic thought in Chongqing and nationwide. It was regarded as Chinese *Declaration of the Rights of Man and of the Citizen* (《人权宣言》). During the Xinhai Revolution(辛亥革命) , Chongqing bourgeoisie established groups, newspapers and periodicals to publicize democratic revolution thoughts and organized armed uprisings. Chongqing bourgeoisie finally overthrew the corrupted feudal rule through the Xinhai Revolution in 1911 and established Chongqing "Shujun Government"

[1] a unit of weight

(蜀军政府) with power in the hands of the bourgeoisie. Although the Xinhai Revolution ended in failure because of the limitations of the bourgeoisie, it ended the feudal society that had been ruling Chongqing for over 2,000 years and opened a new chapter for Chongqing. Since then, Chongqing became the centre of Sichuan bourgeois democratic revolution. In the Second Revolution (二次革命) in 1913, the National Protection War (护国战争) in 1915 and the War of Law Protection (护法战争) between 1917 and 1918, Chongqing appeared as an acting and commanding centre in the historical stage.

Ⅱ.From The May 4th Movement to the Great Revolution

In 1921, the Communist Party of China was founded and the proletariat embarked on the political stage of Chongqing. In 1926, the establishment of "Chongqing Local Executive Committee of CPC" (中共重庆地方执行委员会) symbolized Chongqing democratic revolution entered a brand-new historical stage.

In the Great Revolution period, Chongqing became the centre of the great revolution in Sichuan. CPC Chongqing local party organizations, closely united the left wing of Kuomintang in Chongqing and initiated and led vigorous anti-imperialist and anti-feudal movements in Chongqing and Sichuan. In 1925, they supported the movement that backed on "May 30th Massacre" (五卅惨案) in Shanghai; in 1926, they opposed the struggles led by Kuomintang rightists and nationalists, and they backed on the struggle against the British imperialists by expressing support for "September 5th Massacre" (九五惨案) in Wanxian County (万县) ; they also gained certain victory in the movement to reclaim the Japanese concessions in Wangjiatuo in 1931 and in the opposition against the Japanese to establish consulate in Chengdu in 1936. Between 1926 and 1927, the "Luzhou Uprising" (泸州起义) and "Shunqing Uprisings" (顺庆起义) led by Yang Angong (杨闇公), Zhu De (朱德), Liu Bocheng (刘伯承) from Chongqing Local

Executive Committee of CPC lasted 167 days and dealt a heavy blow to the reactionary warlords and imperialists. Although this uprising ended in failure, it was the first try by the CPC to independently establish revolutionary forces and greatly supported the Northern Expedition (北伐战争) and the National Revolution (国民革命) ; it provided valuable experience and preparation for future uprisings such as the Nanchang Uprising (南昌起义) led by CPC.

In 1927, instigated by Chiang Kai-shek (蒋介石), Sichuan warlord Liu Xiang (刘湘) made appalling "March 31st Massacre" (三三一惨案), Chongqing Local Executive Committee of CPC suffered great sacrifice and great loss. CPC prefectural party committee secretary Yang Angong, minister of the Organization Department Ran Jun (冉钧), Kuomintang leftist leaders Qi Nanxun (漆南薰) and Chen Dasan (陈达三) died as martyrs. However, CPC and its revolutionary forces were like grass that even burned by wildfire. They could still revive when the spring wind blows. CPC Sichuan Provincial Party Committee, Temporary Provincial Party Committee came forward and organized activities many times in Chongqing, and they led Chongqing people in a series of anti-imperialist and anti-feudal revolutionary struggles and anti-Japanese national salvation movement.

During this period, Chongqing administrative system also experienced a series of changes.

On November 22nd,1911, after the establishment of Chongqing Shu Military Government, over 10 military governments in Hunan, Hubei, Jiangxi, Jiangsu, Zhejiang, Yunnan, Guangdong, Guangxi, Shaanxi sent telegrams to Shu Military Government and acknowledged it as "Sichuan political pivot and the governor of it as the representative of Sichuan people." The 57 prefectures and counties that gained independence also sent telegrams to this government to show their obedience to it. When two governments from Chengdu and Chongqing integrated in 1912, Sichuan governor's official residence was set in Chengdu, and Chongqing became a strategic city with military importance. Chongqing assistant government was set up with 54 prefectures, departments and counties in eastern Sichuan under its jurisdiction. When it was cancelled in June 1914, Chuandong Dao (东川道) was set up with 36 counties in eastern Sichuan under its jurisdiction. During the warlord era, Chongqing, as a strategic city with military importance, became a focus of all warlords and was occupied and controlled by Sichuan Army (川军), Yunnan Army (滇军), Guizhou Army (黔军) as well as the Northern Warlords (北洋军阀). This chaos did not end until Liu Xiang unified Sichuan in February 1935 and established Sichuan Government in Chongqing again.

The establishment of Chongqing municipal organization was originated from early 1920s. In July 1921, Liu Xiang took office as commander-in-chief of Sichuan armies and provincial governor of Sichuan. In November, he set Chongqing Commercial Port supervisor's office with Yang Sen (杨森), commander of the second army of Sichuan army as supervisor. This was the beginning of Chongqing municipal organization.

Ⅲ.City and Urban Construction

At that time, the urban area was not set, Chongqing [the urban area of Baxian Chengguan (巴县城关), Yuzhong Peninsula nowadays] and Jiangbei County (江北县) (Yubei District nowadays) where residents concentrated were regarded as the urban area. In 1922, Deng Xihou (邓锡侯), the commander of the third division of Sichuan Army entered Chongqing. In February 1923, Chongqing Commercial Port supervisor's office was changed into Chongqing municipal government by Deng Xihou and he assigned himself as supervisor. In June 1926, Liu Xiang came to Chongqing again as Sichuan rehabilitation supervisor and Sichuan supervisor of border affairs. He changed Chongqing municipal government into commercial port bureau and appointed Tang Shizun (唐式遵), commander of the 32nd division as supervisor. Before long, Tang no longer held the post. Pan Wenhua (潘文华),

commander of the 33rd division, was appointed as supervisor. Pan Wenhua took office in July 1926. He set general affairs, financing, public security and job offices under his bureau. The commercial port area was set tentatively as the municipal administrative area. After Guangdong national revolutionary army made a northern expedition, Liu Xiang was assigned as commander of the 21st army of the national revolutionary army. The Beiyang government assigned him as commercial port supervisor and Chongqing commercial port bureau was changed to city hall. On February 15th, 1929, Chongqing City Hall was changed to Chongqing Municipal Government. Since then, Chongqing was formally established as a provincially administered municipality (namely, ordinary city). In view of its importance, both of Chongqing official posts and the delimitation of its urban area were designed with the standard of a special city. The delimitation of its urban area was set in 1933, and the total surface area of Chongqing was 93.5 square kilometres with a population of 280,449. On October 15th, 1934, the national government decreed. The establishment of Chongqing government was under permission, and it was set as a type B city.

After its establishment, because of its strategic position, Chongqing submitted two applications to the national government in 1930 and 1936 respectively, asking for being ranked as a type A municipality directly under the central government. However, as it could not meet the 3 standards (being a capital city with a population over 1 million and special political and economic circumstances) set by the Municipal Organization Law promulgated by the central government. These two applications before the War of Resistance Against Japanese Aggression were not accepted. However, the political, economic and military importance of Chongqing attracted more and more attention from many aspects. Besides Sichuan warlord Liu Xiang who put his focus on Chongqing, Kuomintang central committee also paid much attention to Sichuan and Chongqing when Nanjing government was established. While pursuing and wiping out the Chinese Workers' and Peasants' Red Army (中国工农红军) between 1934 and 1935, Kuomintang central power began to enter Chongqing, which was regarded as a stronghold to control Sichuan and southwest China. The symbol of this penetration was the station of Nanchang Battalion Staff Committee of the Chairman of the Military Commission of the National Government in Chongqing in January 1935.

The 1920s and 1930s witnessed the intensity of Chongqing municipal construction and great strides towards a modern city. It was also a time that laid foundation for the move of the war capital to the west in the War of Resistance Against Japanese Aggression. The establishment of Chongqing city hall guaranteed unified planning and management for municipal construction. According to the plan, road construction was to drive newly explored area construction. Three major arteries were defined in road construction. Firstly, the central artery was the mountain ridges out of the city; secondly, the southern artery was along the Yangtze River; thirdly, the northern artery was along the Jialing River. When the exploration of new urban area was completed, the 3 major arteries extended to the old city to facilitate renovation of its streets and markets. After the completion of 3 major arteries, several latitude routes that connected the north and the south were built. Modern terminal facilities appeared along the rivers. Urban public services such as postal telecommunications, electric power supply, streetlamps, running water and public transportation were successively set up. Urban area doubled by expanding eastward from the route of Linjiangmen (临江门), Tongyuanmen and Nanjimen to Zengjiayan (曾家岩), Lianglukou (两路口) and Douzibei (兜子背). Adding Jiangbei and Nan’an, the urban built-up area was 10 square kilometres. In the new urban area Lianglukou, Zengjiayan, Caiyuanba (菜园坝), Daxigou (大溪沟), market and new villages appeared, and the old city was greatly transformed. The prosperous area gradually transferred from the coast of two rivers to both sides of traffic arteries, and alleviated the conspicuous contradiction between the narrowness of the urban area and urban development. Chongqing became the earliest city in southwest China to modernize with the highest degree of modernization.

Section Three During the War of Resistance Against Japanese Aggression

Ⅰ.The Chongqing People's War of Resistance Against Japanese Aggression after September 18th Incident

On September 18th,1931, the Japanese brazenly invaded northeast China and created "September 18th" Incident ("九一八"事变). When this news came to Chongqing, people were shocked with indignation, as this year also marked the expiration of the 30-year-lease of Wangjiatuo Japanese Concession. Chongqing people from all walks of life established Chongqing National Association for the Promotion of the Abolition of Unequal Treaties (重庆国民废除不平等条约促进会), People from All Walks of Life in Sichuan Automatically Reclaim the Wangjiatuo Japanese Concession Movement Conference (四川各界民众自动收回王家沱日租界运动大会), Sichuan People's Anti-Japanese National Salvation Congress (四川各界民众反日救国大会), Sichuan People's Anti-Japanese National Salvation Congress Special Committee to Automatically Recover Wangjiatuo Concession (四川各界民众反日救国大会自动收回王家沱租界特组委员会) in succession. They exposed crimes of aggression committed by Japanese imperialists towards the Chinese people and called upon Sichuan and Chongqing people to fight bravely and reclaim Wangjiatuo concession. People from all walks of life went on strikes and held demonstrations and conducted economic blockade in Japanese concession, which dealt a heavy blow to the arrogant Japanese imperialists. Under great pressure of brave Chongqing people, the Japanese aggressors were forced to return Wangjiatuo concession.

In 1932, the "January 28th" Incident ("一·二八"事变) broke out in Shanghai. People from all walks of life in Chongqing organized movements and held Conference by People from All Walks of Life in Sichuan to Urge the Sichuan Army to Send Troops (四川各界民众督促川军出兵大会), Sichuan People from All Walks of Life Urge Sichuan Army to Send Troops to Save the Country Petition Conference (四川各界民众督促川军出兵救国请愿大会) and Sichuan People from All Walks of Life Pay Tribute to Songhu Anti-Japanese Martyrs Conference (四川各界民众追悼淞沪抗日殉国将士大会). They proposed petition to leave Sichuan and fight against the Japanese and paid tribute to martyrs and organized donation campaign to support the 19th Route Army.

After "North China Incident" (华北事变) in 1935, patriotic students in Peiping (北平) held massive "December 9th" Movement ("一二・九"运动) led by underground Party of the Communist Party of China. When news came to Chongqing, students from universities and high schools represented by Chongqing University, East Sichuan Normal College (川东师范学堂), Chongqing Associated School (重庆联中) published telegrams to support Peiping students' patriotic and anti-Japanese struggle. Later, student representatives from over 30 universities and high schools established Chongqing Student Salvation Federation (重庆学生救国联合会) ("Student Federation" in brief). From December 1935 to the following February, Student Federation led Chongqing students to carry out anti-Japanese patriotic campaigns for several times. In March 1936, Student Federation suffered involuntary dissolution by the Chongqing party headquarters of the Kuomintang.

In June 1936, in order to carry out the political view to form a united front by the CPC central committee, Qi Luyu (漆鲁鱼), a member of the CPC secretly established Chongqing National Salvation Association of All Walks of Life (重庆各界救国联合会) ("Chongqing National Salvation Association" in brief). Anti-Japanese and national salvation forces were unified to develop the united front. Under the correct guiding thought, public and underground struggles, legal and illegal struggles were combined. The activities and influence of Chongqing National Salvation Association expanded rapidly. Three underground organizations, Chongqing Student Association for National Salvation (重庆学生界救国联合

会), Chongqing Professional Youth Association for National Salvation (重庆职业青年救国联合会), Chongqing Women's Federation for National Salvation (重庆妇女界救国联合会) were established in succession; one public organization, Chongqing Cultural Association for National Salvation (重庆文化界救国联合会) was also established. The public opinion fronts for Chongqing National Salvation Association were *Business Affairs Daily* (《商务日报》) and *Xin Shubao* (《新蜀报》), on which anti-Japanese national salvation and anti-Japanese national united front policy of the CPC were publicized. Study sessions and reading clubs were held to cultivate young backbones for the anti-Japanese national salvation movements. In the campaign against the establishment of Japanese Consulate in Chengdu in August 1936, in the activities to mourn Lu Xun (鲁迅) 's death in October 1936, and in Suiyuan Resistance (绥远抗战) led by Fu Zuoyi (傅作义) in November 1936, Chongqing National Salvation Association actively organized underground activities such as anti-Japanese national salvation struggles and propagandas, and it fully mobilized anti-Japanese enthusiasm among Chongqing people from all walks of life. After "July 7th Incident" (七七事变) in 1937, public activities were given priority by Chongqing National Salvation Association. By organizing large-scale anti-Japanese commemorations and parades, anti-Japanese dramas and singing in public, literature and art workshops, literature and art associations, wartime knowledge training courses, salvations libraries, civilian literacy classes, civilian night schools, Chongqing National Salvation Association extensively publicized the importance of joint resistance against Japan and possibility of the final victory in the War of Resistance Against Japanese Aggression. Chongqing National Salvation Association also cultivated a large number of youths who plunged themselves to revolution and laid foundation for the recovery and reestablishment of Chongqing local party organizations. From the end of 1937 to the first half of 1938, more than 100 progressive youths were sent by Chongqing National Salvation Association to Yan'an (延安) or the anti-Japanese front (抗日前线). After the establishment of

Chongqing Working Committee of CPC, most members of Chongqing National Salvation Association joined the party and became backbones of CPC organizations at all levels.

Ⅱ.War-time Capital and Republic of China's War-time Capital

When the comprehensive War of Resistance Against Japanese Aggression broke out in 1937, in order to persist in the War of Resistance Against Japanese Aggression and never sign a treaty under coercion, the Kuomintang Government, under the oppression of war, decided to move its capital to Chongqing which was the important crossroad of southwest China and a place of strategic importance with Jianghan area under its control. On December 1st, 1937, the national government declared to handle official businesses the humble new site of Chongqing; on the 7th, the central party headquarters of the Kuomintang's first joint meeting of supervisors after moving to Chongqing was held in Fanzhuang Village (范庄) and it started handling official businesses in Chongqing. In the summer of 1938, as Japanese aggression intensified, Wuhan was in great peril. The Military Commission of the National Government gave urgent orders to Kuomintang central office in Wuhan to move to Chongqing within 5 days. According to this order, party and government offices that moved to Wuhan previously started another large-scale westward movement which was finished in the first ten days of August. Until December 1938, the supreme headquarters of the Military Commission of the National government led by Chiang Kai-shek arrived in Chongqing. Most of the party, government and military organs and their subordinate departments moved to Chongqing. This was the largest-scale westward movement of government agencies in Chinese history. As the Chinese delegation moved to Chongqing and established the Southern Bureau of the CPC Central Committee (中共中央南方局) and the Eighth Route Army Office (八路军办事处) [New Fourth Army

Office (新四军办事处) at the same time] in succession, the central organs of the democratic parties and their principal officials arrived in Chongqing. Chongqing became the political, economic, military, cultural, diplomatic and social centre and activity centre of the Kuomintang area. It became an important arena for Chinese anti-Japanese national united front with cooperation between the Kuomintang and the Communist Party as the basis and all parties involved. Chongqing played an important role as a headquarter, pivot and soul in the political affairs of the country.

On January 3rd, 1942, the allied countries established China theatre headquarter in the world Anti-fascist War with Chiang Kai-shek as generalissimo and American general Stillwell as chief of staff. At that point, the Chinese War of Resistance Against Japanese Aggression was incorporated into the strategic system of the world anti-fascist war. Chongqing became one important supporting point of this strategic system and ascended from commanding headquarter of Chinese anti-Japanese war to the headquarter of world anti-fascist war of allied countries in the far east. Chongqing, the mountain city, "Went beyond Sichuan and became a metropolis that is able to call on the whole country and a cosmopolis in politics, with London, Berlin, Paris, Washington and Moscow as its counterparts".

On May 5th 1939, the national government decided to ascend Chongqing as a type A city directly under the executive council and reorganized Chongqing municipal government by appointing He Guoguang (贺国光), acting director of Chongqing camp as the first mayor of Chongqing after it became a municipality directly under the central government. Meanwhile, the urban area was expanded, and the Ba County government and the Jiangbei County government were moved out of the city to do official businesses. Municipal primary organizations increased from 6 to 12. This was the first time that Chongqing had been a municipality directly under the central government.

In Chiang Kai-shek's proposal, the 38th Executive Meeting of the Supreme Council for National Defence on August 15th, 1940, decided to make Chongqing the war-time capital. On September 6th, 1940, the national government promulgated public proclamations. Chongqing was made as the war-time capital of the national government and was legally determined its political status. It was a sign that Chongqing's political status has been developed to the zenith. It was also an epoch-making event in the history of the establishment of Republic of China. The decision to make Chongqing as the war-time capital also facilitated the improvement and progress of Chongqing municipal construction and gave a play to its function as a central city and accelerated the process of Chongqing modernization and internationalization as well.

Ⅲ.Move to the Interior and Urban Development

With the capital of the National Government moved to Chongqing, a large number of cultural organs, universities, industrial and mining enterprises moved to Sichuan Province. This was the famous "Yichang Evacuation" (宜昌大撤退) in history.

Yichang (宜昌) was an important port of transhipment in the middle and lower reaches of the Yangtze River to Chongqing. Steamers from the lower reaches must go through the Three Gorges and the Chuanjiang River (川江) in Yichang before going to Chongqing. After the National Government declared to move from Wuhan to Chongqing, in the autumn of 1938, a lot of personnel, goods, materials, and equipments were retained in Yichang with the threat of the advancing Japanese army and the bombing of Japanese planes. At this time, it was only 40 days left before the Chuanjiang River enter the dry season, and all the personnel and materials must be sent to Sichuan within these 40 days. Lu Zuofu (卢作孚), who was operating Minsheng Corporation (民生公司), resolutely accepted this arduous task. He worked together with his staff and left no means untried. They worked day and night with all possible speed and fulfilled this impossible task by sending all personnel and materials to Sichuan within 40 days under the Japanese bombardment. Before Yichang was occupied by the Japanese, Yichang port transferred over 1.5 million refugees and 1million goods and materials. The Minsheng Corporation that involved in this transfer lost 16 ships and 116 staff with 61 injured and disabled. This rescue attracted so much attention both at home and abroad that it was regarded as the Chinee version of Dunkirk Evacuation.

Lots of cultural units moved to Chongqing with the National Government, among them were National Central Library, Peiping Palace Museum, Central News Agency, Central Broadcasting Station, Zhonghua Book Company, the Commercial Press, etc. Besides, a large number of schools also moved to the interior—Chongqing, among them over 20 institutions of higher learning, accounting for over 40% of all institutions of higher learning that moved to the interior. This move brought about many students and talents, Xiaba (夏坝) in Beibei District, Xiaolongkan (小龙坎) and Ciqikou (磁器口) in Shapingba District and Baisha Town (白沙镇) in Jiangjin District were 3 school cultural districts that formed in this period.

Table 3-2 List of Universities and Middle Schools that Moved to Chongqing During the War of Resistance Against Japanese Aggression

The name of the school	Original location	New location	Notes
National Central University	Nanking, Jiangsu Province	Songlinpo in Shapingba	
National Central School of Political Science	Nanking, Jiangsu Province	Chongqing South Hot Spring	Later renamed as Central University of Political Science
Private Fudan University	Jiangwan, Shanghai	Xiaba, Beibei	Later changed to a national university
National Jiaotong University	Shanghai	Jiulongpo, Chongqing	
The Army University	Nanking, Jiangsu Province	Shandong, Chongqing	

Continued

The name of the school	Original location	New location	Notes
Ordnance School	Nanking, Jiangsu Province	Ciqikou and Yanggongqiao	
National Institute of Social Education	Nanking, Jiangsu Province	Bishan County	
National Conservatory of Music	Nanking, Jiangsu Province	Qingmuguan, Ba County	
National Jiangsu University	Zhenjiang, Jiangsu Province	Beibei, Chongqing	
National Academy of Arts	Hangzhou	Panxi, Shapingba	
National Shanghai Medical College	Shanghai	Gele Mountain, Chongqing	
National College of Pharmacy	Nanking, Jiangsu Province	Gele Mountain, Chongqing	
Private Chaoyang College	Peiping	Xinglongchang, Chongqing	Became a national college after relocation
National Central Technical College of Industry	Nanking	Shapingba	
Private Wuchang Zhonghua University	Wuchang	Nan'an, Chongqing	
Private Wuchang Cultural Library College	Wuchang	Xiangguo Temple, Jiangbei	
Private Rural Construction College		Xiemachang, Beibei	
National Soochow University Business School	Suzhou, Jiangsu Province	Chongqing	
Shanghai Private Lixin College of Accounting	Shanghai	Chongqing	
Private Regular Art College	Danyang, Jiangsu Province	Deganba, Jiangjin	

Continued

The name of the school	Original location	New location	Notes
National Women's Normal College		Baisha, Jiangjin	
Pre-university Classes set up by the Ministry of Education	Nanjing, Jiangsu Province	Baisha, Jiangjin	
National Nankai Middle School		Shapingba	
National No. 2 Middle School	Jiangsu	Hechuan	
National No. 9 Middle School	Anhui	Deganba, Jiangjin	
National No. 12 Middle School	Hubei	Changshou	
National No. 14 Middle School		Qingmuguan	Later became a middle school attached to the National Central University
National No. 16 Middle School		Yongchuan	
National No. 17 Middle School		Baisha, Jiangjin	
National Overseas Chinese Middle School		Deganba, Jiangjin	

In order to meet the needs of war, lots of industrial and mining enterprises also moved to Chongqing. As a result, an integrated industrial area was formed with Chongqing as the centre. It started from Changshou in the east and reached Jiangjin in the west along the Yangtze River, and it started from Hechuan in the north along the Jialing River, and Qijiang in the south along the Sichuan Guizhou Highway (川黔公路). This integrated industrial area became the industrial lifeline in the wartime. It owned over 200 factories, accounting for 1/3 of all the factories that moved to the interior. Among them were millitary industry, metallurgy industry, machinery industry, textile industry, refining industry, tobacco industry, etc.

Table 3-3 List of Ordnance Industry Enterprises Moved to Chongqing

The name of the factory	Original location	Rename	Notes
Shanghai Steel Works	Shanghai	No. 3 Factory	Incorporated into Steel Works Relocation Committee in January, 1940
Jinan Arsenal	Jinan	No. 30 Factory	
Gongxian Arsenal	Gongxian County, Henan Province	No. 11 Factory	Incorporated into No.1 Factory in 1940
Jinling Arsenal	Nanking	No. 21 Factory	
Arsenal Administration of the Ministry of War	Nanking		
Ammunition Factory of Zhuzhou Arsenal	Zhuzhou, Hunan Province	No. 25 Factory	
Guangdong No.2 Arsenal	Qingyuan, Guangzhou Province	No. 50 Factory	
Steel Works Relocation Committee	Hanyang		
Hanyang Arsenal	Hanyang	No. 1 Factory	
Hanyang Gunpowder Factory	Hanyang	No. 2 Factory	
Artillery Technical Research Division	Nanking	No. 10 Factory	
Artillery Headquarter and Factory	Nanking		
Artillery Division and Ammunition Factory	Nanking		
Guangxi No.1 Arsenal	Guangxi Province	No. 40 Factory	
No. 40 Factory (Preparatory Office of Guangxi Arsenal)	Liuzhou, Guangxi Province		

Continued

The name of the factory	Original location	Rename	Notes
Institute of Applied Chemistry	Nanking		
Baishuiqiao Research Institute	Nanking		
Ballistic Research Institue	Nanking		

Chongqing in the wartime witnessed one of the fastest growths in its history of development. With the expansion of the city, the municipal administration and public causes also saw new developments. In the urban redevelopment, Duyou Street Square (督邮街广场) (Jiefangbei nowadays) was the focus. According to the longtitude and latitude road layout, Datong Road (打铜街), Kaixuan Road (凯旋路), and Zhongxing Road (中兴路) were connected to integrate with the southern city (the lower urban area) so that the upper and the lower urban areas became integrated. A relatively complete road system was initially formed in the old city and facilitated the transfer of the city centre from the lower city to the upper city. The construction of the road system in the new area put focus on the vast areas in the western suburbs. Roads from Fotuguan (佛图关) to Jiulongpo (九龙坡), from Fotuguan to Xinqiao (新桥), from Xiaolongkan (小龙坎) to Yanggongqiao (杨公桥), from Shandong (山洞) to Baishiyi (白市驿) were constructed in succession, which fostered the exploration and development of this area and drove the construction of satellite towns. Meanwhile, roads towards Guangyangba (广阳坝), Shanhuba (珊瑚坝), Jiulongpo and Baishiyi airports were completed in succession, and traffic conditions outside the city was improved. Till the eve of the victory of the anti-Japanese war in 1945, Chongqing had already become the largest industrial and commercial city as well as the cultural, educational, scientific and traffic centre in southwest China with a population of over 1.25 million and an area of 45 square kilometres. The built-up area had expanded to Shapingba (沙坪坝) in the west, the piedmont of Nanshan Mountain (南山) in the east, Dadukou (大渡口) in the south and the Jialing River banks in the north. Several satellite towns were formed around the Liangjiang Peninsula (两江半岛). Chongqing urban area could be divided into 4 parts: central urban area, Jiangbei area along the banks, Nan'an area along the river and Shaci area (Shapingba and Ciqikou area). This laid the foundation for the urban distribution pattern of modern Chongqing.

After the victory of the Anti-Japanese War, Chongqing War-time Capital Construction Planning Committee (重庆陪都建设计划委员会) formulated the *Ten-year Construction Draft Plan of the War-time Capital* (《陪都十年建设计划草案》). This was the first comprehensive project for city construction in the history of Chongqing. Based on careful analysis of the status quo of Chongqing, this draft was made according to the principle which set transportation as priority, sanitation and civilian welfare as secondary, and no bias on the national economy and people's livelihood. With the improvement of people's living standards and enhancement of public efficiency as the objective, the long-term aimless development and hyperinflation situation in Chongqing was adjusted; the prosperity of industry and commerce, the rectification of the city appearance, the planning for future urban development were given priority to. The balanced development of industry and commerce, transportation, social organizations, public housing, urban green space and open space was guaranteed, so were the public facilities. This draft aimed to make Chongqing an industrial and commercial hub, a fine inland harbour, and a modernized metropolis in southwest China. However, the aims of this draft could never be realized under the corrupted Kuomintang Government whose economy was collapsed, whose people were destitute. With the breakout of the civil war, the draft's content ended on paper. However, the strictness and scientificity of this draft provided important reference for future urban construction of Chongqing.

Ⅳ.The Bombing of Chongqing

Since 1938, with its air superiority, Japan conducted savage bombing in the rear area. Chongqing, as the war-time capital, became its main bombing target. The Japanese bombing of Chongqing lasted 6 years and 10 months and it caused the biggest catastrophe in the history of Chongqing.

Picture 3-12 Chongqing City after Bombing

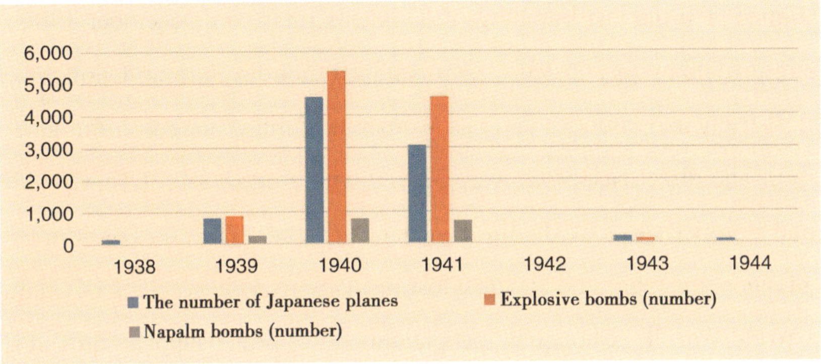

Picture 3-13 The Bombing of Chongqing City

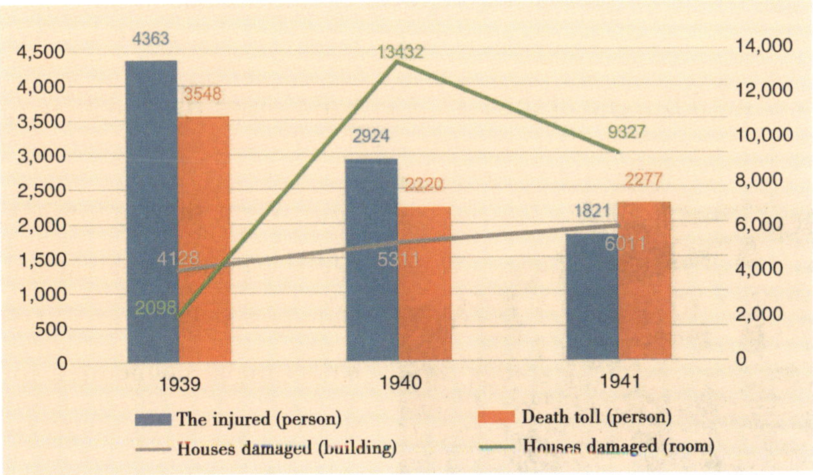

Picture 3-14 The Loss Resulted from Bombing in Chongqing City Between 1939 and 1941

On February 18th, 1938, the Japanese planes bombed Guangyangba and Shichan (石船) in Jiangbei County (Yubei District nowadays) in the suburb. This marked the beginning of the bombing of Chongqing. When the Pacific War broke out, a large number of Japanese armies were transferred, thus the Japanese were forced to stop bombing of Chongqing. Until August 23rd 1943, more than 9,500 planes were involved in the bombing of Chongqing, which bombed the city for over 210 times, killing almost 30,000 civilians, destroying over 30,000 houses and causing tremendous loss of life and property in Chongqing. When the bombing of the city area was stopped, the bombing of rural areas of Chongqing and eastern Sichuan areas continued. Till the last bombing of Kaixian County on December 19th, 1944, the bombing of Chongqing lasted 6 years and 10 months. Among Chongqing city and its 32 districts and counties such as Wanzhou, Fuling, none was immune from the bombing. The direct casualties were 32,829 with a death toll of 16,376, 172,876 refugees and a property loss of 10 billion yuan (1937 ratio). The times of bombing, the length of duration, the range and the great loss resulted from the bombing of Chongqing all rare in World War Ⅱ. Chongqing people defied this brutal suppression and shared a bitter hatred of the enemy and persisted in fighting in the War of Resistance Against Japanese Aggression, thus enabled this heroic city to stand majestically.

Ⅴ Southern Bureau of the CPC Central Committee in Chongqing

Picture 3-15 The Site of Southern Bureau of the CPC Central Committee

When the comprehensive Anti-Japanese War broke out, the Communist Party of China and Kuomintang cooperated for the second time, and the Chinese united front against Japanese aggression took shape. The Chinese Workers' and Peasants' Red Army was renamed as the Eighth Route Army of the National Revolutionary Army (国民革命军第八路军) and established Eighth Route Army Offices in Nanking and Wuhan. When Wuhan was lost in October 1938, the Eighth Route Army Office in Wuhan was moved to Chongqing, and the final office location was set in No.13 Hongyanzui (红岩嘴) and No.50 Zengjiayan (曾家岩). In January 1939, the Central Committee of the CPC decided to establish the South Bureau of the CPC Central Committee in Chongqing with Zhou Enlai (周恩来) as its secretary. With the public and legal Eighth Route Army Office as a shield, this bureau was to lead party organizations secretly in Kuomintang-controlled areas such as Sichuan, Yunnan, Guizhou, Xikang, Hunan, Hubei, Guangdong, Guangxi and Jiangxi as well as those in Hong Kong, Macao and southeast Asia. Zhou Enlai, Dong Biwu (董必武), Lin Boqu (林伯渠), Wu Yuzhang (吴玉章), Wang Ruofei (王若飞), Ye Jianying (叶剑英), Deng Yingchao (邓颖超) permanently stationed in Chongqing as the public representatives of the CPC.

Table 3-4 The Establishment of the Southern Bureau of the CPC Central Committee

Time of establishment	January, 1939
Members	Secretary: Zhou Enlai Members of the Standing Committee: Zhou Enlai, Bo Gu, Kai Feng, Wu Kejian, Ye Jianying, Dong Biwu Committee members: Wu Yuzhang, Xu Teli, Deng Yingchao, Liao Chengzhi, Zhang Wenbin, Liu Xiao, Gao Wenhua
Main organizations	Three departments: the Organization Department, the Publicity Department, the Social Department; two committees: the United Front and Cultural Work; International Studies Office, Jianying Working Group, Nanyang Working Group, Secretariat, etc.
Main responsibilities	On behalf of the CPC Central Committee, it comprehensively led the CPC organizations in the southern regions such as Sichuan and Guizhou, Hong Kong, Macao and Southeast Asia, as well as the people's armed struggle against Japanese aggression in south China and southwest China
Office location	No.70 Jifang Street, moved to No. 13, Hongyanzui after the May 3rd and May 4th bombings

In line with the CPC policy of the Chinese united front against Japanese aggression, the South Bureau of the CPC Central Committee did a lot of work in uniting the progressives, centrists and intellectuals in Kuomintang. It insisted on fighting in the war, keeping united and making progress. It was opposed to surrender, secession, or retrogression. It also conducted reasonable, favorable and moderate struggles against Kuomintang die-hards and made great contribution to the victory of the Anti-Japanese War.

Table 3-5 The Main Middle Parties in Chongqing from 1939 to 1946

The name of the party	Time of establishment	Key leaders
China Democratic League	March 19th, 1941	Zhang Lan, Huang Yanpei, Shen Junru, Luo Longji, etc.
Jiusan Society	May 4th, 1946	Xu Deheng, Pan Shu, Liang Xi, etc.
Federation of Comrades of the Three People's Principles	October 28th, 1945	Tan Pingshan, Wang Kunlun, Chen Mingshu, etc.
China National Democratic Construction Association	December 16th, 1945	Huang Yanpei, Hu Juewen, Zhang Naiqi, etc.
China Democratic Revolution League	1942	Wang Kunlun, Xu Baoju, Wang Bingnan
China Association for the Promotion of Democratic Constitutionalism	February 24th, 1946	Zhang Ximan
China Construction Society	February, 1946	Luo Peilin, Li Wencai, Zhang Zhemin
The Chinese People's National Salvation Association	December, 1945	Shen Junru, Shi Liang, Tao Xingzhi

Section Four During the War of Liberation

Ⅰ. Chongqing Negotiation (重庆谈判) and Political Consultative Conference

In August 1945, Japan announced its surrender. The War of Resistance Against

Japanese Aggression won its final victory. On the one hand, Chiang Kai-shek deployed forces to make preparation for large-scale civil war. On the other hand, he pretended to embrace peace by sending 3 consecutive telegrams to Mao Zedong (毛泽东) on the 14th, 20th and 23rd of August 1945, inviting him to Chongqing to discuss key domestic and international affairs. The central committee of the CPC, after careful analysis, decided to send a CPC delegation with Mao Zedong, Zhou Enlai, Wang Ruofei and others as its members to Chongqing. They arrived in Chongqing at 3 p.m. on August 28th, 1945, and they started Chongqing Negotiation with important historical significance in modern and contemporary Chinese history that lasted 43 days with the Kuomintang authorities. On October 10th, 1945, they signed *Minutes of Talks Between the Government and Representatives of the CPC* (《政府与中共代表会谈纪要》) [Hereinafter referred to as the *Double Tenth Agreement* (《双十协定》)] in Guiyuan (桂园).

According to the 2nd clause of the *Double Tenth Agreement* on the question of political democratization, a Political Consultative Conference is to be held. On January 10th, 1946, the Political Consultative Conference with Kuomintang, CPC, China Democratic League, the Youth Party and independent democrats participated was held in Chongqing national government auditorium. After over 10 plenary sessions within 22 days, repeated struggles and fierce contests among the parties, an agreement was made concerning the following 5 aspects: the program of peaceful nation reconstruction, reshuffle of government, National Assembly, military problems and constitution draft. The greatest achievement of this conference was that it acknowledged policies for peaceful nation reconstruction and denied Kuomintang one-party dictatorship and civil war policy.

As a result, it was warmly welcomed and firmly supported by people. Meanwhile, it also suffered opposition and destruction from Kuomintang die-hards. Even during the conference, Kuomintang spies made Cangbaitang Incident (沧白堂事件) and illegally searched the representative of the conference—Huang Yanpei (黄炎培) 's residence. After the conference, while people from all walks of life in Chongqing were holding a meeting to celebrate the success of the Political Consultative Conference in Jiaochangkou (较场口) on February 10th, Kuomintang spies gathered hooligans and thugs to make troubles and even attacked and injured presidium members such as Guo Moruo (郭沫若), Ma Yinchu (马寅初), Li Gongpu (李公朴) and Shi Fuliang (施复亮) as well as over 60 journalists and members from labour associations. This was the Jiaochangkou Incident (较场口事件) that once shocked China and the world.

Chongqing Negotiation, Political Consultative Conference and Jiaochangkou Incident were important events in modern and contemporary Chinese history. They comprehensively and profoundly reflected the rapid development and changes of the political situation in China after the War of Resistance Against Japanese Aggression. Democracy or dictatorship, peace or civil war, unification or secession, cooperation or separation, all those differences between CPC and Kuomintang were appeared in Chongqing, the war-time capital.

In May 1946, when the Kuomintang government moved back to Nanking, the CPC delegation led by Zhou Enlai and democratic parties moved east to Nanking, too. Those institutions, factories, schools, organizations and a great number of people that had immigrated to Chongqing previously moved back to the eastern cities. The political, economic, military, cultural and social status of Chongqing witnessed relative declination compared with that in the War of Resistance Against Japan period. Even so, Chongqing remained the political, economic, military, cultural and social centre in southwest China. The national government established "Chairman of the Military Commission of the National Government, Chongqing Camp" and "Chairman of the National Government Chongqing Headquarter" "Chongqing Pacification Office of the Ministry of National Defense" "Southwest Military and Political Executive Office" in succession as representative offices of the Kuomintang central committee to control Chongqing and southwest China. In

August 1949, when the Chinese People's Liberation Army (PLA) liberated large areas in north and east China with a rapid pace, the Kuomintang government was like a stray dog. It first moved to Guangzhou, later announced to move from Guangzhou to Chongqing. Before this, on August 24th, Chiang Kai-shek, together with Huang Shaogu (黄少谷), Jiang Jingguo (蒋经国), Yu Jishi (俞济时) and others, had already flown to Chongqing. Representatives in charge of the party, government and army in southwest provinces were gathered to attend a meeting planning southwest defence and vainly attempted to review the old dream of "revival" during the War of Resistance Against Japan with Chongqing as the base. However, with the changing of time, the nature of war fundamentally changed, and Chongqing never became a base for the remnants of Kuomintang for "revival". On the contrary, Chongqing became its burial ground.

Ⅱ.Chongqing Social Economy— on the Verge of Breakdown

Under the reactionary rule of the Kuomintang, the economic and cultural prosperity during the War of Resistance Against Japan period saw serious retrogression or even stagnation. The Kuomintang government had already mired in political, military, social, financial and monetary pathology. Money squeezed; factories went bankrupt; transportation disrupted; foreign goods flooded; commerce recessed; prices soared; currency devalued; workers unemployed and went bankrupt, and civilians lived in poverty. The Kuomintang had lost political, economic and social basis for its further rule. In opposition to Kuomintang civil war policy, dictatorship, the squeeze and plunder of common people from the imperialism, feudalism and bureaucrat capitalism, the people of Chongqing, with its glorious revolutionary tradition, all fought resolutely against Kuomintang reactionary rule under the leadership of CPC. The "Anti-hunger, Anti-civil-war, Anti-persecution" (反饥饿、反内战、反迫害) struggle organized by the majority of young students, the "Anti-pressgang, Anti-donation, Anti-rent" (抗丁、抗捐、抗租) struggle organized by the peasants and the armed uprisings in upper and lower east Sichuan led by CPC underground organizations, all dealt heavy blows to the Kuomintang reactionaries.

Ⅲ. The Struggle of East Sichuan Underground Party (川东地下党)

After the victory of the War of Resistance Against Japanese Aggression, the Southern Bureau of the CPC Central Committee attached great importance to the development of the underground party. In March 1946, the CPC Chongqing Municipal Committee was rehabilitated. When the Southern Bureau was moved to the east, the party's east Sichuan temporary working committee was established in October 1947 with the CPC Chongqing Municipal Committee as its subordinate. Faced with a severe situation, people in east Sichuan conducted arduous struggles and made great sacrifice under the leadership of east Sichuan underground party. *Tingjin Newspaper* (《挺进报》) —a municipal party committee newspaper was destroyed and 133 party members and civilians were arrested and sacrificed their lives.

To cooperate with the PLA's struggles in frontline battlefield, east Sichuan underground party hastened their preparation for armed struggle. Between 1947 and 1948, the party's east Sichuan temporary working committee led armed uprisings in Fengjie, Daning (Wuxi) and Wushan in lower east Sichuan and Huaying Mountain uprising in upper east Sichuan in succession. In November 1947, the party's east Sichuan temporary working committee established East Sichuan Democratic Allied Forces Lower East Sichuan Guerrilla Column [later renamed as East Sichuan Guerrilla Column of CPC (中国共产党川东游击纵队)] in Lutangping (鹿塘坪), Liuping Village (六坪村), Jiangkou Town (江口镇). On January 7th, 1948, the guerrilla held armed uprisings and attacked the administrative office at Xining Village (西宁乡) in Wuxi County, Nanxi Town (南溪镇) in Yunyang County and won a decisive victory. Under Kuomintang regular army's converging attack from the north to the south, the guerrillas were transferred towards Hongchiba (红池坝) in Wuxi, but they were surrounded by Kuomintang. The uprising was failed with the sacrifice of political commissar Peng Yongwu (彭咏梧). In August 1948, in the name of Southwest Democratic Allied Force, east Sichuan temporary working committee launched Huaying Mountain uprising in advance. Wang Pu (王璞), as the secretary of the committee, led this uprising. He also led Daishi (代市) and Guange (观阁) uprisings in Guangan (广安), Sanxi (三溪) uprising in Wusheng (武胜), Fulong (伏龙) uprising in Yuechi (岳池), Jinzituo (金子沱) uprising in Hechuan and Zhengjing (真静) uprising in Wusheng successively. He dedicated himself in different counties and commanded battles in person. The insurrectionary army attacked administrative offices in villages and towns, opening the granaries to help the poor, and being very popular with the public. Kuomintang mobilized military police from Chongqing to suppress. Owing to the great disparity of strength between the enemy and our forces, all uprisings failed. The party organizations in uprising areas were destroyed, as many as 400 to 500 party members and revolutionary masses sacrificed their lives. The two uprisings in upper and lower east Sichuan played a positive role in embracing the liberation in east Sichuan and Chongqing.

Ⅳ. The "November 27th Massacre" ("一一·二七"血案)

Kuomintang established concentration camps in Cinder Cave (渣滓洞) and White Residence (白公馆) prison site in Gele Mountain (歌乐山) in Chongqing as a place to lock up communists, revolutionary progressives and political criminals. Revolutionaries such as Ye Ting (叶挺), Xu Xiaoxuan (许晓轩), Huang Xiansheng (黄显声) and anti-Japanese patriots were once imprisoned here. On the eve of Chongqing liberation, communists such as Jiang Zhujun (江竹筠), Xu Jianye (许

建业), Yu Zusheng (余祖胜), Luo Guangbin (罗广斌), Song Yiyun (宋绮云) and revolutionaries such as general Yang Hucheng (杨虎城) were all imprisoned in these two concentration camps.

In August 1949, Chiang Kai-shek arranged the massacre of communists and revolutionaries in Cinder Cave and White Residence in person. On September 6th, general Yang Hucheng and his son Yang Zhengzhong (杨拯中) were murdered in the reception area in Songlinpo (松林坡). On October 28th, Chen Ran (陈然), the secretary of *Tingjin Newspaper*, together with other 9 people, were murdered in Daping. On November 14th, 30 people including Jiang Zhujun were murdered secretly in the broadcasting station Lanya (电台岚垭) which is the former Sino-American Cooperative Organization.

On November 27th, Kuomintang created a larger-scale bloody massacre, the "November 27th Massacre" that shocked both China and the world. At 4 p.m. or so, Kuomintang spies started the massacre of the revolutionaries in White Residence prison site in batches. This massacre lasted till deep night. Meanwhile, the PLA had reached the southern bank of the Yangtze River of Chongqing. The spies were in a hurry to flee, and massacre in batches turned to holocaust. They concentrated revolutionaries that has not been murdered in the cells downstairs and strafed crazily with American machine guns and carbines. Nearly 200 communists and revolutionaries were murdered on this day, only 35 survived.

Ⅴ.Liberation of Chongqing

On October 1st, 1949, the People's Republic of China was founded. Since then, wiping out the remnants of Kuomintang and shattering Chiang Kai-shek's conspiracy to set up a southwest regime became the top priority of the PLA. Before the founding of PRC, CPC had planned the liberation of the southeast by sending the Second Field Army and He Long (贺龙) Legion of the First Field Army to the southwest and establishing the Southwestern Bureau of the CPC Central Committee (中共中央西南局) with Deng Xiaoping (邓小平) as the first secretary. Subsequently, Central Military Commission and Mao Zedong made specific plans for the liberation of Southwest China from strategic and tactic perspectives. In August 19th 1949, Liu Bocheng (刘伯承) , the commander of the Second Field Army of PLA and Deng Xiaoping, the political commissar, ordered *the Basic Command for the Second Field Army to Fight in Sichuan and Guizhou* (《第二野战军向川黔进军作战的基本命令》) and mainly completed the strategic deployment to march towards the southwest.

On November 1st, 1949, PLA launched a strong offensive towards southwest in the thousands of miles front from the Yangtze River in the north and the borders of Hunan, Guangxi and Guizhou in the south. Xiushan, Youyang and Qianjiang were liberated successively. They broke through the Wujiang River (乌江) natural barrier and liberated Nanchuan on 24th, thus cutting through Chongqing portal. Meanwhile, the fifth legion and the tenth army of third legion of the Second Field Army, marched into Guizhou from Hunan and liberated Guiyang, Zunyi successively. They continued their triumphant pursuit towards the north, northwest and southwest of Guizhou to chase the fleeing enemy and cut off the route of retreat of the Kuomintang army in Sichuan and Shaanxi areas. On November 26th, Liu Bocheng and Deng Xiaoping issued the order to quickly wipe out the enemy on the south bank of the Yangtze River and take over Chongqing whenever possible. The army branched out into three columns and surrounded Chongqing City from Fuling, Nanchuan and Qijiang. On 27th

Picture 3-16 The Liberation of Chongqing on November 30th, 1949

and 28th, Jiangjin, Shunjiangchang (顺江场) and Yudong that were in Chongqing peripheral were taken over. The army marched towards the city of Chongqing and easily broke through the line of defence along the Yangtze River. Chiang Kai-shek realized the situation was not in his favour, so he fled to Chengdu in a hurry from Baishiyi airport in the early morning of November 30th. In the afternoon of November 30th, 1949, the 5 barracks of the 11th, 12th and 47th army of the Second Field Army of the PLA marched into Chongqing city, and Chongqing declared liberation.

Section Five After the Founding of People's Republic of China

Ⅰ.The Period of Southwest Region

1.The Establishment and Consolidation of the New Republic

After the liberation of Chongqing, in order to strengthen military control, establish new social order, develop social productive forces and manage southwest China as a whole, the CPC central committee, referring to other regions' experience, established an administrative division at the regional level in the southwest, and Chongqing became a municipality directly under the Southwest Military and Political Commission. From 1951 to 1952, Ba County, Beibei City, Qijiang County, Changshou County, Jiangbei County were assigned to Chongqing successively. In June 1952, 5 districts and 1 county were under Chongqing jurisdiction. In 1953, Southwest Administrative Committee was established in Chongqing. Later, the Central Committee decided to make 10 administrative regions into municipalities directly under the central government, including Chongqing. This was the second time that Chongqing had been a municipality in history. In the same year, Ba County, Qijiang County and Jiangbei County were assigned to Jiangjin Prefecture in Sichuan, and Changshou County was assigned to

Fuling Prefecture in Sichuan.

The Southwestern Bureau of the CPC Central Committee, the head office of southwest party and military institutions, the Southwest Military (Administrative) and Political Commission and the Southwest Military Command were all established and stationed in Chongqing, which became the only municipality and station of the party and military institutions in southwest China after liberation.

Under the direct leadership of the Southwestern Bureau of the CPC Central Committee and Southwest Military and Political Commission, the takeover of Chongqing was completed successfully. The CPC Chongqing Municipal Committee, the municipal people's government, the people's governments at all levels and various mass organizations were established in succession. Faced with social disorder in the initial period after the founding of the PRC, according to the deployment of the Central Party and the Southwestern Bureau of the CPC, Chongqing carried out the work to suppress counter-revolutionaries, to ban reactionary sectarian organizations, to prohibit opium, and to crack down on prostitution.

In its suppression of counter-revolutionaries, on January 18th, 1950, within 10 days after the establishment of Chongqing Municipal Public Security Bureau, 1,315 criminals including various counter-revolutionaries and other criminals were arrested citywide. On March 13th, 1951, Chongqing conducted a major hunt for counter-revolutionaries and arrested 4,296 counter-revolutionaries and seized 14 guns and 2,656 bullets, hundreds of reactionary files, commission orders and registers, together with 458 liang gold, 6,872 silver dollars and some American and Hong Kong dollars that were to be used in counter-revolutionary activities.

In the ban of reactionary sectarian organizations and repatriation of the old military and political personnel, Chongqing Police Headquarters, Chongqing Military Control Commission and Chongqing Public Security Bureau issued *Procedures for the Registration of Demobilized Officers and Men of Chiang's*

Bandit Army, *Proclamation of the Dissolution of Illegal Party and Caucus Organizations*, *Promulgation of Chongqing Municipality's Interim Measures on the Registration of Social Organizations* successively, and received response from some order registrants. Till April 1951, 11,660 people participated in the registration of illegal parties and caucus organizations. 37,800 people announced to withdraw from reactionary sectarian organizations. Meanwhile, 432 ringleaders of the reactionary parties were arrested, together with 709 reactionary officers, 413 despotic landlords, 138 bandits and 564 leaders of reactionary caucus. In the aspect of housing, severance and employment of stragglers and disbanded soldiers, by 1950, 22,751 of Chiang's officers and soldiers were disbanded, together with 296 officials of the old government, 2,164 refugees, 9,206 stragglers and disbanded soldiers. Besides, by the end of 1952, 20,685 refugees and beggars were accepted in asylums.

In the prohibition of opium and the crack down on prostitution, Chongqing Municipalty discussed and passed *Regulations of Chongqing Anti-smoking and Anti-drug Commission* (《重庆市禁烟禁毒委员会组织规程》) and issued *the Proclamation on the Complete Prohibition of Opium* (《关于彻底禁绝鸦片烟毒的布告》). In October 1950, Chongqing Anti-Opium and Anti-Drug Commission started working. By the end of 1951, 22,515 cases were broken; over 30,000 liang illegal drugs were burnt; 27 flagitious drug dealers were executed by shooting; 16 drug dealers were sentenced to death with a reprieve, and over 1,000 drug dealers were sentenced. In 1952, Chongqing launched larger scale mass anti-drug activities within the municipality and broke 115 group cases and 2,887 single cases. 3,148 big drug dealers were arrested in succession. 21,908 liang illegal drugs of various kinds, 43,944 liang raw materials to make drugs, and 6,109 machines to make drugs as well as a large quantity of firearms and ammunition were seized. The total number of drug traffickers who registered in these activities amounted to 9,878. Chongqing municipality also took in and remoulded prostitutes. By the end of 1952, over 6,000 prostitutes were taken in.

Besides, to strengthen the new republic, the Chongqing Municipality also conducted the Rectification Movement (整风运动) among party members and cadres. Through the works mentioned above, Chongqing social order witnessed rapid improvement and the new regime of people was strengthened.

2.The Construction of New Chongqing

In March 1950, Chongqing Municipal Party Committee made a clear guideline for the work in a period of time thereafter. It was production oriented, production recovery and development, the turning of a consumer city into a production city, the construction of a new people's and productive Chongqing. Faced with this arduous and onerous task, Chongqing Municipal Party Committee and Chongqing Municipal People's Government, under the correct and direct leadership of the Southwestern Bureau of the CPC Central Committee and Southwest Military (Administrative) and Political Commission, united people from all walks of life and overcame all kinds of difficulties and rapidly fulfilled all kinds of democratic reforms such as rent reduction and deposit return, land reform, urban democratic reform, marriage and judicial reform.

Rent Reduction and Deposit Return Movement (减租退押运动) arose the enthusiasm of over 120,000 peasants in the city. It reduced a burden of 33.47 billion (old currency) for the peasants and laid foundation for land reform. From February 1951, land reform was carried out throughout the city by means of publicity and education, the organization of peasant associations, the division of class status, the evaluation of farmland and production, the registration and confiscation of landlord's lands and allotment. By the end of March 1951, 3,266,469 farm implements, 13,978 farm cattle, 1,460, 269 furniture and 377, 734 houses were confiscated and expropriated. 6,466 despotic landlords were crack down.

Urban democratic reform was mainly the reform of industrial and mining enterprises. From March 1950 to March 1953, state-run industrial and mining enterprises, private industrial and mining enterprises, construction and porterage experienced democratic and productive reforms. In the reform of the state-run factories, anti-bureaucratic and anti-commandism activities were conducted. Unreasonable old systems were abolished. Various democratic organizations and new production management system were established. In the reform of private enterprises, by means of cost calculation, salary reduction, redundant personnel reduction, unreasonable old system abolishment, waste reduced and production enhanced, and guild organizations strengthened and workers' enthusiasm for production enhanced. In the reform of porterage work, unreasonable feudal exploitation such as guild transfer, share transfer, by-business and bonus deduction distribution were all abolished. Pseudo guilds and branches were dissolved. Feudal head system was abolished, and handling organizations and procedures were simplified. Feudal heads were dealt a blow. "Preparatory Committee of Chongqing Longshoremen's Union" (重庆市码头工人公会筹委会) and "Preparatory Office of Chongqing Transportation Company" (重庆市搬运公司筹备处) were established, and port handling order was stabilized.

Picture 3-17 The Commencement Date of the Construction of Chongqing Working People's Culture Palace on July 1st, 1951. This picture shows the Foundation Stone Laying Ceremony.

Besides, Chongqing also carried out marriage and judicial reform, Campaign to Resist the American Aggression and Aid Korea, the Movement Against the "Three Evils" (三反)[1] and the Movement Against the "Five Evils" (五反)[2]. Remarkable achievements were made in the restoration and development of the national economy, the promotion of

[1] "Three evils" refer to corruption, waste and bureaucracy within the Party, the government, the army and mass organizations, and this movement lasted from 1951 to 1952.

[2] "Five evils" refer to bribe, tax evasion, theft of state property, cheat on labour and materials, theft of national information.

culture and education, and improvement of municipal utilities. All the achievements mentioned above laid foundation for the transition from new democracy to socialism.

During this period, according to the guideline to build a new people's and productive Chongqing, taking Chongqing urban geographic characteristics, distribution of productivity and characteristics of residential settlements into consideration, the principles of urban development were determined. That is "Large Dispersion and Small Concentration" (大分散、小集中) and "Westward Development" (向西发展). With areas in western Chongqing such as the triangle area of Da Ping, Yang Jiaping (杨家坪) and Shiqiaopu (石桥铺), Shapingba, Ciqikou, Xiaolongkan area, Dadukou area and Zhongliang Mountain (中梁山) area as the focus, with urban roads and industrial construction as the guide, the layout of Chongqing avoided scattering everywhere. The development of western new areas was promoted. In 1951, Chongqing Municipal People's Government designed the overall layout with the triangle area of Daping, Yangjiaping and Shiqiaopu as the centre of new Chongqing, with the thousands of meters around the triangle area as the new urban area. Three central areas were arranged in the northeast, southwest and northwest of the triangle area. They were northeast economic centre along the original urban area in Liangjiang Peninsula, Jiangbeicheng, Guanyinqiao (观音桥) in Jiangbei District and Danzishi (弹子石), Longmenhao (龙门浩) in Nan'an District, southwest industrial centre in Dadukou, Lijiatuo (李家沱) and Yudong (鱼洞) area, northwest culture centre in Shapingba, Ciqikou and Xiaolongkan. The professional division exerted important influence on the development of Chongqing new western regions and function divisions among cities.

Ⅱ.Municipality Directly Under the Provincial Government

On June 22nd, 1954, the CPC Central Committee decided to abolish regional administrative agencies and merge some provinces and cities. Chongqing merged into Sichuan Province and was changed from a municipality directly under central government to a city under the jurisdiction of Sichuan Province. In 1955, Nantong Mining Area (南桐矿区) was established. Seven districts including the central District, Jiangbei District, Shapingba District, Jiulongpo District, Nan'an District, Beibei District and Nantong Mining Area were under Chongqing administration. In 1959, Ba County and Qijiang County in Jiangjin District of Sichuan, and Changshou County in Fuling District of Sichuan were assigned to Chongqing. In 1965, Dadukou District in Chongqing was established. In 1974, Shuangqiao District (双桥区) in Chongqing was established. In 1976, Jiangbei County in Jiangjin District of Sichuan was assigned to Chongqing. In 1983, the State Council decided to cancel Yongchuan District and 8 counties within its administration. Yongchuan, Dazu Tongliang, Hechuan, Bishan, Jiangjin, Rongchang and Tongnan were assigned to Chongqing. Between 1992 and 1993, Yongchuan County, Jiangjin County and Hechuan County were cancelled, and Yongchuan City, Jiangjin City and Hechuan City were established. They were under direct jurisdiction of Sichuan Province, but they were managed by Chongqing. Nantong Mining Area was renamed as Wansheng District (万盛区). In 1995, with the approval of Sichuan Provincial Government, the jurisdiction of Chongqing was adjusted to 11 districts, 3 county-level cities under the administration of Chongqing instead of Sichuan and 7 counties. Yubei District and Banan District were newly established, and Ba County was cancelled. The Central District was renamed as Yuzong District.

1.The First Five-Year Plan

Under the guidance of the party's general line, Chongqing carried out Agricultural Cooperative Movement (农业合作化运动), and Chongqing started the socialist transformation of agriculture, handicraft industry and capitalist industry and commerce, and Chongqing achieved smooth transition from new democracy to socialism.

Picture 3-18 The Completion of the Auditorium of the Southwest Administrative Committee in March 1954

Chongqing's First Five-Year Plan for the development of the national economy, which was implemented in 1956, laid the preliminary foundation for Chongqing modern industry. The scale of industrial capital construction was increased, and concentrated investment was made in energy industries such as electric power, coal and natural gas; reconstruction and extension was made in metallurgical industrial enterprises such as iron and steel industry; chemical industry, textile industry, food industry and other light industries all saw rapid development. The industrial development was fast and the production capacity increased; Chongqing industry became more prominent in Sichuan Province. The distribution of industrial productivity has changed, and new industrial power plants were opened up in Zhongliangshan (中梁山), Nanping (南坪), Daojiao (道角), Shimen (石门) and Qiaojiaotuo (窍角沱) ; a batch of machine industries and textile industries were built in Baisha of Jiangjin, Laifeng (来凤) of Bishan, Yulong (玉龙) of Dazu and Yongchang Town (永昌镇) of Yongchuan. Longxihe (龙溪河) Step Hydro-power Station and Nantong Coal Mine Industrial Area were key zones of development, and thus the past geographical distribution of industry along the river was improved. The modern economic structure was taking shape. In 1957, the proportion of industry value in the gross output value of industry and agriculture increased to 85.70%, and the ratio of heavy industry in industry was 44.03%. The First Five-Year Plan also facilitated sustainable development of agriculture, transportation, urban infrastructure, as well as cultural and educational undertakings, which brought about profound changes in Chongqing politics, economy, and culture. However, the guideline to “set heavy industry as priority” in the First Five-Year-Plan also exerted a negative impact on Chongqing industrial structure, energy consumption and environment.

2.Keep Forging Ahead in Twists and Turns

The establishment of the socialist system and the completion of the First Five-Year Plan provided prerequisite for the overall socialist construction in Chongqing. However, owing to international, domestic, subjective and objective factors, in “Great Leap Forward” (大跃进) and the Movement of People’s Communes (人民公社化运动), the guiding principle to rush for quick results in economic construction and the left-deviationist mistakes with unrealistic production targets, arbitrary orders, the tendency toward boasting and exaggeration and the practice of equalitarianism in the name of communism as its main features, resulted in serious damage to productivity. People lived a hard living. In the field of ideology, under the wrong policy of “expanding class struggles”, Rectification Movement, Anti-Rightist, struggle against right deviations and socialist education movement in urban and rural areas (城乡社会主义教育运动) came one after another. These movements and their errors brought about great losses and negative impacts. In the “Cultural Revolution” which started in 1966, Chongqing became one of the severely afflicted areas. When the “Gang of Four” (四人帮) were crushed, by means of reforming from the bottom, bringing order out of chaos, overcoming the shackles of left-leaning thought, Chongqing finally got out of trouble and rose from the bottom and strode forward to the era of reform and opening-up.

3.The Strategic Area Construction in National Defence

Almost at the same time with the "Cultural Revolution", the CPC Central Committee decided to initiate the grand Strategic Area Construction in National Defence[1]. Chongqing was the largest central city within the scope of this construction, and thus shouldered great responsibility.

From the second half of 1964 to the late 1970s, a boom for the Strategic Area Construction in National Defence emerged around Chongqing. In September 1964, the state established the Strategic Area Construction in National Defence Planning Group in Chongqing area, compling *Plan for Chongqing Area in the Strategic Area Construction in National Defence* (《重庆地区三线建设规划》), proposing an industrial layout project with Chongqing as the centre. Later, from 1964 to 1966, 58 enterprises and public institutions, together with 43,488 staff related to 15 central ministries migrated in large-scale internally to Chongqing. They came from 12 provinces and cities such as Beijing, Shanghai, Nanjing, Liaoning and Guangdong. Till 1975, the number of migrated staff reached its peak 435,000, accounting for a quarter of Chongqing urban population. From the second half of 1964 to 1967, 59 grand backbone projects and supporting projects were constructed or reorganized or expanded. These projects included the reorganization and expansion of ordnance industry, the new construction of ship, electronic and aerospace projects, the supporting construction of metallurgy, chemical and mechanical industries, and the new construction and expansion of transportation projects.

The Strategic Area Construction in National Defence brought about major development opportunities for Chongqing. The construction of a large batch of industrial projects in the peripheral regions and the building and the opening to traffic of trunk railways like Chuanqian (川黔) and Xiangyu (襄渝) improved the structure and layout of Chongqing industrial economy. Modern industrial system

[1] This construction refers to the large-scale infrastructure construction of national defence, science, technology, industry and transportation carried out by the government of the People's Republic of China in 13 provinces and autonomous regions in central and western regions of China for war preparedness.

was built up. Meanwhile, the gradual rise of a batch of small towns formed 4 town clusters in Changshou, Qijiang, Ba County and Beibei; Nantong Mineral Area (Wansheng Economic and Technological Development Zone nowadays) formed in the 1950s. A modern town system with different functions and sizes was shaped. That initially established the current pattern of Chongqing satellite cities.

After more than a decade of construction, Chongqing initially had established a relatively complete production system of national defence; the industrial structure and layout has saw gradual improvement; the traffic has been gradually developed; a town system with reasonable layout had been formed; a large number of scientific and technological talents have been brought in. This further laid the foundation of the industrial economy. However, influenced by the "Cultural Revolution" and the guiding ideology of the "left", the plan and layout of the Strategic Area Construction in National Defence was not reasonable; the proportion of light and heavy industries was severely out of balance, and thus did not booster local economy. This brought about great difficulties to the adjustment of enterprises established in the strategic areas and negative impacts on the development of local national economy.

4.Bring Order out of Chaos

When the "Gang of Four" was crushed in October 1976, Chongqing's work to bring order out of chaos was severely impeded by the long-term influence of ideology of the "left" and "two whatevers" (whatever Chairman Mao decided or directed) and wandered forward. In the wake of a national debate about the standard of truth in 1978, the party's basic line and guiding ideology were reoriented to the correct path of Marxism-Leninism. According to the deployment of the Central Party Committee and Sichuan Provincial Party Committee, Chongqing made an overall rectification from political, organizational, economic, educational, scientific and technological perspectives.

In early 1983, 145,535 unjust convictions were rectified. All of them were left over from "Cultural Revolution" and history, and they were related to movements of underground party, Anti-Hu Feng case, Anti-Rightist, struggle against right deviations and "Four Clean-ups" Movement. 150,000 relevant personnel were involved in the implementation of the policy. 20,936 carders whose cases were filed and investigated in the "Cultural Revolution" were redressed and rehabilitated; remedial work was done on the 1,017 people who were persecuted to death; redressing and rehabilitating works were done on major local cases in Chongqing and policies were implemented. Redressed and rectified "NO.1 Case" that involved 31 defectors from the middle-class and upper-class insurrection, Latent Spy Case in the early days of Liberation and Persecution Case of the Insurgents.

In the wake of the reform and opening-up, the national economy began to resuscitate. All walks of life gradually embarked on the correct track.

Ⅲ.Cities Specifically Designated in the State Plan and Reform of the Comprehensive Urban Economic System

1.Direct Planning by the State

In the early 1980s, after breakthroughs made in rural reform, reform of urban economic system were put on the agenda. Chongqing, as the economic centre in the southwest and an important production base of conventional weapons, had a complete range of industries, but the management system was very complex.

In February 1983, the Central Government approved Chongqing as a pilot city for urban economic system reform and direct planning by the state was implemented. Chongqing was listed in the State Plan as a provincial independent planning unit. The Central Government pointed out "the choice of Chongqing as a pilot city for urban economic system reform is an important decision made by CPC Central Committee and the State Council on the current reform work in

China. To do a good job in this pilot city is of great importance to further invigorate and develop the economy of southwest China. To explore a new way to combine military production with civilian production and organize economic zones centred around large cities."

The main rights enjoyed by Chongqing as a city specifically designated in the state plan are listed as follows. The state implemented a separate plan for Chongqing; in nationwide industrial and agricultural production, transportation, post and telecommunications, fixed-asset investment, purchase, sale, distribution and allocation of major commodities, distribution and allocation of energy and major materials, export and import trade, financial credit, labour wages, science and technology as well as various social undertakings, set separate account for Chongqing. Granted economic management authority to Chongqing equivalent to that of a province, on the premise of ensuring the national plan and the provincial plan, Chongqing had the right to make overall arrangements for the city's production, construction, circulation and distribution. Provincial enterprises and institutions in Chongqing were decentralized to Chongqing for administration.

Direct planning by the state, as a breakthrough of comprehensive pilot reform in Chongqing, played a leading role in the reform. It effectively drove and promoted the reform of other aspects, and it reduced the division of departments, the division of urban and rural sectors, the division of military and civilian within Chongqing economy, and it enhanced the vitality of the city and enterprises.

2.The New City-Guide-County System (市带县) of Urban and Rural Integration

Before 1983, there were 9 districts and 4 counties under Chongqing jurisdiction. The population in Chongqing was 6.6 million. In February 1983, when Chongqing gained the right as a comprehensive economic system reform pilot, the Stated Council approved to cancel the prefectural administrative office in

Yongchuan District of Sichuan. 8 counties under its jurisdiction were assigned to Chongqing. They were Yongchuan, Dazu, Tongliang, Hechuan, Bishan, Jiangjin, Rongchang, Tongnan. The new city-guide-county system was introduced. After this merger, Chongqing has 9 districts and 12 counties under its jurisdiction with a population of 13.94 million.

When the new city-guide-county system was implemented, Chongqing Municipal Government printed and distributed *the Decision on Several Issues Concerning the Improvement of City-Guide-County System* (《关于搞好市带县若干问题的决定》). According to this decision, the districts' and counties' authority of economic management was expanded; the technical and economic exchanges and cooperation between urban and rural areas were strengthened; the development of township enterprises was supported. Chongqing made a beneficial exploration for the development of urban and rural economic integration.

3.Macroeconomic System Reform and State-Owned Enterprise Reform

In macroeconomic field, Chongqing first carried out financial and monetary system reform as well as price reform.

In the financial system reform, the practice of unified collection and expenditure under the planned economy was changed. Fiscal revenue and expenditures should be distributed in proportion to the growth of the whole province. Surplus income share was practiced. Districts and counties also made corresponding adjustments.

In the monetary system reform, a fundraising and financing network was established. A variety of financial organizations were developed, such as the establishment of city credit cooperative, city financial services, postal savings service and securities company, the promotion of the settlement of commercial bills, the development of trust deposit investment business, buyer seller credit and financial leasing, etc. The credit fund management system was reformed.

In the price reform, focus was put on the formation mechanism of price conversion. The prices of most industrial consumer goods were liberalized; the market mechanism was introduced; the management of central and local enterprises at different levels took initial shape. A new price pattern with the coexistence of multiple forms such as the nation setting the price, the nation guiding the price and the market regulating the price was formed. In the middle of 1990s, a price system that was compatible with the socialist market economy was initially established.

Later, reforms were made in circulation system, investment system and state property management system.

In microeconomic field, a crucial battle for the reform of the state-owned enterprises was waged. This reform started from decentralization and surrender part of the profits and gradually implemented various forms of pilot reforms of the economic responsibility system such as asset management system, system of contracted responsibility, rental system, stock-holding system to enhance the vitality and competitiveness of enterprises. Meanwhile, new ways of military industry system reform were actively explored. Chongqing played an exemplary role for the whole county in its grasp of military and civilian integration as well as the development of the production of civilian goods. Civilized national consumer product brands such as “CHANGAN AUTO” and “Jialing Motorcycle” emerged. Before 1997, the year when Chongqing became a municipality directly under the central government, Chongqing rural reform and urban reform went hand in hand. A market economy was gradually established.

Ⅳ.Chongqing: A Municipality Directly under the Central Government

1.The Municipality of Chongqing

In early 1992, Deng Xiaoping put forward some ideas to bridge the development gap between the coastal areas and the inland areas in his south tour talks. Later, the Party Central Committee made a strategic decision to open to the outside world from the coast to the river, along the border, along the highways, the railways, and airlines as well as into inland. It also made a strategic decision on the key development of the Yangtze River. Two major initiatives to implement this strategic decision were the development and opening of Pudong and the construction of the Three Gorges Project. From the "Ninth Five-Year Plan", the Central Government attached more importance to the development of the inland, and it made adherence to the coordinated development of regional economies and gradual bridging of the development gap among regions as the national economic and social development guidelines and strategic tasks. The central and western development strategy was established. The Yangtze River Economic Belt that crossed the east, central and west regions with a population of several hundred million was the carrier of this development strategy. Chongqing became the perfect pivot of the central and western development strategy.

Chongqing is located in the upper reaches of the Yangtze River, at the junction of three provinces—Yunnan, Guizhou and Sichuan respectively. In the Yangtze River Economic Belt and the southwest economic zone, Chongqing plays the role of a hub that connects the east with the west and transfers from left to right. This is the unique geographical advantage of Chongqing. Meanwhile, Chongqing is also an important regional centre in the southwest. After the War of Resistance Against Japanese Aggression and several decades of development in the Strategic Area Construction in National Defence, Chongqing boasted rich industrial categories and sound industrial systems. It had become the economic centre and transportation hub in southwest China and in the upper reaches of the Yangtze River. Thus, to separate Chongqing from Sichuan province was an idea that was put forward in the 1980s. With the acceleration of the development strategy of the central and western regions of China, and the resettlement of the Three Gorges Project, the Central

Government began to conduct a careful evaluation on Chongqing.

In August 1996, after careful research and repeated argumentation by the CPC Central Committee and the State Council, Chongqing was established as the 4th municipality directly under the central government after Beijing, Tianjin and Shanghai. To ensure the smooth implementation of this important decision, the CPC Central Committee and the State Council approved in September the request of Sichuan Province to entrust Chongqing to administer Fuling City, Wanxian City and Qianjiang Area (“two cities and one area”). On September 15th, Chongqing officially exercised management functions on “two cities and one area” on behalf of Sichuan.

On February 27th, 1997, Premier Li Peng, on behalf of the State Council, proposed to National People’s Congress (NPC) *Proposal for the Establishment of Chongqing Municipality Directly under the Central Government* (《关于提请审议设立重庆直辖市的议案》). He pointed out that “In order to give full play to the role of Chongqing as a major economic centre, to further promote the economic and social development of eastern Sichuan, southwest China and the upper reaches of the Yangtze River, and to be conductive to the construction of the Three Gorges Project, to the unified planning, arrangement and management of immigrants in the reservoir area, and at the same time, to solve the problem that Sichuan Province and its administrative area under its jurisdiction was too large to manage”. It is decided to establish Chongqing as a municipality directly under the central government. On March 14th, this proposal was approved at the Fifth Session of the Eighth National People’s Congress. On June 18th, Chongqing held the opening ceremony of the being listed as a municipality directly under the central government. The establishment of Chongqing as a municipality directly under the central government symbolized that the economic and social development of Chongqing entered a new historical period.

After the establishment of Chongqing as a municipality directly under the central government, Fuling City, Wanxian City and Qianjiang Area in Sichuan Province were cancelled, and the administrative areas under their jurisdiction were incorporated into Chongqing Municipality. In 2011, Shuangqiao District and Wansheng District were cancelled and were incorporated into Dazu District and Qijiang District respectively. Till 2018, there were 26 districts, 8 counties and 4 minority autonomous counties under Chongqing jurisdiction.

Picture 3-19 Opening Ceremony of Chongqing Municipality on June 18th, 1997

Picture 3-20 The Conference Venue of the Opening Ceremony of Chongqing Municipality on June 18th, 1997

2."314" Overall Deployment

In March 2007, the General Secretary of the CPC Central Committee, President Hu Jintao attended Review by the Chongqing Delegation at The Fifth Session of the Tenth National People's Congress and delivered an important speech. Standing at the height of overall situation and strategy, Hu Jintao navigated Chongqing development by setting three orientations—strive to build Chongqing as an important role of growth in the western region, an economic centre in the upper reaches of the Yangtze River and a municipality that coordinates urban and rural development; one grand objective—take the lead in realizing the goal of building a well-off society in an all-round way in the western region; four tasks—increase efforts to promote agriculture through industry, to foster rural development with urban development, and make steady headway in the construction of a new socialist countryside; to transform the pattern of economic growth effectively, and accelerate the pace of adjustment and reform of old industrial bases; to focus on improving people's well-being and actively build a harmonious socialist society; and to comprehensively strengthen urban construction and improve the level of urban management.

3.Embark on a New Journey to Comprehensively Build Socialist Modernization

In January 2016, during his visit to Chongqing, the General Secretary of the CPC Central Committee, President Xi Jinping pointed out that Chongqing is an important strategic fulcrum of western development, the joint of the "Belt and Road Initiative" and the Yangtze River Economic Belt ("two points" orientation) ; Chongqing is to be built into an inland open highland and a beautiful land with green mountains and clear water ("two lands" objective). In March 2018, when attending the Review by the Chongqing Delegation at the First Session of the 13th National People's Congress, president Xi Jinping gave important instructions by proposing two objectives: "the promotion of high-quality development" and "the creation of high-quality life" ("two high" objectives). Meanwhile, he also gave important instructions on fostering a sound political environment and emphasized that "leading cadres should stress political ethnics". In April 2019, General Secretary Xi Jinping visited Chongqing again and suggested that Chongqing should "Play a supporting role in promoting the western development in the new era and play a leading role in promoting joint construction of 'Belt and Road Initiative' and play an exemplary role in promoting green development of 'the Yangtze River Economic Belt'." The strategic position of Chongqing was strengthened again. A new development blueprint was made for Chongqing in the national regional development and opening to the outside world.

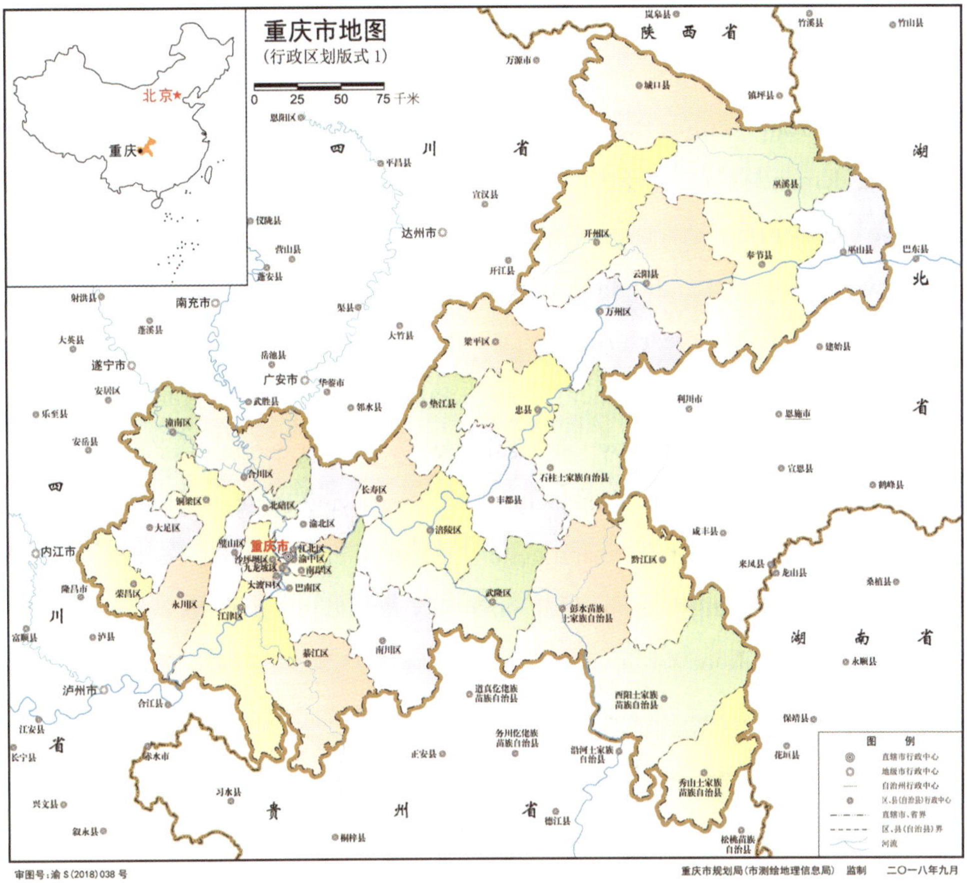

Picture 3-21 Administrative Division Map of Chongqing (2018)

After the 19th National Congress of the CPC, under the guidance of Xi Jinping Thought on Socialism with Chinese Characteristics for the New Era, in order to fully implement the spirit of the 19th National Congress of the CPC in Chongqing, in January 2018, at the First Session of the Municipal People's Congress, Chongqing Municipal Party Committee and Government, combined with the reality of Chongqing and set out to achieve the next five years' objectives by fighting "Three Critical Battles" and fulfilling "Eight Action Plans". "Three Critical Battles" refer to resolutely guard against and defuse major risks, take targeted measures for poverty alleviation and pollution prevention. "Eight Action Plans" refer to the implementation of an innovation-driven development strategy led by big data intelligence, rural revitalization strategy, infrastructure construction improvement, military-civilian integration strategy, invigoration of the city with science and education, strengthening the city with talents, construction of an inland open highland, demand-oriented assurance and improvement of people's livelihood and ecological priority for green development. "Eight Action Plans" focus on the long-term development and highlight three-year-duration, while "Three Critical Battles" aim at winning in three years. According to the requirements of each item and each list, Chongqing is to complete them one after another and year by year. It will strive to build a beautiful and happy Chongqing with quality economic development, more dynamic institutions and mechanisms, better living standards for the people, more orderly social governance and better ecological environment. Built up on this momentum, Chongqing is embarking on a new journey to comprehensively build socialist modernization.

Table 3-6 Administrative Divisions of Chongqing in 2017

Name of the place	The population of permanent residents (10,000)	District government residence	Total area (km^2)	Administrative division code	Zip code
Yuzhong District	64.95	Qixinggang Street	23	500103	400010
Wanzhou District	160.74	Chenjiaba Street	3,453	500101	404000
Fuling District	114.08	Lizhi Street	2,941	500102	408000
Dadukou District	33.27	Xinshancun Street	103	500104	400080
Jiangbei District	84.98	Cuntan Street	221	500105	400020
Shapingba District	113.39	Qinjiagang Street	396	500106	400030
Jiulongpo District	118.69	Yangjiaping Street	431	500107	400050
Nan'an District	85.81	Tianwen Street	262	500108	400064

Continued

Name of the place	The population of permanent residents (10,000)	District government residence	Total area (km^2)	Administrative division code	Zip code
Beibei District	78.62	Beiwenquan Street	751	500109	400700
Qijiang District	107.84	Gunan Street	2,747	500110	400800
Dazu District	76.39	Tangxiang Street	1,434	500111	400900
Yubei District	160.25	Lianglu Street	1,457	500112	401120
Banan District	100.58	Longzhouwan Street	1,823	500113	401320
Qianjiang District	46.20	Chengxi Street	2,390	500114	409700
Changshou District	82.43	Puti Street	1,421	500115	401220
Jiangjin District	133.19	Jijiang Street	3,216	500116	402260
Hechuan District	136.06	Nanjin Street	2,343	500117	401520
Yongchuan District	109.61	Zhongshanlu Street	1,579	500118	402160
Nanchuan District	56.43	Dongcheng Street	2589	500119	408400
Bishan District	72.52	Bicheng Street	915	500120	402760
Tongliang District	68.72	Bachuan Street	1,341	500151	402560
Tongnan District	68.23	Guilin Street	1,585	500152	402660
Rongchang District	70.10	Changyuan Street	1,077	500153	402460
Kaizhou District	169.12	Hanfeng Street	3,964	500154	405400
Liangping District	66.40	Liangshan Street	1,888	500155	405200
Wulong District	41.44	Furong Street	2,892	500156	408500

Continued

Name of the place	The population of permanent residents (10,000)	District government residence	Total area (km^2)	Administrative division code	Zip code
Chengkou County	18.63	Gecheng Street	3,289	500229	405900
Fengdu County	59.56	Sanhe Street	2,899	500230	408200
Dianjiang County	67.67	Guiyang Street	1,517	500231	408300
Zhongxian County	70.80	Zhongzhou Street	2,187	500233	404300
Yunyang County	89.66	Shuangjiang Street	3,636	500235	404500
Fengjie County	75.33	Yong'an Street	4,098	500236	404600
Wushan County	46.23	Gaotang Street	2,955	500237	404700
Wuxi County	39.10	Baichang Street	4,015	500238	405800
Shizhu Tujia Autonomous County	38.65	Nanbin Street	3,014	500240	409100
Xiushan Tujia and Miao Autonomous County	49.13	Zhonghe Street	2,453	500241	409900
Youyang Tujia and Miao Autonomous County	55.65	Zhongduo Street	5,168	500242	409800
Pengshui Miao and Tujia Autonomous County	50.64	Hanjia Street	3,897	500243	409600

Chapter Four Economic Development

Section One Agriculture

Chongqing boasts a long history of agriculture. As early as the Ba State period that was 2,000 years ago, "5 cereals [1] were already planted and 6 domestic animals were already raised"("土植五谷，牲具六畜") *(Huayang Local Chronicles—the Local Chronicle of the Ba State*). People also started to breed silkworms and plant hemp and tea. During the Qin and Han dynasties, agriculture in Chongqing area developed with the building of water conservancy projects. In villages, ponds were already dug for comprehensive utilization such as to conserve water and to irrigate farmlands. New iron farming tools began to be used and popularized. Rice was widely cultivated in flat areas. "There were rice fields in the north of Jiangzhou County, which provided rice for the emperor's kitchen", and the surplus grain was distributed far down to the lower reaches of the Yellow River. In the Han Dynasty, pigs, chicken, ducks and fish were already bred, and lotus root, water chestnut, tangerines and litchi were planted. Jiangzhou became the water wharf in Bashu area for material distribution, and its agricultural and side-line products were exported to other places. During the Tang and Song Dynasties, the reclamation of agricultural lands expanded from flat areas and river valleys to hilly areas. Advanced methods such as the building of terraces were created. Terraces appeared in the Tang Dynasty. In the Song Dynasty, record had that "farmlands are cultivated in the hills, and it is hard to count by acres". Rice and wheat became the

[1] rice, two kinds of millet, wheat and beans

main cereal crops. Cash crops such as tea, fruit, tung tree, mulberry and medicinal herbs were widely cultivated. Double-cropping rice was planted along the Yangtze River. In the Ming and Qing Dynasties, a large number of immigrants from Hunan, Hubei, Jiangxi and Guangdong immigrated to east Sichuan, and they brought with their relatively advanced production technology as well as sweet potato, citrus, grapefruit, white pig and other special varieties. Food production developed rapidly; rice planting area saw gradual expansion. Rice produced in Chongqing and its periphery areas were exported to other areas and shipped down the river in an endless stream. In the Qing Dynasty, Chongqing had already become the largest entrepot trade city in the middle and upper reaches of the Yangtze River. Goods from southeast provinces and grain, firewood, local specialties from Sichuan were mainly distributed here.

After the Opium War, imperialist forces gradually penetrated the interior. In the 16th Year of Guangxu in the Qing Dynasty, *Sino-British Yantai Treaty Amendment* listed Chongqing as an open commercial port. In the following year (1891), Chongqing opened its port to the outside world. Its natural economy, which had lasted for thousands of years, began to disintegrate. Peasants expanded the production of silkworm, hemp, medicinal materials, bristles, etc. The commodity rate of agricultural products increased, and commercial production was developed. In the 1930s, modern farms for the purpose of commodity production appeared in Chongqing, but traditional agriculture still dominated. Feudal land ownership seriously restricted the development of social productive forces. In the later period of the War of Resistance

Picture 4-1 Raw Materials for Fuling Pickled Mustard Tuber(涪陵榨菜)—Greengrocery Root

Against Japanese Aggression, Chongqing's economy began to decline seriously, and its agricultural production lagged behind. Depression and dilapidation plagued villages and peasants lived an extremely hard life. Till 1949, a sharp decline in production was seen in the city, and the gross value of agricultural output was only 1.421 billion yuan.

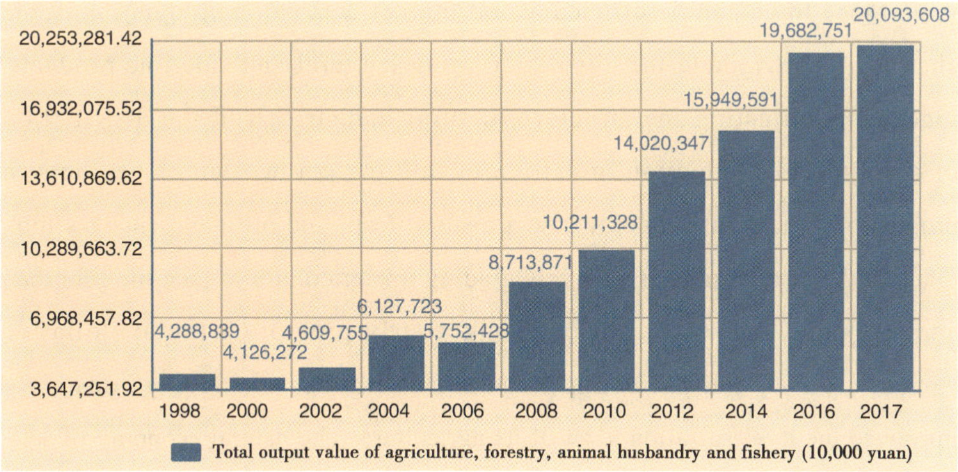

Picture 4-2 Total Output Value of the City's Agriculture, Forestry, Animal Husbandry and Fishery after Municipalization

After the founding of the People's Republic of China, Chongqing vigorously built water conservancy projects, rehabilitating old canal weirs, promoting the construction of bay ponds in mountains, small reservoirs and electromechanical irrigation works, carring out large-scale fundamental construction of farmlands. Meanwhile, Chongqing also dedicated to the promotion of agricultural science and technology and the reform of farming techniques, increasing the construction of agricultural machinery stations, making efforts to popularize advanced technology and to reform cultivating methods for grain and oil crops, strengthening the application of agricultural machinery, introducing and using improved farm tools, further shaking off the shackles of feudal land ownership, liberating rural productive forces. After the reform and opening-up, Chongqing, as the country's first comprehensive economic reform pilot city, carried out economic restructuring centred on the household contract responsibility system in rural areas, and Chongqing reformed old systems such as the "integration of politics and society" in people's commune and the exclusive purchase and selling of agricultural and side-line products. In 1983, regions and prefecture-level cities were merged. Following the law of economy, Chongqing attached importance to economic efficiency and market demand, employing multiple channels to invigorate the circulation of agricultural and side-line products, vigorously adjusting the structure of rural industries and the distribution of agricultural production, greatly arousing the enthusiasm of peasants in production. The rural economy saw a historic leap, and profound changes took place in the countryside. By actively guiding its agriculture to take the suburban and ecological development path, vigorously promoting the exploitative agriculture [1], and promoting large-scale farming, Chongqing constantly improved the modernization level of its agriculture. The natural economy of self-sufficiency and semi-self-sufficiency was transformed to commodity economy on a larger scale in rural areas. The rural economy developed in an all-round way, in 1985, with the total planting area of crops in the city amounting to 3,214,717 hectares, among them, cereal crop accounting for 2,748,498 hectares, 9,489,700 tons, oil crops accounting for 176,866 hectares, 181,200 tons. Vegetable production adopted advanced technology such as plastic mulching, producing early, fresh and tender vegetables for the cities. Vegetable planting area amounted to 140,569 hectares. From 1986 to 1997, the city's agricultural structural adjustment adhered to "Two Stabilities, Three Developments

Picture 4-3 Fengjie Navel Orange

[1] It refers to the development of unused land resources and the development of new agricultural productivity.

Picture 4-4 Changshou Shatian Pomelo

and One Path" (namely, stabilize grain production and stabilize vegetable production; develop township enterprises and develop animal husbandry; develop forestry and fruit industry; regard leading products, excellent and special new products and backbone enterprises as the leader, and implement the path of agriculture, industry and commerce management) to develop rural economy. After Chongqing became the municipality directly under the central government in 1997, according to the principle to"transform and improve the primary industry, expand and optimize the secondary industry, accelerate the development of the tertiary industry", the city's agriculture and rural economy developed rapidly.

From the beginning of reform and opening-up to the time before Chongqing became a municipality, the primary industry in Chongqing accounted for a large proportion of the GDP. In 1978, 1986, 1996, the ratio was 34.6%, 32.5% and 21.9% respectively. The structure of agricultural industry was not scientific.

After 40 years of reform and adjustment, in 2017, the structure of the primary, secondary and tertiary industry in Chongqing was optimized for 6.9: 44.1: 49. The agricultural economy has transformed from agriculture as its priority before municipalization to industrial integration and development, and agricultural industry structure was remarkably optimized. According to the resource endowment of Chongqing, under the policy of "Never Relax Food Production, Actively Develop Diversified Economy" , Chongqing Party Committee and Government formulated the *Comprehensive Agricultural Zoning of Chongqing* (《重庆市综合农业区划》) (1987, 1999). The "Three Major Agricultural Projects" ("三大工程") were listed as important tasks and strategic measures for rural economic development in the 1990s. The "Three Major Agricultural Projects" referred to the comprehensive development project of 3 million mu[1] winter paddy fields, comprehensive transformation project of 2 million mu slope barren land and vegetable basket project. The "Three Unique" (三绝) agricultural products were vigorously promoted in Chongqing, namely, ratooning rice, semi-arid cultivation, and fish cultivation in rice fields. The "Three High" (三高) agriculture with high-yielding, high-quality and high-efficiency was developed, and agricultural industrialization management was explored. Strategic adjustments of agricultural and rural economic structure were carried out; the "Three Hundred Projects" (三百工程) were started and implemented, namely, the one-million project of agricultural industrialization in 2001, the construction project of one hundred strong economic towns in 2003, and the one-million rural labour transfer and employment project in 2004. Chongqing also adhered to the policy of "Give more, Take less, Let loose" (多予、少取、放活), implementing the policy of "One Exemption and Three Subsidies" (一免三补), promoting the development strategy of "One Circle and Two Wings" (一圈两翼) in 2006, alleviating poverty through industrial development, and carring out "Hundreds of Projects" (千百工程) to promote the construction of new socialist countryside. In 2008, the Ministry of Agriculture and Chongqing Municipality started the co-construction of urban and rural modern agricultural demonstration zones; and in 2009, the co-construction of national modern animal husbandry demonstration zone started. The Fourth Party Congress of Chongqing proposed to vigorously develop profitable agriculture with characteristics and proposed to synchronously develop the "Four Modernizations", namely, industrialization, urbanization, informatization and agricultural modernization. A series of important initiatives to promote agricultural developments and rural reforms drove the rural modernization in Chongqing.

---

[1] a unit area in China, 1 mu≈667 m^2

Despite natural disasters and the fluctuation of markets, agriculture and rural economy saw sustainable and healthy development. Agricultural production conditions were gradually improved; agricultural structure was continuously optimized; agricultural and rural reforms were deepened; high-quality agricultural products grew rapidly; the level of agricultural modernization had been greatly improved, and steady progress was made in agricultural production. Chongqing also actively promoted the building of new socialist countryside, through a serious of policies to increase peasants' income such as industrial development, the transfer of rural surplus labour force employment, peasant's burden reduction and rural poverty alleviation. Peasants' income saw continuous growth, and dramatic changes took place in rural areas and the living standard of peasants was greatly improved. The per capita disposable income of permanent rural residents increased from 126 yuan in 1978 to 12,638 yuan in 2017.

Nowadays, Chongqing is an important production base of agricultural products such as grain and oil, citrus, sericulture, tobacco, medicinal materials, tung oil, pickled mustard tubers and hogs in China. Profitable agriculture with characteristics has seen continuous development. Featured agricultural products are well known. Fuling mustard tuber, together with French pickle and German red cabbage are regarded as "Three Famous Pickles in the World". Fengjie navel orange, which is comparable to Washington navel orange, is one of the "Four Famous Oranges" in China. Liangping pomelo once won the national pomelo category Jinjiang Cup (金江杯) and it is one of China's "Three Famous Pomelos". Changshou Shatian pomelo was awarded "National Excellent Fruit" for many times. Reforms such as shared ownership of financial subsidies for agricultural projects, agricultural guarantee system, primary supply and marketing cooperatives are implemented. Family farms, peasants' cooperatives and leading agricultural enterprises are developing vigorously. The work to improve rural drinking water, comprehensive environmental improvement, renovation of the dilapidated houses, poverty alleviation is making steady headway. A number of beautiful and liveable demonstration villages have been built. In 2017, five national-level poor counties and regions with a population of 160,000 were lifted out of poverty. The total output value of the city's agriculture, forestry, animal husbandry and fishery amounted to 200.936 billion yuan. Grain crop yield was 11,671,500 tons. Vegetable yield was 19,471,800 tones, and fruit yield was 4,459,400 tons. The number of hogs was 20,132,800. The number of poultry was 250,000,000. The number of cattle and sheep available for slaughter was 557,400 and 3,295,400 respectively. The import and export trade volume of agricultural products amounted to 1.307 billion US dollars.

Section Two　Handicraft Industry

Picture 4-5　The Production of Grass Cloth in Rongchang

In the Neolithic sites excavated in Chongqing area, a large number of stone hoes, stone axes, stone sickles and other production and hunting tools were unearthed. In the Xia (夏) and Shang (商) Periods, bowls, pots, basins and other rough pottery utensils could be made. In the period of the Ba State, copper weapons, pottery, iron axes and textiles and other products were produced. The manufacture of copper ware has reached a certain level. There were "tiger pattern" and "palm pattern" on the utensils. The decorations were unique with strong national characteristics. In the Qin and Han Dynasties and afterwards, with the introduction of new technology and the popularization of iron tools, the handicraft industry in Bayu area, such as silk, linen, wine-making, metal smelting, casting, construction, ceramics, papermaking and so on, saw further development. “Huangrun Fine Cloth” (“ 黄润细布 ”) produced in Rongchang was woven with hemp, which was smooth, fine and soft. It was once used as a tribute and was marketed overseas along the “Southern Silk Road”. From the Northern Song Dynasty to the Southern Song Dynasty, ceramic production was very common and became an important household handicraft industry. The porcelain industry in Huangjueya (黄桷垭) area in Nan’an was very prosperous. Eleven porcelain workshops were excavated in the vicinity of the Tushan Lake (涂山湖). Thousands of pieces of porcelain were collected. These porcelains were mainly black glaze porcelain, which were regular in shape and varied in style. Among them, the obsidian varnished black glaze porcelain was regarded as “divine skill”. It was one of the treasures of the world heritage.

In the Ming Dynasty, Tutai Iron Mining Area of Qijiang (綦江土台铁矿区) had become an important iron base in Sichuan Province. After the middle of the Ming Dynasty, coal mining, iron smelting, textiles, glass, paper making, printing, wine-making and salt boiling were gradually developed and expanded in scale. In the 1st year of Tongzhi (同治) (1862) of the Qing Dynasty, the first glass workshop in Chongqing produced products such as window glass, bright tiles and opium smoke hoods by local methods. Rongchang porcelain industry was also well developed. From Xianfeng Period (咸丰) to Guangxu Period (光绪) in the Qing Dynasty, many famous kilns were found in this county. They were Zhongxing kiln (中兴窑) , Mozi kiln (磨子窑) , Laoxing kiln (老兴窑), Chongxing kiln (崇兴窑) , Wanxing kiln (万兴窑) and Xiaxing kiln (下兴窑). They could produce products with high craft value such as coloured glaze and carved ornaments, cinnabar vases and hexagonal cinnabar mounds. Till the 31st year of Guangxu (1905) in the Qing Dynasty, more than 10 local glass workshops had been developed in Chongqing. In the same year, Cheng Chongchu (陈崇初), a

Picture 4-6 Bamboo Weaving with Characteristics

Chongqing native, returned after studying in Japan and set up Fuchuan (富川) Paper Company in Wangjiatuo, Nan'an, producing matchbox papers. It was the first modern papermaking factory in Sichuan Province that embraced transition from manual production of paper to machine production. Around the Opium War, the traditional individual handicraft industry rapidly developed to workshops, factories and shops. The production of goods was accelerated. Local governments began to hold training centres for workers. A number of handicraft enterprises developed towards modern industry were founded. Some enterprises introduced advanced production equipment from abroad and coastal areas, and they produced cotton cloth, food, iron, copper, porcelain and craft decoration products. The handicraft industry along Chaotianmen and Xiaoshizi (小什字) was very prosperous. Place named after the handicraft industry such as the Da Tong Street [1] (打铜街), Da Tie Street [2] (打铁街) and Mu Huo Street (木货街) [3] appeared. Merchants and customers from all over the country gathered. Eight guildhalls and thirteen gangs were formed. Chongqing market prospered. Zhao Xi (赵熙), a poet in late Qing Dynasty, once wrote a poem like "The glow of lights is like a rainbow, and the water trend turns from west to east. The Bazi State was a strategic place, and this big city presses Yuwang Palace like a mountain. Beyond the buildings, vitality, singing and dancing, the sound of the river drum in the dusk. As a land of wealth in Sichuan since ancient times, red candles in pavilions intoxicate the spring breeze." This

[1] "Tong" means copper. "Da Tong Street" is a street where coppersmith gathered with their tools for making copper.
[2] "Tie" means iron.
[3] "Mu Huo" refers to handicrafts made of wood.

became the realistic portrayal of Chongqing at that time.

Picture 4-7 Liangping Bamboo Curtain

Traditional craftsmanship has been preserved. They are Liangping bamboo curtain craft, dragon lantern colour and biding craft, Hechuan walnut slice craft, Hechuan inkstone craft, Yilu (艺庐) micro-engraving craft, dragon and phoenix candle craft, old bacon process craft, papermaking craft of Langxi (朗溪) bamboo bridge and paper bamboo craft. Fan making craft [Rongchang Folding Fan (荣昌折扇)], pottery firing craft [Rongchang Pottery Making Craft (荣昌陶器制作技艺)], weaving craft of grass cloth, lacquer painting [Chongqing Lacquer Painting (重庆漆器髹饰技艺)], fermented soya bean brewing craft [Yongchuan Fermented Soya Bean Brewing Craft (永川豆豉酿制技艺)], traditional craft of making pickles [Fuling Traditional Craft of Making Picked Mastard Tuber (涪陵榨菜传统制作技艺)] and the craft to make Tujia stilted building (土家族吊脚楼营造技艺) were listed as the representative items of national intangible cultural heritage.

Section Three Industry

In the end of the 19th century and early 20th century, Chongqing modern industry developed on the basis of some large handicraft factories and workshops. After the signing of the *Sino-British Yantai Treaty Amendment* in the 16th year of Guangxu (1890) in the Qing Dynasty and *Sino-Japanese Treaty of Shimonoseki* (《中日马关条约》) in the 21st year of Guangxu (1895), Britain, Japan, America, France and Germany invaded Chongqing successively. They set up consulates, lease lands, foreign trade banks, industrial and mining enterprises, aggressively promoted

Picture 4-8 Gun Assembly Machine in Chongqing Arsenal During the War of Resistance Against Japanese Aggression

foreign goods and plundered raw materials. The invasion of foreign capital contributed to the disintegration of the feudal economy, created conditions for the emergence and development of national capitalism. In the 17th year of Guangxu (1891) in the Qing Dynasty, Chongqing was officially opened as a port and became the earliest modern industrial city in western China. In 1891, Senchang Match Company (森昌洋火公司) established factories in Wangjiatuo and Daxikou (大溪口). They were the earliest modern industrial enterprises in Chongqing, as well as the earliest matchmaking factories in China. In the early 20th century, cotton and silk reeling industries were booming. Jihouxiang Cloth Factory (吉厚祥布厂), Zhenhua Company (振华公司), Fuchuan Weaving Factory (富川织布厂) were established successively. With the marked improvement of production technology, Chongqing became Sichuan's cotton weaving centre and silk reeling industry centre based on capitalist handicraft workshops. On the eve of the War of Resistance Against Japanese Aggression, industrial production sectors such as coal mining, metallurgy, textile, food, leather, cigarette, soap, medicine, cement, electric power were formed, and a rudimentary modern industry was established. In 1937, with the breakout of the War of Resistance Against Japanese Aggression, the national government moved its capital to Chongqing. More than 400 factories along the coast and in the middle and lower reaches of the Yangtze River were relocated. Therefore, a great deal of new machinery and industrial capital was transferred to Chongqing, together with technical talents and management experience. Chongqing industry developed rapidly. A comprehensive

Picture 4-9 Old Factory Area of Chongqing Iron and Steel Company (CISC) in the 1970s

Picture 4-10 The First Microcomputer Production Line in Southwest China Put into Production in January 1986

industrial structure with machinery, light textile, metallurgy, mining, power as the main body was formed. Chongqing became the largest industrial base in Kuomintang-controlled areas. A large army of more than 200,000 workers in the fields of arsenal, machinery, smelting, coal, textile, chemical industries, shipping, postal and telecommunications were developed and formed, and they made great contributions to support the War of Resistance Against Japanese Aggression. In 1945, after the victory of the War of Resistance Against Japanese Aggression, the national government "returned" to Nanjing. Some bureaucratic capital and national capital industries followed. Chongqing industry began to shrink. The military industry and heavy industry that served in the wartime gradually transferred to light textile industry that was needed by the market.

After the founding of the People's Republic of China, Chongqing has always been a key city in national economic construction. In the initial post-liberation period, the city's central task was to resume production with the focus on restoring the steel, machinery, textile and other industries. In 1950, Chongqing Iron and Steel Corporation rolled out the first heavy rail of the PRC and began to produce rails in batches. It made important contribution to the construction of Chengdu-Chongqing Railway. In 1951, Chongqing special steel plant produced the first batch of seamless steel pipes in China, filling a big gap in China's industrial products. In this period, the state invested nearly 70,000,000 yuan to establish a batch of backbone enterprises such as the Mining Machinery Factory (矿山机器厂), No.2

Electrical Machinery Plant (第二电机厂), Southwest Pharmaceutical Factory (西南制药厂), Dongfeng Chemical Plant (东风化工厂), Xinhua Printing House (新华印刷厂) in Shipingqiao (石坪桥), Xiaolongkan and Hualongqiao. In the period of the "First Five-Year Plan", projects such as Songzao Mining Bureau (松藻矿务局), Chongqing Power Plant, Changshou Power Plant, ferroalloy Factories, and boil factories were constructed and reconstructed. Open Hearth Workshop of Chongqing Iron and Steel Company, Chongqing Air Compressor Factory, 601 Dyeing and Weaving factory, Chongqing Thermos Bottle Factory were established. The industrial production capacity of Chongqing was greatly enhanced, and a socialist industrial system was initially established. In the period of the "Second Five-Year Plan", influenced by the "Great Leap Forward", "Unrealistic Production Targets" and "Arbitrary Orders" industrial production saw sharp decline. In 1960, according to the guideline of "adjustment, consolidation, enrichment and improvement", Chongqing industry carried out adjustment with enterprise structure adjustment as the main content. During this period, general mechanical industries were established in Shimen, Shangqiao (上桥) and Shuichuan (水川); chemical industries were established in Zhongliangshan, Lijiatuo and Jingkou; agricultural machinery manufacturing industries were developed in Xiemachang (歇马场) and Haitangxi (海棠溪), and the production capacity in coal, steel, textile, food and paper industries was further expanded. In 1964, the oil ditch gas mine went into operation; the first Bayu gas pipeline was built; oil industry was added as a new industry. In the period of the "Third Five-Year Plan", due to the disturbance and destruction of the "Cultural Revolution", Chongqing industry saw continuous decline. During the period of the "Strategic Area Construction in National Defence" between 1966 and 1975, the state invested 4.2 billion yuan in the construction of a number of arms, ships, electronics, aerospace and nuclear enterprises and research institutes in Chongqing. It relocated and rebuilt numerous supporting enterprises in the national defence industry, among which were Southwest Aluminium Processing

Picture 4-11 Automobile Industrial Park in Liangjiang New Area (两江新区)

Picture 4-12 A Corner of Automobile Production in Liangjiang New Area

Plant, Sichuan Automobile Factory, Southwest Synthetic Pharmaceutical Factory, Changjiang Rubber Factory, Yiping (一坪) Chemical Plant, East Sichuan Natural Gas Mining Industry, etc. It played a good role in consolidating national defence and improving the distribution of industrial production in Chongqing.

Since reform and opening-up, the industrial adjustment of the whole city further strengthened its support for agriculture, the development of light textile industry, the compression of capital construction and the adjustment of the usage of investment. In 1983, Chongqing became the first pilot city for comprehensive economic reform. Its industry was centred on invigorating enterprises. Through the expansion of enterprise autonomy pilot, the implement of factory director (manager) responsibility system, the establishment of economic responsibility system, the reform of distribution system, these measures mobilized the enthusiasm of the enterprises and the staff. Chongqing industry entered a new period of stabilized, coordinated and sustainable development. Between 1976 and 1985, key industries such as Sichuan Vinylon Factory, Heavy Forging Plant, Chongqing Shipyard, Sichuan Diesel Engine Plant, were established in succession. In 1985, the total industrial output value of Chongqing reached 6.616 billion yuan. Five major industries were formed, including machinery, chemical industry, metallurgy, textile and food industry. Industrial categories were relatively complete, and their supporting capacity was stronger. After the Third Plenary Session of the Eleventh

Central Committee of the Communist Party of China, the central government proposed a strategy shift for the ordnance systems, namely, "Military Civilian Integration, Peacetime and Wartime Integration, Military Priority and Civilian Support of the Army". Chongqing national defence industry gave full play to its advantages and embarked on the road of military civilian integration. Between 1980 and 1985, the total output value of Chongqing national defence industry increased by 27% annually. In 1985, the output value of civilian goods reached 888 million yuan. A batch of marketable pillar products were formed. In 1986, Chongqing became a comprehensive industrial city in southwest China and in the upper reaches of the Yangtze River, and one of the three industrial centres with an industrial output value of over 10 billion yuan in central and western China. Chongqing was the 7th oldest industrial base in China. Its industrial categories such as machinery, metallurgy, textile, chemical industry, food, and instrument industry were relatively complete. Before municipalization, Chongqing had become one of the three hundred billion industrial centres in central and western China.

Since 1986, Chongqing's industrial development has been divided into two stages and six "Five-Year Plan" periods. They are the difficult exploration stage from the "Seventh Five-Year Plan" to the "Ninth Five-Year Plan", and the benign development stage from the "Tenth Five-Year Plan" to the "Twelfth Five-Year Plan". The "Seventh Five-Year Plan" period witnessed the exploration of the reform of the state-owned enterprise system and the volatile development of the industrial economy; the "Eighth Five-Year Plan" period witnessed the deepening of comprehensive reform and the acceleration of the development of the industrial economy; the "Ninth Five-Year Plan" period witnessed the overcoming of difficulties in the reform of state-owned enterprises and the stepping out of difficulties in the industrial economy; the "Tenth Five-Year Plan" period witnessed basic rationalization of system and mechanism and the sound development of industrial economy; the "Eleventh Five-Year Plan" period witnessed the acceleration of industrial restructuring and the development of industrial economy on a fast track; the "Twelfth Five-Year Plan" period witnessed the expansion and strengthening of the information industry and the promotion of coordinated development of the industrial economy. Especially after Chongqing became a municipality directly under the central government, it grasped major opportunities such as Three Gorges migrants, West Region Development of China, comprehensive trials on urban-rural integration, establishment of Liangjiang New Area, national central city construction, the promotion of the Belt and Road Initiative, the development of the Yangtze River Economic Belt, and it transformed and upgraded old industrial bases. Under the guidance of the Scientific Outlook on Development and the new development concept, Chongqing adhered to the new road of industrialization. Its industrial structure was more diversified, and risk-resistance capacity of the industries was gradually enhanced. The industrial layout transformed from blooming everywhere to intensive development. The level of development has been comprehensively raised. The mode of development was gradually shifting from investment-driven to innovation-driven, and the support for industrial development was further strengthened. The ownership structure transformed from state ownership to the coexistence of state ownership, private ownership and foreign ownership. The stability of development was increased. The industrial development direction transformed from traditional manufacturing to intelligent manufacturing, and the level of informatization improved constantly.

In recent years, Chongqing has developed in accordance with the positioning given by the state, such as an important central city of the country, an economic centre in the upper reaches of the Yangtze River, an important modern manufacturing base of the country, a comprehensive transportation hub in the southwest and an inland open highland. It accelerated the transformation and upgradation of the economic structure, and gradually changed the mode of economic growth from extensive and epitaxial growth into intensive and endogenous growth. The old industrial base was bursting with vigour and vitality. An industrial pattern with two-wheel drive by automobile and electronics, multi-point support by equipment, chemical medicine, materials, energy and consumer goods was formed. A platform system of Industrial Development Zone led by Liangjiang New Area was constructed. It is the largest electronic information industry cluster in the world and the largest automobile industry cluster in China. In 2018, the city's total industrial output value reached 599.77 billion yuan, an increase of 1.1% over the previous year. The added value of industries above designated size increased by 0.5% over the previous year. In terms of sub industries, the added value of the automobile industry decreased by 17.3% compared with last year; the motorcycle industry decreased by 0.3%; the electronics industry increased by 13.6% and the equipment industry increased by 4.8%; the chemical industry increased by 1.5% and the pharmaceutical industry increased by 9.3%; the material industry increased by 11.0%; the consumer goods industry increased by 1.9% and the energy industry increased by 1.7%.

Strategic emerging industries were booming. The innovation-driven development, which led by intellectualization of big data, was making further progress, and the engine of high-quality economic development has gained stronger momentum. The added value of high-tech industry increased by 13.7% year on year, contributing 411.7% to the growth of industries above designated size. The added value of strategic emerging manufacturing increased by 13.1%, contributing 495.2% to the growth of industries above designated size, and it became the main driving force of the city's industrial growth.

Table 4-1 Output of Major Products of Industries Above Designated Size in 2018

Name of product	Yield	Year-on-year growth (%)
Automobile (10,000)	205.04	–27.5
New Energy Vehicle (10,000)	2.43	33.0
Industrial Robot (set)	2,917	68.8
Laptop (10,000 set)	5,730.23	–3.8
Printer (10,000 units)	1,589.48	9.5
Integrated Circuit (10,000 pieces)	54,062.26	16.7
Liquid Crystal Display (LCD) (10,000 pieces)	14,261.06	56.2

Section Four Commerce and Trade

Chongqing is located at the confluence of the Yangtze River and the Jialing River. Since ancient times, it has been an important water terminal for material distribution because of the advantages of those two rivers. In the period of the State of Ba, the Ba people established a city on the north bank of Guiting (龟亭) [Dongsunba (冬笋坝), Xiaonanhai (小南海), Banan District nowadays]. This is the earliest market in Chongqing. During the Warring States period, the Bashu Area had economic contacts with all ethnic groups in the Southwest. Lacquerware, ironware, farm implements, silk and other commodities in Bashu area began to be

Picture 4-13 Chongqing Chaotianmen Wharf in the Late Qing Dynasty

shipped to all parts of the Southwest. During the Qin and Han Dynasties, owing to the unification of currency, weights and measures, the exchange and circulation of commodities were more convenient. At the end of the Western Han Dynasty, Jiangzhou became the most prosperous place for commerce and trade in southwest China and one of the starting points of the "Southern Silk Road" (Sichuan, Yunnan, Myanmar and India ancient road). In Bashu area, silk and local special products are exported in large quantities, and glass products, amber and jadeite are imported in large quantities. During the Tang and Song Dynasties, agriculture, ceramics, textiles, wine-making and paper industries developed, and Yuzhou trade flourished. A grand scene of traders on the boats in the two rivers from busy to noon was formed. By the Song Dynasty, Chongqing became the largest transit trade city in southwest China. Cloth, silk, grain, salt, tea, medicinal materials and other commodities mainly produced in the upper reaches of the Yangtze River were sold in large quantities through Chongqing for re-export in the middle and lower reaches of the Yangtze River. At the same time, the towns along the Minjiang River (岷江), the Tuojiang River and the Jialing River, the main tributaries of the Chuanjiang River, and the small towns along the main traffic arteries had developed in succession. In the 61st year of Kangxi (1722) in the Qing Dynasty, Chongqing was the largest and famous trade city in China with entrepot trade as the main body in the upper reaches of the Yangtze River. The "Chongqing-Hankou-Suzhou" route of the Yangtze River had become the main channel for the exchange of rice, wood, salt, cotton, cloth and foreign groceries in

Picture 4-14 British Swire Bank Delivers Goods to Chongqing

the upper reaches of the Yangtze River. In the 8th year of Xianfeng, Hankou was opened as a treaty port, foreign cloth and yarn began to penetrate Chongqing. The varieties and batches of commodities exported from Chongqing began to increase, mainly tea, grass cloth, bristles, pickled mustard tubers, medicinal materials, etc.

After Chongqing was opened as a treaty port. British Swire bank and Jardine Matheson established branches in Chongqing. Customs brokers such as "Swire Chongqing" and "Investment Promotion Reentry" were established to handle foreign trade business. A large number of foreign goods were transported to Chongqing, and then sold to the hinterland of the upper reaches of the Yangtze River in exchange for a large number of silver and local special products. The throughput of goods and materials increased greatly. In 1891, the total value of Chongqing trade was 13 million liang of silver, and the annual value of imported foreign goods was 11 million liang of silver. From the opening of Chongqing as a treaty port in 1891 to the Xinhai Revolution in 1911, Chongqing commodity trade developed rapidly. In the late Qing Dynasty, there was a saying that "There were two rivers up and down, thirteen gangs in the left and right" (上下两条江，左右十三帮) in Chongqing. Later, this kind of organization further developed into a standardized trade association. By 1901, twelve trade associations had been established to run the business of cotton, cotton yarn, salt, wine, paper, sugar, silk goods, groceries and other commodities. By the end of the 19th century, Chongqing had become the largest commercial city in the upper reaches of the Yangtze River and the largest trade port in southwest China with more than 20 industries, such as cotton, salt, wine, sugar, silk goods, groceries, medicine materials, etc. There were more than 50 foreign banks and stores in Chongqing, and the urban market continued to expand, and the commercial industries continued to increase. The salt industry, money industry, piece goods industry and cotton yarn industry had become the four major commercial groups.

After the Xinhai Revolution, the division of goods became more and more detailed, forming new industries such as transportation, electricity, hardware, chemical industry, kerosene, general merchandise, textiles, stationery, etc. With the increase of merchants from other places, merchants from all over the country set up guildhalls in Chongqing to organize the circulation of commodities. At the beginning of the 20th century, there were nine guildhalls, including Guangdong guildhall, Fujian guildhall, Huguang guildhall, Jiangxi guildhall, Shaanxi guildhall, Shanxi guildhall, Zhejiang guildhall and Yungui guildhall. With the rapid growth of import and export trade, trade associations, provincial guilds, affiliated firms and brands, constituted the main channel for trade circulation. Foreign business companies and foreign banks, foreign goods distribution network and local goods acquisition network were formed with Chongqing as the centre. Chongqing became a commercial centre of Sichuan Province and started to be geared to the world. With the expansion of the scale of commodity distribution, commerce in Chongqing flourished day by day. By the middle 1930s, there were 57 trade associations and more than 130 business groups in Chongqing.

After the outbreak of the War of Resistance Against Japanese Aggression, the national government moved its capital to Chongqing, and a number of industrial and commercial enterprises across the country moved to Chongqing. The commerce, industry and mining, transportation, post and telecommunications, finance and other undertakings in Chongqing all developed greatly, and it became the largest commercial city in the rear area during the war. Chongqing grew rapidly from a regional industrial centre in Sichuan and southwest China to a commercial centre in the rear area during the wartime. Commercial enterprises, industries and commercial capital increased; market facilities and market system gradually improved; a relatively complete commercial system was formed in Chongqing, which initially became the economic centre and material distribution centre in the upper reaches of the Yangtze River and southwest China. In addition, Chongqing was also a foreign trade centre in the rear area during the war. The four major companies in Sichuan dealing with traditional export materials were also headquartered in Chongqing, which monopolized the export business of bristles, tung oil, raw silk, wool, tea and so on in the rear area. Chongqing, as an important trading port during the war, foreign goods were also transported to other areas from here.

After the founding of the People's Republic of China, commerce and trade industry in Chongqing developed rapidly and completed the transition from a socialist which planned economy to socialist market economy, the transition from the direct operation and management of the state to the macro-control by the state, the transition from the monopoly of the public ownership with emphasis on the state-owned economy to the common prosperity and development of the economy under multiple forms of ownership. The period from the liberation of Chongqing in November 1949 to 1952 was the period of economic recovery in Chongqing. The government took over factories, banks, warehouses, public places, receiving employees and a batch of real estates, materials and equipment, creating conditions for the recovery and development of the economy. By confiscating the bureaucratic capital, the national commercial economy was established and developed. After February 1950, Chongqing began to rectify finance, stabilize prices and further adjusted industry and commerce. During the "Three-Year Recovery" Period ("三年恢复"时期), its commerce recovered and developed to some extent. From 1953, Chongqing entered the period of building a planned economy and began to implement the "First Five-Year Plan". In order to carry out the general line of the transition period,

Picture 4-15 Jiefangbei Business District

Chongqing carried out socialist transformation of agriculture, handicraft industry, capitalist industry and commerce. After the construction of the "First Five-Year Plan" period, the total retail sales of commodities reached 1,080.61 million yuan in 1957. From 1958, Chongqing entered the "Second Five-Year Plan" period. In this period, the objective economic law was ignored, and the subjective will of the people was overstated, which led to the blind pursuit of high speed in economic construction and the mistakes of three-year "Great Leap Forward" since 1958.

The "Three Difficult Years" from 1959 to 1961 made the material even more scarce and the market supply more difficult. In 1961, the eight-character policy of adjustment, consolidation, enrichment and improvement began to be implemented in the national economy. After the adjustment from 1961 to 1965, major economic imbalance was fundamentally reversed, and the economic situation was improved comprehensively, and a new round of development begun. Social purchasing power and commodity supply were basically balanced, and people's living standards were significantly improved. In the second half of 1966, the "Cultural Revolution" began. Commerce in Chongqing was affected. The Time-honoured Brands were regarded as "four old" and were renamed. Urban and rural markets were closed. The market supply was increasingly tight. The enterprise management was chaotic. The variety of business operation was reduced. The flavours disappeared and services were simple and hard.

After reform and opening-up, Chongqing commerce developed unprecedentedly, and the reform of the circulation system deepened year by year. With the coordinated development of various economic components, a new open circulation network has been gradually established. The pattern of big market, big circulation and big trade began to form. In the field of circulation, a commodity circulation system with public ownership plays a dominate role. Diversified economic components, diversified modes of operation and diversified channels of circulation that suitable for economic development were gradually established. A market circulation pattern with retail and wholesale sales as the main business was formed and developed rapidly. A number of large-scale market carriers of various categories and levels, including means of production and living, wholesale and retail, domestic trade and foreign trade, comprehensive and professional, were established. A diversified circulation system was gradually formed, and the scale of social circulation was expanded year by year. The market system was gradually improved, and remarkable achievements was made in the market construction.

After Chongqing became a municipality directly under the central government, the municipal Party Committee and the municipal government firmly seized the effect of municipality, the opportunity to develop the western region and the resettlement of the Three Gorges immigrants, and focused on the strategic goal to accelerate the development, which enrich the people and build a commercial centre in the upper reaches of the Yangtze River, and established the concept of "Circulating and invigorating the city with commerce" (流通活市、以商兴市), and developed commercial circulation as a leading industry. With the growth of consumer goods market, the scale continued to expand, and the business centre framework took initial shape. The reform was deepened; the commodity trading market developed rapidly; the modern circulation mode was advanced by leaps and bounds; market subjects was diversified; the opening-up and development promoted competition; commercial brands were on the increase; industrial management was strengthened, and the relocation and construction of immigrant enterprises in the Three Gorges Reservoir Area was completed successfully. In 1997, the city's total retail sales of consumer goods exceeded 50 billion yuan, reaching 56.8 billion yuan. It took seven years to reach 106.8 billion yuan in 2004, exceeding 100 billion yuan. Fundamental changes took place in the circulation system, circulation subject, circulation channel, management system and operation mechanism. The commercial structure has been continuously optimized; the system was being perfected; the business circle was flourishing; the market and the commercial business were booming;

the business service industry was developing in a healthy and orderly way; the commercial economic strength was significantly improved; the regional circulation was transformed into an open pattern of commerce and trade that was transregional and open to the whole country and the world.

In 2017, the city's total retail sales of social consumer goods reached 806.767 billion yuan; the wholesale and retail trade volume was 688.604 billion yuan; the catering and accommodation industry was 118.163 billion yuan. The consumption structure has been constantly upgraded; hot consumption continued to grow; online retail sales grew rapidly; the contribution to economic development has been stable. At the end of the year, the number of enterprises above designated size exceeded 8,000, reaching 8,046. Traditional commerce was still the third largest industry except industry and other service industries. The tax revenue of the city's commerce and trade service industry was 38.39 billion yuan, accounting for 13.8% of the total tax revenue of the city and contributing nearly 10% to the tax growth. In 2017, Chongqing pilot free trade zone was launched, and 692 projects were introduced, and a total value of 300.75-billion-yuan contracts (agreements) were signed, and 11,700 new enterprises were registered.

The development trend of trade and service industry was good. With the innovative development of e-commerce, there were many consumption highlights in the business circle. In 2017, there were 12 business circles with a retail sales volume of 10 billion yuan. The exhibition economy has been upgraded. In 2017, the direct revenue of the exhibition industry was 15.28 billion yuan, and it was awarded the title of "The Most Influential Exhibition (Award) Destination in 2017" and "The Top Ten Exhibition City in China" . Clothing consumption brand was prominent; catering and accommodation and residential services brands developed rapidly. 54 city-level agritainment gathering areas, 54 city-level food streets, 41 green hotels and 156 diamond-grade restaurants were built. 38 Time-honoured Brands were identified in Chongqing, and the title of "The Capital of Noodles in China" was awarded to Chongqing. The service trade grew rapidly. In 2017, international service outsourcing reached $2.1 billion, ranking the first among cities in the central and western regions. The comprehensive pilot zone for cross-border e-commerce was further promoted. The import, export and settlement of cross-border e-commerce reached 17.1 billion yuan. The cultivation of new growth areas in foreign trade was accelerated. In 2017, the city's total import and export value was $66.604 billion, including $24.005 billion for import and $42.599 billion for export. Among the world's top 500 enterprises, 279 settled in Chongqing, and 5,604 complete vehicles were imported, ranking the first in the new batch of import ports of complete motor vehicles in inland China for two consecutive years. The circulation system was improved, and the standardization and informatization level of the city's commerce and logistics was constantly improved, and the number of standard pallets in the market was more than 1 million.

Section Five　Communications and Transportation Industry

Chongqing is connected to Sanshu (三蜀) in the west, Han and Mian (汉沔) in the north, Yunnan and Guizhou (滇黔) in the south, and Hunan and Hubei (荆襄) in the East. Located in the upper reaches of the Yangtze River and in the east of Sichuan Basin, Chongqing boasts the world-famous Three Gorges of the Yangtze River, hills, mountains, platforms, flat dams and other landforms, and most of the roads are distributed between hills, mountains and rivers. With convenient water transportation, Chongqing has the longest inland waterway routes and it is the most extensive water transportation hub in China. The Yangtze River, the Jialing River, the Wujiang River and their tributaries run through the whole region, forming a natural waterway, which is the largest inland river network in western China. The advantage as a waterway transportation has always made Chongqing a transportation hub in the western region.

Ⅰ.Water Transportation

In ancient times, the Ba People lived near the mountains and rivers. They were good at handling boats, and the transportation of wooden boats was developed. During the Qin and Han Dynasties, there were four waterways in Jiangzhou leading to the whole country. During Tang and Song Dynasties, Yuzhou Port (渝州港) became a transportation port of "million hus of ships" ("万斛船") [1]. It was called "Controlling the two rivers, transporting the millet of the three rivers (the Jinghe river, the Weihe river and the Luohe river) and it is very convenient" (控两江之会, 漕三川之粟, 城为便利). There were 4 waterways leading to Chang'an (Xi'an nowadays). Hezhou (Chongqing Hechuan nowadays), which controlled the three rivers (Jialing River, Fujiang River and Qujiang River), was known as the "Important Capital of Bashu" (巴蜀要津) and one of the starting points for transporting Sichuan grain by water. In the Song Dynasty, the wartime water transportation network with Chongqing as the main hub was established to resist the attack of the Mongolian army for 40 years. The Yuan Dynasty attached great importance to the construction of post stations and built a network of water and land post stations with Chaotianmen as the hub in Chongqing. During the Ming and Qing Dynasties, the number of water and land stations increased, and Chongqing port became the centre of the water transportation network in Sichuan.

Picture 4-16 In 1919, Wanxian (nowadays Wanzhou), several boatmen rowed across the river.

[1] "Hu" is a unit of measurement in ancient China.

Picture 4-17 Chaotianmen Wharf in the 1920s

Picture 4-18 Crooked Bottom Boat (歪屁股船) in the Wujiang River

After Chongqing was opened as a treaty port, the water transportation of Chuanjiang River developed rapidly. Flag ship (挂旗船) (a long-distance wooden cargo ship chartered by foreign companies with the national flag of a foreign country) transport came into being. The number of Lijin vessels (厘金船) (Chinese civilian vessels that have to pay Lijin to local authorities) that entered and left Chongqing port for freight transportation increased. The number of import and export commodities transported through Chongqing increased dramatically. After the Opium War, the invasion of imperialist powers deepened step by step. In the 24th year of Guangxu in the Qing Dynasty (1898), Archibald John Little, an Englishman, purchased the "Lichuan" (利川) ship in Shanghai, and he sailed up to Chongqing for a trial voyage on the Chuanjiang River. This was the beginning of Chuanjiang river cruise. In the 34th year of Guangxu in the Qing Dynasty (1908), Chuanjiang steamship company was established in Chongqing. In the following year, the company's "Shutong" (蜀通) ship arrived in Chongqing. In 1990, it started the regular voyage between Chongqing and Yichang, which was the first Chinese commercial liner on the Chuanjiang River. In the modern era, the shipping industry in Chongqing was on the rise. Lu Zuofu, a patriotic industrialist, created a small passenger ship called "Minsheng" (民生) and sailed the Hechuan-Chongqing route, opening up and developing the shipping business of the Jialing

River and the Yangtze River. From 1927 to 1935, ship docks such as Chaotianmen, Jialingmen (嘉陵门), Qiansimen, Taipingmen (太平门) and Jinzimen (金紫门) were successively built in Chongqing port area. In 1938, the first mechanized wharf was built in Jiulongpo, Chongqing Port. After the outbreak of the War of Resistance Against Japanese Aggression, inland rivers became the main transportation routes. As the middle and lower reaches of the Yangtze River were successively occupied, the shipping industry vigorously expanded the routes of the upper reaches of the Yangtze River and its tributaries; it connected the northwest and southwest regions through combined transportation by land and water. In ensuring the transportation of military supplies and civilian supplies in the rear area, the shipping industry was greatly developed.

Picture 4-19 "Minsheng ship" of Minsheng Company

In the early days after the founding of the People's Republic of China, Chongqing shipping industry played a leading role in restoring production and developing economy. After the opening of Chengdu-Chongqing Railway in 1952, Chongqing Jiulongpo Wharf was transformed into the first mechanized wharf of combined transportation by water and land in Southwest China, which has been expanded many times to become the largest port area of combined transportation by water and land in Southwest China. The Lanjiatuo (兰家沱) and Maoertuo (猫儿沱) combined transport ports were built to realize the mechanization of port operation. The Ministry of Communications carried out Chuanjiang waterway regulation project for many times and completed the Fujiang River three-block stone ship locks, realizing the electrification of navigation marks, mechanization of stranding beach and comprehensive night navigation of Chuanjiang waterway.

Along the Yangtze River, Chaotianmen, Jiulongpo, Lanjiatuo, Maoertuo, Wanxian (Wanzhou District nowadays), Fuling and other mechanized wharf berthing areas were constructed and expanded successively, the water transport enterprises in Yongchuan, Wanxian, Fuling, Qianjiang and other areas all realized motorization. In 1980, Chongqing port was officially opened to the outside world, and foreign trade and water transport were launched. Minsheng Steamship Company was rebuilt, and the state-owned Chongqing Yangtze River Steamship Company, Sichuan Chongqing Steamship Company and Chongqing Water Transportation Company were successively established. By 1996, the Chongqing's inland waterway mileage had reached 2,429 kilometres with 6,153 transport vessels carrying 39 million water transport passengers, and passenger turnover was 5.752 billion passenger-kilometres.

Picture 4-20 Chaotianmen Passenger Terminal in the 1990s

Picture 4-21 The Jiangyu Passenger Ship Passing Qutang Gorge in the 1990s

Since 1986, significant progress had been made in the regulation and construction of Chongqing waterway. Major tributaries of the Yangtze River, such as the Daning River, the Meixi River, the Xiaojiang River and the Jialing River were regulated successively. A civilized model waterway for the Jialing River was build, and the projects of the aviation and

Picture 4-22 Golden Cruise

electrical hubs of the Fujiang River, the Jialing River and the Wujiang River were completed. With the continuous development of port construction, technical renovation was carried out in key operation areas such as Jiulongpo, Lanjiatuo and Maoertuo successively. Wanxian Pailou (万县牌楼), Fuling Lychee Garden (涪陵荔枝园), Fengjie Guanmiaotuo (奉节关庙沱), Zhongxian Xiadukou Trestle (忠县下渡口栈桥), Yunyang Xiaonanmen (云阳小南门) and other passenger terminals were constructed. By improving the loading and unloading process and the technical level of loading and unloading process, the port capacity can be further expanded. By 1996, the Chongqing's water freight volume reached 24.91 million tons and the freight turnover reached 16.025 billion tons. The volume of cargo entering and leaving the major ports reached 4.92 million tons and 5.84 million tons respectively.

With the successful impoundment of the Three Gorges Project, the situation of the waterway below Chongqing was fundamentally improved. The shipping cost was greatly reduced, creating conditions for the 10,000-ton-class fleet to go directly to Chongqing. In 1997, the total length of the Yangtze River main and branch river wharf was 63.57 kilometres with 931 berths; the port throughput was 19.034 million tons of cargo and 30.938 million passengers. After Chongqing had become a municipality directly under the central government, Chongqing made a breakthrough in waterway transportation, with a great development in ship tonnage and passenger and freight volume. With the large-scale development

Picture 4-23 Guoyuan Port Area (果园港区)

of shipping capacity and the successful completion of the migration transport task in the Three Gorges Reservoir area, and the waterway container transportation and waterway roll on transportation developed rapidly. From 2000 to 2005, Chongqing port infrastructure entered the stage of reconstruction of Three Gorges Reservoir Area. 72 berths and 64 container terminal projects were started successively. In 2005, the first phase of Chongqing Cuntan International Container Terminal Operation Area, the largest in Southwest China, was completed and put into trial operation. Chongqing became the largest waterway transportation hub in southwest China.

In 2017, the city's inland waterway mileage reached 4,472 kilometres, including 1,917 kilometres of grade waterway. The coastline of the wharf reached 78.53 kilometres and the number of port berths was 1,101. The improvement of port facilities promoted Chongqing passenger ships towards touristy, comfortable and multi-functional development and promoted Chongqing passenger transport towards touristy, sightseeing and leisure transport development and promoted Chongqing cargo ships towards large-scale, special and medium-sized development. In 2017, the entire water transportation system handled 185 million tons of freight volume, 212.6 billion tons of freight turnover, port cargo throughput of 197 million tons, container handling weight of 16.639 million tons and 8.66 million passengers. The turnover volume of waterway freight was 212.572 billion ton-kilometres, accounting for 63% of the city's overall traffic and freight turnover throughout the year. The proportion of goods in the surrounding areas transferred through Chongqing port was 45%. More than 90% of the city's foreign trade materials

Picture 4-24 Cuntan (寸滩) Port Container Terminal

were transported by water.

Ⅱ.Land Transportation

1.Road Transportation

Picture 4-25 Ancient Plank Road in the Three Gorges

The land transportation in Chongqing was relatively backward at first. During the Qin and Han Dynasties, the people of Bashu dug river valleys along the Yangtze River, the Jialing River, the Qujiang River, the Fujiang River and other major waterways for boat hauling and access roads. During the Tang and Song Dynasties, with Chongqing as the centre, there were Micang Road (米仓道) and Yangba Road (洋巴道) connecting Sichuan and Shaanxi in the northeast; there were north Chengdu-Chongqing Road and south Chengdu-Chongqing Road leading to Chengdu in the west; there was Shixi Road (奭溪道) connecting Sichuan and Guizhou in the south; there was an avenue extending to Wanzhou in the east. During the Yuan, Ming and Qing Dynasties, Chongqing's folk roads were further developed. Along the road, there were post stations and Tangpu (塘铺), among which Chaotianyi (Chaotianmen in Chongqing nowadays) connected several folk roads, and it was the general hub of folk roads.

Hidden in the mountains of Qinba (秦巴), there were ancient and long salt roads. The main ones that originated from or passed through Chongqing were Sichuan Ancient Salt Road, Zhenping (镇坪) Ancient Salt Road and Sichuan-Hubei Ancient Salt Road. The Sichuan Ancient Salt Road, which was divided into Sichuan-Hubei Ancient Salt Road, Sichuan-Hunan Ancient Salt Road, Sichuan-

Guizhou Ancient Salt Road and Sichuan-Yunnan Ancient Salt Road according to the region, was a large comprehensive transportation network gradually formed since the Warring States period. Originated from east and south of Sichuan and Chongqing, it had a great impact on the intersection areas of Sichuan, Chongqing, Hubei, Hunan and Guizhou. Zhenping Ancient Salt Road started from Daning saltworks in Wuxi County in the south and went northward along Daning River and turned over Jixinling (鸡心岭), the main ridge of Daba Mountain, and then it entered Zhongbao Town (钟宝镇) for transportation. Sichuan-Hubei Ancient Salt Road, originated from the ancient saltworks of Ningchang (宁厂), Wuxi County, was known as the "Silk Road" in the south by scholars.

Picture 4-26 Zhenping Ancient Salt Road, Starting from Daning Saltworks in Wuxi County

The construction of Chongqing highway began in the warlord era of separatism, and each highway basically extended along old folk roads. In 1927, Liu Xiang, the warlord of Sichuan Province, set up Yu-Jian General Administration of Road in Chongqing to be responsible for the construction of Yu (Chongqing) -Jian [Jianyang (简阳)] Road (the first main highway in Sichuan Province). In 1928, Tongliang County Road Bureau operated automobile transportation business from the county to Anju (安居) Highway, which was the earliest automobile transportation business in Chongqing. These roads were built by various defensive areas, without unified plans, unified standards, distinction of county roads, provincial roads or national roads. In 1933, after the opening of Chengdu-Chongqing highway, Sichuan Highway Administration established Chengdu-Chongqing Traffic Operation Management Office in Chongqing to monopolize cross-county long-distance bus passenger and freight transportation.

Picture 4-27 A lady on a Chinese-style Sedan Chair

During the War of Resistance Against Japanese Aggression, Chongqing, as the war-time capital of the national government, became the hub of the international channel connecting the southwest and northwest provinces. With the rapid development of land transportation, 425.9 kilometres of roads were built in the city. The Han-Yu Highway from Chongqing to Hanzhong in Shaanxi was newly built. The Sichuan-Guizhou and Sichuan-Hunan highways were renovated along the whole line, forming a rear road transportation network with Chongqing as the hub, Chengdu-Chongqing, Sichuan-Guizhou, Sichuan-Hunan and Han-Yu highways as the backbones, connecting other highways in the southwest and northwest, and connecting Yunnan-Vietnam, Yunnan-Myanmar and other international routes. In 1949, the total length of Chongqing highway was 836.5 kilometres.

After the founding of the People's Republic of China, Chongqing successively resumed the construction of highways and bridges which damaged in the wartime, and it renovated and reconstructed the original trunk roads of Sichuan-

Picture 4-28 Crowded Buses in Chongqing in September 1945

Picture 4-29 Rickshaw Pullers on the Streets of Chongqing

Picture 4-30 Chongqing Freight in the Republic of China

Guizhou, Sichuan-Hunan and Chengdu-Chongqing, and it built highways in river areas, townships and counties along the southern Chongqing highway. The state-owned southwest transportation company and Chongqing Branch of Sichuan transportation company were successively established to transform the private automobile industry. Changdian Highway (长垫公路), Yuchang Highway (渝长公路), Laidong Highway (来东公路), Baishiyi-Maoheshan Highway (白市驿至帽合山公路), Beibei-Yuechi Highway (北碚至岳池公路), were completed and opened to traffic successively, and the district and county automobile transportation industry, as well as the car transport industry in various regions, also developed accordingly. After the Third Plenary Session of the Eleventh Central Committee of the Communist Party of China, road construction in the vast rural areas reached a climax. In 1985, the Chongqing's highway mileage reached 19,377 kilometres. The road surface developed from low level to medium level, then to sub high level and to high level. With national highway 210 (Baotou-Chongqing-Nanning), 212 (Lanzhou-Chongqing), 319 (Xiamen-Chongqing, Chengdu) and 8 provincial roads as the framework, many county and township roads, special roads as the network of the external and internal highway network were initially formed.

Since 1986, Chongqing highway construction has developed rapidly. In 1989, the first-class automobile highway from Hongqihegou (红旗河沟) to Shuangfengqiao (双凤桥) was completed and opened to traffic. The total length was 22.8 kilometres. It was transformed into the airport expressway with

Picture 4-31 Chongqing Shuijiang-Wulong Section of Baotou-Maoming Expressway

the highest technical standard in Chongqing at that time. It was known as "The First Road in Yuzhou". In 1990, the construction of Chongqing section of Chengdu-Chongqing expressway started with a total length of 114 kilometres. It was known as "The First Road in the Southwest". Since then, the construction of the expressway advanced rapidly. By 1996, the total mileage of highways in Chongqing was 26,892 kilometres, of which 16,675 kilometres were grade highways. There were 157,200 civilian vehicles, 374.1 million highway passengers with the volume of passenger transportation as 11.324 passenger-kilometres. The highway freight volume was 202.14 million tons, and freight turnover was 5.945 billion ton-kilometres.

Since Chongqing became a municipality directly under the central government, the pace of highway construction in the city has been accelerated, and the highway traffic construction began to develop in a coordinated way with the combination of the main road network, the main branch network and the capillary network. From 1997 to 2005, Chongqing-Changshou Expressway, Changshou-

Picture 4-32 Chongqing-Suining Expressway—an Expressway Surrounded by Forests

Picture 4-33 Fengjie Section of Shanghai-Chengdu Expressway

Fuling Expressway, Chongqing-Guizhou Expressway phase I, Chongqing-Hechuan expressway, Liangping-Wanzhou Expressway, Baotou-Maoming Expressway Chongqing Section, were successively completed and opened to traffic, becoming an important part of the main framework of the "one ring with five beams" expressway. In 2000, the municipal party committee and the municipal government proposed the construction of "eight-hour to Chongqing" (八小时重庆) with 922 kilometres of new highways. In 2002, Chongqing began the construction of roads connecting 36 counties to each other. In 2005, the "Eleventh Five-Year Plan" of Chongqing proposed for the first time that Chongqing traffic construction in 2010 should complete 2,000 kilometres expressway ahead of schedule with "two ring expressways and eight highways", and a rural road network covering 42 districts and counties should be constructed. From 2003 to 2005, 31,000 kilometres of rural roads were newly built or upgraded. 620 towns and 2,292 villages were built with asphalt roads or cement roads, and 1928 villages had access to roads. This is the largest construction of rural roads in Chongqing since the founding of the People's Republic of China. In 2013, Fengjie-Wuxi Expressway was completed and opened to traffic, indicating that all districts. Counties in the city were connected by expressways or high-grade highways, and "Four-hour to Chongqing" (四小时重庆) was fully realized. During the "Twelfth Five-Year Plan" period, Chongqing accelerated the construction of major highways based on "internal and external connectivity" (内畅外联), successively launching the construction of the new 1,000-kilometre and the fourth 1,000-kilometre expressways. More than 20 projects were started, including the Yangtze River expressway, the Jiulongpo-Yongchuan expressway, and the construction of 1,200-kilometre expressways began smoothly. In the west, Chongqing took the lead in launching the village access project to make all the villages accessible and rural roads available to all villages. In 2017, the mileage of Chongqing highways that opened to traffic was 147,900 kilometres, with a network density of 179 kilometres per 100 square kilometres,

Picture 4-34 Huangjuewan Flyover

533 million road passengers, 28.554 billion kilometres of passenger transport turnover, 950 million tons of road freight transport and 106.896 billion tons of freight turnover. There were 673 highway tunnels with a length of 702,100 linear meters, 8,277 administrative villages with smooth roads, and the patency rate was 100%. 6,316 villages with smooth roads were removed and merged, and 100% of townships and towns and 97.6% of administrative villages had access to buses.

2.Railway Transportation

Railway transportation is the latest and fastest-growing form of transportation in Chongqing. The main railway lines were built after liberation, and quickly became the main channel of long-distance passenger and freight transportation. In the first year of Xuantong in the Qing dynasty (1909), the construction of Yichang-Wanxian section of Chuan-Han (川汉) Railway was started. In May 1911, the 3rd year of Xuantong in the Qing Dynasty, the Qing government, under the coercion of foreign powers, announced that the main railway lines were "all state-owned" and signed contracts with banks from the United Kingdom, the United States, France and Germany to borrow money to build roads, granting those four countries the rights to build this railway to offset debts, which aroused Railway Protection Movement in

Picture 4-35 The Opening of Chongqing-Wanzhou High-speed Railway Officially on November 28, 2016

Sichuan. The construction of Chuan-Han Railway only completed 17.3 kilometres in Hubei before meeting its premature death. In 1928, Beichuan Minye (北川民业) Railway Co., Ltd. started the construction of Beichuan Railway. It is the first railway in Sichuan Province. In 1937, the construction of the Chengdu-Chongqing Railway started in seven sections. To the eve of liberation in 1949, only 34% of the budget work was completed within two phases of construction. In 1943, Tianfu (天府) Mining Co., Ltd. produced 110-horsepower locomotive, which was called the "first self-made locomotive in China" by *Ta Kung Pao* (《大公报》) at that time. In 1949, three railway branch lines were built in Beichuan (北川), Daihuang (戴黄) and Qijiang, with a mileage of about 100 kilometres.

After the founding of the People's Republic of China, the Chengdu-Chongqing Railway, which is the first trunk railway of the PRC, was built in the case of a hundred wastes waiting for prosperity. On July 1st, 1952, the Chengdu-Chongqing Railway was opened to traffic, which fundamentally changed the structure of Chongqing's transportation. Since then, the focus of Chongqing's external transportation shifted rapidly to railway transportation. From the 1960s to the 1970s, the Sichuan-Guizhou Railway and Xiangyang-Chongqing Railway were successively opened to traffic, and Tongxi (铜西), Sili (四梨), Licai (梨菜) and north-south railway lines were newly built, initially forming a radial railway network. In the 1980s, Chongqing railway vigorously carried out the electrification expansion and transformation, and after the transformation, the transportation capacity of Chengdu-Chongqing Railway was more than

Picture 4-36 Chongqing High-speed Railway

doubled. In 1985, the length of three main railway lines of Chengdu-Chongqing, Sichuan-Guizhou and Xiangyang-Chongqing reached 455 kilometres. Within the city, there were two railway branches from Sanjiang (三江) in Qijiang County (Qijiang District nowadays) to Nantong Mining Area, Wansheng (Wansheng Economic and Technological Development Zone nowadays), Xiaonanhai to Lishuwan (梨树湾), and 117 special lines for factories and mining enterprises with a total length of 425 kilometres (under the administration of the branch bureaus). Chongqing Railway Branch handled 24.386 million tons of freight and 24.383 million passengers. Chongqing and Chengdu became two hubs of southwest railway network. Since 1986, with the rapid development of railway transportation in Chongqing, an unprecedented breakthrough in the construction of high-speed railway has been achieved. People's travel became more convenient; universal railway network was improved; external channels were gradually opened; the hub construction was continuously speeding up; the hub operation was more efficient; the quality of the road network was continuously improving, and the service level continued to improve. After Chongqing became a municipality directly under the central government, the implementation of Chongqing railway network plan was accelerated. In 1997, the construction of Dazhou-Wanzhou Railway was started. In 2004, the passenger train was officially launched. The length of main line was 157 kilometres, which formed a comprehensive transportation network of combined transportation by water and land with the Yangtze River shipping. It was a direct channel for goods and passengers to reach the river and the sea. In 2001, the construction of the Chongqing-Huaihua Railway was started. In 2007, the passenger transport line was opened to traffic,

Picture 4-37 Chongqing North Railway Station

with a total length of 625 kilometres. It was one of the landmark projects of the western development strategy. In 2007, the construction of Suining-Chongqing Railway was started, and it was officially opened to traffic in 2006. The total mileage of operation was 165 kilometres, and the designed speed was 140 kilometres per hour, and the maximum designed speed of reserved double-tracking railways was 160 kilometres per hour, which was the highest designed speed in southwest China at that time. Chongqing North Railway Station was built and put into use, and Chongqing was gradually establishing its status as a national railway hub. In 2008, the railway operating mileage in Chongqing reached 1,258 kilometres and doubled that when Chongqing became a municipality directly under the central government in 1997. With the launch of Chengdu-Chongqing Electric Multiple Unites (EMU) (成渝动车组) in 2009, Chongqing railway transportation entered a period of rapid development. Chongqing successively opened "five fixed" freight trains ("五定"班列) from Chongqing to Guangzhou, Shenzhen and other coastal ports, opening "China-Europe (Chongqing)" railway freight trains, making great efforts to improve its railway freight capacity, giving full play to the role of "China-Europe (Chongqing)" strategic channel. Chongqing has become one of the national railway logistics bases. The dream of combined transport by sea and land and international direct transportation has come true. Chongqing trains have driven from inland to the world. Chongqing further accelerated the construction of a network of major railway channels to the outside world, building Chengdu-Chongqing High-speed Railway, Lanzhou-Chongqing High-speed Railway, Chongqing-Guizhou Railway, Chongqing-Huaihua Double-tracking Railway, accelerating the project of Zhengzhou-Wanzhou High-speed Railway and the eastern ring line, a railway hub of Chongqing, and actively building a "double-cross-shaped" major railway channel to the outside world. In 2017, the city's railway operation mileage reached 2,371 kilometres, and a railway network of "one hub, ten trunk lines and two branch lines" with the main city as the center was basically formed. The railway passenger transport volume was 63.49 million; the passenger transport turnover was 19.696 billion passenger-kilometres; the freight traffic volume was 18.0838 million tons; the freight transport turnover was 17.413 billion ton-kilometres. The key role of railway in the city's comprehensive transportation system was further strengthened, which has made outstanding contributions to the regional economic and social development.

Ⅲ.Air Transportation

In 1929, Guangyangba Airport (广阳坝机场) was built in Chongqing. It was an earthen airport that was made after bulldozing 200 mu of land into a flat dam. In 1931, Air China opened the route from Hankou to Chongqing, and then extended to Chengdu, Guiyang and Kunming. In 1933, Air China built Chongqing Shanhuba Airport (珊瑚坝机场), which was the first airport built by civil aviation in China. Since then, it successively built Baishiyi Airport, Jiulongpo Airport and Dazhongba (大中坝) Airport, etc. It successively operated air services to Hankou, Chengdu, Guiyang, Kunming, Hong Kong, Luzhou, Yibin, Leshan, Lanzhou, Jiuquan (酒泉), Hami (哈密), Hanzhong, Baoji (宝鸡), Zhijiang (芷江), Liuzhou, Guilin (桂林), Xi'an, Guangzhou and other domestic cities, serving as the connection point of air transportation between major cities in the southwest and major cities in the middle and lower reaches

Picture 4-38 The "Shanhuba" in November 1945. Located in the urban area and in the heart of the Yangtze River. It was an airport during World War II, which would be submerged when flood came.

of the Yangtze River. At the same time, it operated air services with foreign cities such as Hanoi in Vietnam, Lashio and Yangon in Myanmar, Dinjan and Calcutta in India, Almaty in Soviet Union, forming a large rear civil aviation network with Chongqing as the center. Before liberation, Chongqing had seven major airports. They were Liangshan Airport, Guangyangba Airport, Coral Dam Airport, Dazhongba Airport, Baishiyi Airport, Jiulongpo Airport and Xiushan Airport, and more than 40 air-harbors, temporary airports, standby airports and glide airports in Chenjiaba (陈家坝), Wanxian County, Jiushiba (旧市坝), Tongliang, Dengyunqiao (登云桥), Dazu, and other airports in Wanxian County, Beibei, Yongchuan, Hechuan, Bishan and Jiangjin.

In 1941, the Kuomintang Government set up the American Volunteer Group of Chinese Air Force and appointed American Colonel Chennault as the commander of the group. The overall combat command centre was in Chongqing. Under the command of Colonel Chennault, the air force repeatedly hit the Japanese armies. Its team emblem and shark-head fighters were well-known all over the world. "Flying Tigers" became a household name. During the War of Resistance Against Japanese Aggression, Sino-Italian Nanchang Aircraft Factory moved to Haikongdong (海孔洞), Conglin Town (丛林镇) in Nanchuan County (Wansheng Economic and Technological Development Zone nowadays), which laid a foundation for the start of the aviation industry in China. After the founding of the People's Republic of China, Chongqing air transport industry witnessed further development. In 1950, the People's Republic of China launched its first regular flight route — Tianjin-Beijing-Wuhan-Chongqing route. During the period of resisting the US aggression and aid Korea, most flight personnel and aircraft equipment of Civil Aviation Administration of China (CAAC) were concentrated in Chongqing, which became an important airport in China. In the middle and late 1950s, Chongqing was reduced to a civil aviation terminal. Since then, Baishiyi Airport was expanded into a secondary airport, and Chongqing became a southwest general aviation base.

In the 1980s, the construction of Chongqing Jiangbei Airport began. With the rapid development of civil aviation in Chongqing, air passenger capacity and freight volume doubled. In 1985, Chongqing already operated air services to 11 cities including Beijing, Shanghai, Chengdu, Kunming, Guiyang, Guilin, Changsha, Xi'an, Nanjing, Wuhan and Guangzhou, becoming one of the three major airports (Chengdu, Kunming, Chongqing) in southwest China. By 1996, there were 66 cities that were officially navigable with Chongqing, including 3 international (regional) cities. The airport handling capacity was 2.42 million passengers and 44 thousand tons of goods.

After Chongqing became a municipality directly under the central government, Chongqing had become an important modern manufacturing base in China with the rapid development of its industrial economy. Since the 18th National Congress of the Communist Party of China, the State Council and the Central Military Commission promoted the reform of low-altitude airspace management, listing the general aviation industry as a strategic emerging industry, establishing Liangjiang Aviation Investment Group and Liangjiang Aviation Industrial Park, forming the development trend of "two wings flying together" for transportation aviation and general aviation. After more than ten years of construction and development, Chongqing Jiangbei Airport has become one of the three major aviation hubs in southwest China. It was equipped with advanced wireless communication and navigation, approach instrument landing, navigation lighting, aviation meteorological services and other systems. Its flight support capacity has been continuously enhanced, and it has taken the lead in opening a direct flight to Europe in the

Picture 4-39 Terminal 3 of Chongqing Jiangbei Airport

western region. With the completion and operation of Wanzhou Wuqiao Airport (万州五桥机场) and Qianjiang Zhoubai Airport (黔江舟白机场), Chongqing realized the airport layout of "one big airport and three small airports" and became an aviation hub city in southwest China. In 2016, Chongqing was listed by the National Development and Reform Commission as the only pilot city in the whole navigation industry chain in China. In 2017, there were three civil airports in the city, of which Jiangbei Airport was 4F Class airport, Wanzhou Airport and Qianjiang Airport were 4C Class airports. The city's civil aviation transport took off and landed 314,700 aircraft. Civil aviation throughput was 27.76 million, and passenger turnover was 37.761 billion people per kilometre. The cargo volume of civil aviation was 132,600 tons, and the freight turnover volume was 195 million tons kilometre, with a passenger throughput of 39.66 million and a cargo and mail throughput of 369,000 tons. In 2017, Chongqing opened the largest number of intercontinental long-distance routes since Chongqing became a municipality directly under the central government. Chongqing made a breakthrough in direct flights to the east and west coasts of Northern America. An aviation network covering major port cities in Europe, America, Oceania and Asia has been established, and Chongqing was listed by the National Development and Reform Commission as one of the first 26 comprehensive pilot zones for aviation development again.

Ⅳ.Modern Stereoscopic Public Transport System

The main urban area has formed a multi-form and multi-level stereoscopic urban public transport system with boats on the river, cable cars and elevators on the slope, cars and rail transit on the ground, and cableways across the river in the air.

1.Cableway Construction

Picture 4-40 Chongqing Wanglongmen Cable Car Constructed in the 1950s.

From 1978 to 1986, in addition to the first cable car passenger line — Wanglongmen (望龙门) cable car passenger line, Chongqing successively built a passenger cable car at Lianglukou (两路口), a cable car for both passengers and goods at Longmenhao (龙门浩), a cable car for passenger transport at Xiyanguan in Changshou (长寿西岩关) and a cable car for passenger transport at the southern and northern side of Chaotianmen. Buses, trolley buses and passenger cable cars formed the prototype of the public transport system with Chongqing characteristics as a mountain city. From 1986 to 2005, in combination with the geographical characteristics as a mountain city and a river city, Chongqing made great efforts to strengthen the construction of stereoscopic public transport; Chongqing built passenger cableways on the Jialing River and the Yangtze River with remarkable achievements. In 1980, the construction of the Jialing River Passenger Ropeway started building, opening the prelude to the development of stereoscopic urban public transport in Chongqing. In 1982, the Jialing River Passenger Ropeway was put into trial operation. In 1987, the Yangtze River Cableway Project was completed and put into trial operation. In 1987, the

Picture 4-41 Chaotianmen Cable Car Officially Opened to Traffic in 1984

Picture 4-42 The Yangtze River Cableway

municipal government decided to build Shangxin Street (上新街) to Nanshan Park Tourist Cableway. The construction of this cableway began in 1992, and it was completed and put into operation in 1993. In 1997, Jinyun Mountain (缙云山) Tourist Cableway was completed and put into operation.

2.Construction of Passenger Elevator and Escalator

The tunnel of Kaixuan Road (凯旋路) in Yuzhong District is a 186-step-stone terrace with a length of about 100 meters and a height difference of about 35 meters. It is an important passage with a shorter distance between the upper and lower half of the Central District of Chongqing (Chongqing Yuzhong District nowadays). In 1985, the municipal government decided to build the Kaixuan Road Passenger Elevator. In 1986, Kaixuan Road Passenger Elevator was completed and put into operation. In 1991, Chongqing Passenger Ropeway Company, Chongqing Jialing Enterprise Company and Hong Kong Riritong Investment Co., Ltd. jointly invested in the construction of escalators at Lianglukou. The construction was started in 1992 and was officially put into operation in 1996.

Picture 4-43 Lianglukou Escalator

3.Bridge Construction

After the founding of the People's Republic of China, Chongqing successively built a number of large-scale highway bridges, such as Hechuan Fujiang Bridge (合川涪江大桥) and Qijiang Bridge, among which 48 were 100-meter-long bridges. Various large-span modern bridges have gradually replaced the old stone

Picture 4-44 The Jialing River Bridge, Chongqing-Macao Bridge and Light Rail Line 3 Bridge

Picture 4-45 Qiansimen Bridge

arch bridges. In 1959, the second Yangtze River bridge, Chongqing Baishatuo (白沙沱) Yangtze River Bridge, was built to connect Chengdu-Chongqing railway and Sichuan-Chongqing railway. In 1997, five Yangtze River bridges, namely Fuling Yangtze River Bridge, Wanxian Yangtze River Bridge, Fengdu Yangtze River Bridge, Jiangjin Yangtze River Bridge and Chongqing Lijiatuo (李家沱) Yangtze River Bridge, were completed and opened to traffic successively. Later, Gaojiahuayuan (高家花园) Bridge of the Jialing River, Dafosi (大佛寺) Bridge of the Yangtze River, Egongyan (鹅公岩) Bridge, Masangxi

Picture 4-46 Chaotianmen Bridge

Picture 4-47 Panlong (盘龙) Flyover in Nan' an

(马桑溪) Bridge, Zhongxian Bridge, Wushan Bridge, Huanghuayuan (黄花园) Bridge of the Jialing River, Ma'anshi (马鞍石) Bridge, Beibei Bridge, Hechuan Bridge, Shimen Bridge and Gaojiahuayuan Bridge were constructed and opened to traffic in succession. In 2017, there were 11,500 highway bridges and 845,000 linear meters in the city.

4.Rail Transit Development

In 1995, the *Plan of Chongqing Rail Transit Network* (《重庆轨道交通线网规划》) involving five rail transit lines with a length of 117 kilometres was included in the *Overall Urban Planning of Chongqing (1996-2020)* [《重庆市城市总体规划 (1996 — 2020 年) 》] ; it approved by the State Council, and rail transit gradually entered the public life. In 2000, the first phase of Chongqing Rail Transit Line 2 was fully started. In 2002, the *Plan of Chongqing Urban Rapid Rail Transit Network* (《重庆市城市快速轨道交通线网规划》) involving 354-kilometre "six lines and one ring" was redefined, and later it was adjusted to "nine lines and one ring" . In 2004, Chongqing Rail Transit Linc 2, the first rail transit line in Chongqing, was put into operation. It was the first urban rail transit in

Picture 4-48 Chongqing Rail Transit Line 6

western China. In 2016, the city's rail transit operation lines including line 1, line 2, line 3 and line 6 (including the branch line of line 6), among which line 1 and line 6 were metro, line 2 and line 3 were light rail. The line network covered 9 districts in the main city of Chongqing, with 117 stations and 213.3 kilometres operation mileage. In 2017, the total operation mileage of rail transit in the city was 264 kilometres, including 166 kilometres of subway and 98 kilometres of monorail. The passenger capacity of rail transit was 743 million.

During the "Thirteenth Five-Year Plan" period, Chongqing transportation will further accelerate the construction of railway corridors and will build a "double-cross-shaped" high-speed railway network, a number of railway trunk lines and park railway special lines. Chongqing will strengthen the construction of railway passenger and freight hub and will form a "three mains and two auxiliaries" (三主两辅) passenger transport hub pattern. Chongqing will speed up the construction of key highways and will form a network of "three-ring expressways, twelve radiant expressways and multiple lines". Chongqing will further enrich and improve the construction of provincial export channels and will vigorously carry out road network renovation projects. Chongqing will improve the airport layout and will form the "one big four small" airport system and will make the development of civil aviation an important driver of economic transformation. It will accelerate the construction of the shipping centre in the upper reaches of the Yangtze River and will build an inland shipping system with "one trunk, two branches, four hubs and nine key points" as the backbone and shipping clusters as the support. It will build a logistics hub of railway, public and water intermodal port; it will form four hub ports: the main city Guoyuan, Jiangjin Luohuang (江津珞璜), Fuling Longtou (涪陵龙头) and Wanzhou Xintian (万州新田). By 2020, Chongqing will basically become a comprehensive transportation hub in southwest China and will build a modern comprehensive transportation system with "unimpeded, convenient, interconnected, comfortable, safe, economic, and green" characteristics, which will meet the economic and social development of Chongqing and the travel needs of the people. [1]

---

[1] This paragraph describes the period up to 2019.

Chapter Five　Culture and Tourism

Section One　Culture and Art

Chongqing is an ancient city with a long history and a famous cultural city with glorious revolutionary tradition. In the pre-Qin (先秦) Period, the Ba people were brave and were good at fighting, singing and dancing. While engaging in productive labor and constant war, they left behind the Ba Culture in the Bronze Age (青铜时期), which was the cultural form that combined the Yin and Zhou Culture (殷周文化) as well as the southern clan culture. During the Spring and Autumn Period and the Warring States Period, the Ba people were famous for their singing and dancing. "Xialibaren" (下里巴人) was a ballad sung by the Ba people. Yang Xiong (扬雄) of the Western Han Dynasty called it the "local song of the Ba people" (巴人土歌). In the Han Dynasty, the ancient Ba people's war dance was favoured by the feudal emperors, especially the founding emperor Liu Bang (刘邦). At that time, the Ba people's war dance was equipped with four kinds of music, namely, *The Song of Maoyu* (《矛渝本歌曲》), *The Song of Antai* (《安台本歌曲》), *The Song of Annuyu* (《安弩渝本歌曲》) and *The Song of Xingci* (《行辞本歌曲》). In the Wei and Jin Dynasties, the "Bayu Dance" was changed into the "Zhaowu Dance" (昭武舞) and the "Xuanwu

Picture 5-1　The War Dance of the Ba People

Dance" (宣武舞), in which stage performance and singing were combined. In the heyday of the Tang Dynasty, Zhuzhi Songs (竹枝歌) were popular in Chongqing. It was an art form evolved from the Ba ballads and reflected the life and love of the working people in the Bayu areas. With the vigorous development of formative arts, the sculptures of Dazu Cliff Statues (大足摩崖石刻) distinguished themselves mainly with high relief and shallow relief, and fully combined various forms of expression such as round sculpture, high relief, shallow relief, line carving and openwork carving, with rich changes and vivid plots. On Fuling White Crane Ridge Inscription (白鹤梁石刻), records of dry-water season and numerous poems since the Tang Dynasty were engraved, with more than 30,000 words in total and high attainment of calligraphy. It is the earliest and most numerous hydrological inscriptions about dry-water season with the longest duration in the world. It is referred to as the "First Ancient Hydrological Station in the World" by experts on the preservation of cultural relics.

From the "song and dance of the Ba People" (巴人歌舞) in ancient times, "Xialibaren" in the Spring and Autumn period, the "Bayu Song and Dance" (巴渝歌舞) in Qin and Han Dynasty and the "Zhuzhi Songs" in the prosperous Tang Dynasty, people got to know that the music, rap, juggling and lantern festival rose in the later generations were forms of song and dance with music and they were the results of the development and mutual integration of songs, dances, drums and music. With the art of Ba as the center, this art combined the charm

Picture 5-2 Xiushan Lantern Dance (秀山花灯舞)

Picture 5-3 Hand Waving Dance of Tujia Nationality (土家族摆手舞)

of Ba and Chu opera (巴楚戏曲), Quyi (曲艺) [1], song and dance, acrobatics and integrated them into an art category with local style, which provided a good soil and open space for the development of various arts after the Song Dynasty. During the reign of Baoqing (宝庆) and Shaoding (绍定) (1225-1233) in the Southern Song Dynasty, Chongqing was already a commercial and trade center in eastern Sichuan with developed water and land transportation as well as a variety of flower fairs, temple fairs and lantern fairs. Since the Ming and Qing Dynasties, local operas represented by random play (乱弹) [2] became popular. With the establishment of merchant trade circulation and commercial guilds, temples such as Yuwang Temple (禹王庙), Wenchang Palace (文昌宫), Tuzhu Temple (土主庙) and Wanshou Palace (万寿宫) were built in various places. Some guilds in Chongqing and clan ancestral temples set up theatrical buildings to provide opportunities and places for opera performances. The performing arts also spread to the city from the countryside. As the gateway of Yunnan, Guizhou, Sichuan and Tibet, Chongqing area attracted numerous merchants from south and north, and

[1] It refers to Chinese folk-art forms, including ballad singing, story-telling, comic dialogues, clapper talks, cross talks, etc.

[2] a general term for Chinese opera melodie

the opera art was also flourishing. During the Daoguang Period (道光) of the Qing Dynasty, Huqin Opera (胡琴戏) from Hubei Province was introduced. In Xianfeng Period, Han Opera (汉调) was introduced, followed by Qin Opera (秦腔), Chu Opera (楚剧) and Beijing Opera (京剧). Together with local high-pitched opera, various local operas were integrated. By communicating with, learning from and complementing each other, Sichuan opera was further developed.

On July 7th, 1937, the War of Resistance Against Japanese Aggression broke out . Chongqing became the war-time capital of the nationalist government as well as the military, political, economic and cultural center of the rear area. A large number of factories, schools, government agencies and social organizations in coastal areas and enemy-occupied areas moved to Chongqing, and famous people from all walks of life also gathered in Chongqing. Most military schools of the state army, navy and air force, scientific research institutions and academic, cultural and artistic organizations settled in Chongqing. The Southern Bureau of the CPC Central Committee represented by Zhou Enlai, held high the banner of the anti-Japanese national united front and attracted a large number of elites from domains of domestic culture, arts, science and education, and foreign friends to Chongqing, and it jointly created a new situation of anti-Japanese war culture. With the prosperity of art activities, a large number of outstanding artists, such as Guo Moruo (郭沫若), Mao Dun (茅盾), Lao She (老舍), Yang Hansheng (阳翰笙), Hong Shen (洪深), Tian Han (田汉), Cao Yu (曹禺), Xia Yan (夏衍), Xu Beihong (徐悲鸿), created many fine works of art, which can be regarded as a

Picture 5-4 Drama Still of *Quyuan* (《屈原》)

milestone in Chinese art history. *Qu Yuan* (《屈原》), *Flower of Tang Di* (《棠棣之花》) by Guo Moruo, *Spring and Autumn of the Heavenly Kingdom* (《天国春秋》) by Yang Hansheng, *General Mobilization* (《全民总动员》) by Cao Yu and more than 10 plays participated in the drama festival and Chongqing fog season grand public performance for several consecutive years. Chongqing established the All-China Art Resistance Association and All-China Cartoon Resistance Association and held more than 220 exhibitions of various paintings. China Film Studio, the Central Film studio and China Education Film Studio moved to Chongqing and produced 16 feature films, such as *Blood in the Lonely City* (《孤城喋血》), *Loyal Soul* (《热血忠魂》), *Eight Hundred Heroes* (《八百壮士》) and *March of Victory* (《胜利进行曲》) , with 103 newsreels and science and education films. All showed in Britain, the United States, the Soviet Union, France and Southeast Asia, which greatly inspired and shocked the people of the world. These works expressed the spirit of patriotism and internationalism, as well as the heroic and unyielding fighting spirit of the Chinese nation and promoted people's confidence and determination to fight to the end.

After the founding of the People's Republic of China, literary and art workers from the old liberated areas and young literary and art workers from Beijing and Shanghai came to Chongqing, where they formed a team with local literary and art workers capable of literature and art. More than 2000 excellent works have been created successively, such as *Forty Year's Wish* (《四十年的愿望》), *Longquan Cave* (《龙泉洞》), *A Carpenter* (《一个木工》) and *Sister Jiang* (《江姐》). They were deeply loved by the masses and won more than 300 awards in national and provincial performances and exhibitions. Since the reform and opening-up, the mass cultural activities have been active, and the mass cultural undertakings have been greatly developed. A three-level mass cultural network at the municipal, district, county and township levels has been basically formed. Since it became a municipality directly under the central government, Chongqing has

Picture 5-5 Opera Still of *Sister Jiang*

enjoyed a fruitful harvest of literary and artistic creation. It accelerated the pace of cultural legislation, making achievements in theoretical research, accelerating the pace of cultural facilities construction, making more active foreign exchanges, improving the efficiency of public cultural services continuously, diversifing cultural activities. Sichuan Opera *The Story of Shanhua* (《山花传》), *The Dream of a Lady from the Ba County* (《巴女梦》), *The Dragon and Phoenix Gorge* (《龙凤峡》), *Gold* (《金子》), *Lady Nvjiao in Tushan Mountain* (《涂山女娇》), opera *Goddess in Wushan Mountain* (《巫山神女》), drama *Driftwood Man* (《漂木人》), children's drama *Wonderful Flower in Blood Pool* (《血泊奇花》) were created. The Opera *Goddess in Wushan Mountain* won the first prize in the opera category of "Five-One Project Award" (五个一工程奖) in China, and Sichuan Opera *Gold* won the gold medal of the first Sichuan Opera Festival in China. The special collection library of Chongqing library was completed and partially opened, and a number of cultural facilities such as Chongqing Theater, Hall of Resistance Against Japanese Aggression (抗战大礼堂) and Shengli Theater (胜利剧场) were gradually reconstructed. A number of key projects such as Chongqing Grand Theater, Guotai Art Center (国泰艺术中心), Hongyan Soul Square phase II project and Gele Mountain Martyrs Cemetery Exhibition Center, Chongqing Sichuan Opera Art Center, New Chongqing Museum of Natural History, Exhibition Hall of Hongyan Revolutionary Memorial Museum, China Three Gorges Museum in Chongqing, namely, Chongqing Museum were started and completed successively.

In recent years, with benefiting the people through culture as the theme, the reform and innovation as the driving force, Chongqing firmly grasped the leadership of ideological work and promoted the coordinated development of cultural undertakings and cultural industries, making new breakthroughs and achievements in cultural reform and development of Chongqing. In 2017, the original dance drama *Du Fu* (《杜甫》) won the highest award of Chinese Dance — "Lotus Award". The humanities documentary *China-Russia Book Route* (《中俄书途》) won the excellent project award of "2016-2017 China-Russia Media Exchange Year"; three works of the movie *Bloody Battle on the Xiangjiang River* (《血战湘江》), the TV drama *Desperate Guard Division* (《绝命后卫师》) and the radio drama *Baby Back Home* (《宝贝回家》) won the "Five-one Project Award" of the Publicity Department of the CPC Central Committee; six micro videos such as *Orchid Season* (《兰草时节》) won national awards; three works such as *Landscape in the Dark* (《黑暗中的风景》) won the excellent award of radio and television program award of China Radio, Film and Television Award; *Revolutionaries* (《革命者》) was rated as excellent TV drama script by

Picture 5-6 Sichuan Opera Still of *Gold*

Picture 5-7 Luo Zhongli's Oil Painting *Father*

the former State Administration of Press, Publication, Radio, Film and Television. In 2017, 829 villages and towns (streets), 4,598 villages (communities) comprehensive cultural service centers were upgraded. 9 district and county libraries and 9 district and county cultural centers were newly built, rebuilt and expanded. 900,000 live satellite households were connected. 31 Alpine radio stations were reconstructed and expanded, and other major infrastructure projects of radio and television were completed, making sure that the rich and colourful culture benefited people. 38 districts and counties purchased 36,000 episodes of public mobile culture from the society and screened more than 120,000 films benefiting the people. The quality and efficiency of the cultural industry has been improved. The cultural and creative park of Eling No.2 Factory (鹅岭二厂文创公园) and Yidu Cultural and Creative Park (艺度创文创园) have been completed and put into use; 37 characteristic cultural clusters have been formed; 5,000 cultural enterprises have been gathered, and the annual output value has exceeded 10 billion yuan. For the first time, the number of cultural market entities exceeded 100,000, and the output value of cultural industry exceeded 200 billion yuan. Chongqing actively integrated into the Belt and Road Initiative and promoted cultural trade development through cultural exchanges. Chongqing cultural delegation participated in the Volga Festival; Chongqing library cooperated with Russian Presidential Library, Samara State Library and Minsk State Library of Belarus; Chongqing Art Museum and Belarus National Art Museum exchanged artists. Chongqing assisted and supported Chongqing bonded port area and Chongqing Gangrong Cultural Industry Co., Ltd. in developing foreign cultural trade. In 2017, the city launched 374 cultural exchange projects with Hong Kong, Macao and Taiwan as well as foreign countries.

Picture 5-8 *Return and Complement*

Section Two Sports Culture

Since ancient times, there have been martial arts, wrestling, horse riding, archery, weightlifting and other sports activities in Bashu Area, mainly for performance or comparison of skills. There have also been dragon dance, lion dance, dragon boat race, mountain climbing, kite flying, rope skipping, chess and other items for leisure and entertainment according to seasons and customs. Ancient Ba people created the technique of guiding Qi, which later generations called "Qigong" (气功). It has been passed down to this day and has become an important item for the masses to practice martial arts, keep fit and drive away diseases. In the late Warring States period, there were sword, broad axe, spear, dagger-axe, axe and other weapons in Bashu, and Chinese Martial Arts began to develop. During the period of the Republic of China, warlords attached great importance to and advocated martial arts and frequently set up arena to compete.

At the beginning of the 20th century, with the introduction of modern sports, sports such as track and field, swimming, ball games, gymnastics, boxing, bodybuilding gradually developed. During the War of Resistance Against Japanese Aggression, Chongqing began to develop aviation sports, such as paragliding, parachute tower parachuting, aviation model, which was the earliest area in China

Picture 5-9 Mass Sports and Fitness

to carry out such projects. Martial arts experts from all over the county came to Chongqing, promoting the introduction of boxing schools and the development of martial arts skills, and the performance of large-scale national skill competitions was active. After the founding of the People's Republic of China, the number of sports in Chongqing further increased. In the 1950s, fencing, shooting, motorcycles, military camping and other items were added. In the 1970s, track and field, swimming, football and shooting became key sports, and new sports such as roller skating, shuttlecock, croquet, judo and chess were developed. Competitive sports flourished.

Since Chongqing became a municipality directly under the central government, Chongqing sports have ushered in a new period of development. The reform of sports made initial achievements. With the reform of football system as the breakthrough, the reform of training system and competition system was strengthened, and the socialization of mass sports management and the materialized development of individual sports associations were promoted. Mass sports developed vigorously; the number of people participating in sports activities continued to increase and the scope of their participation expanded. In 1983 and 1986, Chongqing was awarded as the "Hometown of Track and Field" (田径之乡) twice in China, and the physical quality and health of the citizens improved greatly. In 2017, Chongqing hosted more than 70 major events such as Chongqing International Marathon, World Cup rock-climbing competition, as well as a series of mass sports activities such as the 7th Chongqing National Fitness Games and the 4th Chongqing Senior Citizen Games. Chongqing International Marathon attracted 30,000 athletes from 30 countries and regions. The competitive level has been constantly improved. By 2005, it had won 16 world champions, 65 Asian champions and 197 national and army champions in international and domestic competitions, and it set 24 world records. In 2017, Chongqing hosted

Picture 5-10 Rafting on the Aiyi River

21 international and domestic sports events. Chongqing athletes won 50 gold medals, 25 silver medals and 51 bronze medals in international and domestic sports events. Chongqing Contemporary Lifan Football Club won the 10th place in China Super League and Chongqing Real Estate Weiqi Team won the 6th place in China Weiqi First-class League. Developed from scratch, sports scientific research provided scientific and technological services for competitive sports and updated training concepts and innovated training methods. From small to large, the sports industry has gained good social benefits in developing sports competition market, sports fitness and entertainment market and intangible assets. In 2017, the total output value of sports industry was 30.915 billion yuan, with an added value of 14.394 billion yuan, accounting for 0.8% of the city's regional GDP. The total output value and added value of sports service industry were 21.361 billion yuan and 10.896 billion yuan respectively, accounting for 69.1% and 75.7% of the total output value and added value of the city's sports industry respectively. The achievements of legal system construction were fruitful, and normative documents such as *Regulations of Chongqing Municipality on National Fitness*（《重庆市全民健身条例》）, *Implementation Opinions on Accelerating the Development of the Fitness and Leisure Industry*（《关于加快发展健身休闲产业的实施意见》）, *Implementation Plan of the 13th Five-Year Plan for Youth Sports*（《青少年体育“十三五”规划实施方案》） were issued, which further improved the level of sports management and administration in accordance with the law. In 2017, the reform and development of sports venues effectively promoted the free and low-cost opening of 69 large sports venues and 5 small and

medium-sized sports venues in the city. 230 new sports projects for farmers were built, and 1,196 new sports projects for farmers were updated, and 17 new sports fitness squares for farmers and more than 300 community fitness sites were built.

Section Three Tourism

Ⅰ.Tourism Resources

1.Scenic Spots and World Natural Heritage Sites

There are 36 national and municipal scenic spots in Chongqing, including 7 national scenic spots and 29 municipal scenic spots.

1) National Scenic Spots

(1) Three Gorges Scenic Spot of the Yangtze River (Chongqing Section)

The Three Gorges scenic area of the Yangtze River (Chongqing Section) includes Fengjie-Baidicheng, the Qutang Gorge, the Wuxia Gorge, the Shennv Creek (神女溪), the Daning River Small Three Gorges, the Madu River Small Three Gorges (马渡河小三峡), Dachang Ancient Town (大昌古镇) and other areas. The majestic Three Gorges of the Yangtze River is famous for its magnificence, wonder, danger, beauty and seclusion.

Picture 5-11 Red Leaf of the Wushan Gorge

(2) Jinyun Mountain Scenic Spot

Jinyun Mountain Scenic Spot is located in the West Bank of Wentang gorge of the Small Three Gorges of Jialing River, Beibei District, Chongqing, with an altitude of 350-950 meters. Together with the Small Three Gorges of the Jialing River and Hechuan Diaoyucheng, it was designated as a national level natural scenic spot. The reserve is rich in plant resources, some of which have an ancient origin, and there are many rare and endangered plants. The national level protected rare plants include dove tree, silver fir, Taxus, Alsophila, etc. The national level protected rare animals include grass owl, golden pheasant, Eurasian eagle-owl, etc.

(3) Jinfo Mountain Scenic Spot

There are three wonders in Jinfo Mountain Scenic Spot: Karst World Natural Heritage, Biodiversity and Buddhist culture. It has original and unique natural features, magnificent and strange rock mass modeling, mysterious and deep cave palace, unpredictable meteorological landscape, breath-taking and exciting cliff plank road, and historic Tang Dynasty temples. Integrating mountains, water, forests, springs and caves, it is a combination of masculinity, strangeness, danger and beauty. It has been rated as National Scenic Spot, National Nature Reserve, National Forest Park, National Natural Heritage, National Popular Science Education Base, National AAAAA Scenic Spot and National Civilized Scenic Spot. In 2014, it was listed as a World Natural Heritage.

Picture 5-12 Rhododendron Sea in Jinfo Mountain

(4) Simian Mountain Scenic Spot

The Simian Mountain System is called "inverted mountain" in geology because it is surrounded by mountains. Located in Jiangjin District, Chongqing, the Simian Mountain boasts four characteristic landscape resources, and they are fantastic mountains, magnificent waters, red stones and profound cultural heritage. The most famous among them are Love Ladder; the highest waterfall in China — Wangxiangtai Waterfall with a height of 158 meters and a width of 48 meters; China's largest heart-shaped landscape with the name "the World's Best Heart-shaped Landscape" and "the World's First Colorful Waterfall".

(5) Furong River Scenic Spot

The Chongqing section of the Furong River is a national key scenic spot, with a length of 35 kilometres and a typically large "U-shaped" canyon as the main part. In the scenic area of the Pinghu Gorge in Wulong section of Chongqing, the river is green and blue; the trees on both sides are vigorous; the roots are in various shapes; water birds fly; stalactites hang; springs flow; green shadows whirl. These all making the most beautiful scenery of the Furong River. In Furong River Scenic Area, the national first-class rare animal, Francois's Leaf Monkey can be observed at close range, and the macaque are seen in groups.

(6) Tiankeng Difeng (天坑地缝) Scenic Spot

Located in Xiaozhai Village (小寨村), Jingzhu Township (荆竹乡), Fengjie County, Chongqing, this scenic spot is closely connected with the Qutang Gorge with the world-famous Three Gorges of the Yangtze River in the north. It faces the famous Daning River and the Small Three Gorges across the river, with Tujia and Miao Autonomous Prefecture of Enshi in the south. It connected with Zhangjiajie (张家界), a famous national scenic spot, and it connected with Longping (龙坪) ancient human cultural relics of Wushan Temple in the east. It includes six scenic spots: Tiankeng, Difeng, the Longqiao River (龙桥河), the Migong River (迷宫河), the Jiupan River (九盘河) and Maocaoba (茅草坝).

(7) Tanzhang Gorge (潭獐峡) Scenic Spot

Tanzhang Gorge scenic spot is located in the southeast of Wanzhou District, Chongqing. With a total area of 69 square kilometres, it includes 32,100 mu of forest area. It is integrated with Wangerbao (王二包), a municipal nature reserve with rare animals and plants and the "Kingdom of Insects" in the Three Gorges Reservoir area. The canyon, ground fissure, secluded pool and karst cave in this scenic area are quite distinctive. It is a resort for leisure, vacation, scientific research and exploration in the Three Gorges Reservoir area.

2) Municipal Scenic Spots

Table 5-1 Basic Information of Municipal Scenic Spots

The serial number	The name of the scenic spot	Application area (km^2)	Planned area (km^2)	Approval time of Chongqing government	Approval time of Sichuan government	Approval time of Chongqing municipality directly under the central government	Notes
1	Dazu Stone Carvings Scenic Spot	84.00	115.50		August, 1989	April, 1999	During the 9th Five-Year Plan
2	Nanshan-Nanquan Scenic Spot	92.50	75.00		August, 1989	April, 1999	During the 9th Five-Year Plan
3	Tongjing Scenic Spot	11.00	14.50		August, 1989	April, 1999	During the 9th Five-Year Plan
4	Xiaonanhai Scenic Spot	30.00	27.10		January, 1995	April, 1999	During the 9th Five-Year Plan
5	Hongchiba Scenic Spot		357.80		January, 1995	April, 1999	During the 9th Five-Year Plan
6	Bamboo Sea Scenic Spot	119.00	92.40		January, 1995	April, 1999	During the 9th Five-Year Plan
7	Qinglong Waterfall Scenic Spot		60.10		January, 1995	April, 1999	During the 9th Five-Year Plan
8	Xiaoxi Scenic Spot	25.00	24.00		January, 1995	April, 1999	During the 9th Five-Year Plan
9	Heishan-Shilin Scenic Spot	60.00	101.10	January,1992		April, 1999	During the 9th Five-Year Plan

10	Heishishan-Gunziping Scenic Spot	125.00	179.50	October, 1995		April, 1999	During the 9th Five-Year Plan
11	Bayue Mountain-Western Hot Spring Scenic Spot		51.00	January,1992		April, 1999	During the 9th Five-Year Plan
12	Changshou Lake Scenic Spot	58.70	245.20	January,1992		April, 1999	During the 9th Five-Year Plan
13	Dingming Mountain-Canal Scenic Spot	16.00	65.00	January,1992		April, 1999	During the 9th Five-Year Plan
14	Gele Mountain Scenic Spot	14.20	51.00	June, 1990		April, 1999	During the 9th Five-Year Plan
15	East Hot Spring Scenic Spot	58.70	57.20	June, 1990		July, 2000	During the 9th Five-Year Plan
16	Tanzhang Gorge Scenic Spot		76.00			July, 2000	During the 9th Five-Year Plan
17	Zhangguan-Baiyan Scenic Spot		49.10			July, 2000	During the 9th Five-Year Plan
18	Wujiang Gallery Scenic Spot		120.00			July, 2000	During the 9th Five-Year Plan
19	Tiansheng Sanqiao Scenic Spot		50.00			July, 2000	During the 9th Five-Year Plan
20	Mingyue Mountain Scenic Spot		118.10			July, 2000	During the 9th Five-Year Plan

Continued

The serial number	The name of the scenic spot	Application area (km^2)	Planned area (km^2)	Approval time of Chongqing government	Approval time of Sichuan government	Approval time of Chongqing municipality directly under the central government	Notes
21	Longquan Scenic Spot		74.00			October, 2000	During the 9th Five-Year Plan
22	Ganjinggou Scenic Spot	191.00	65.20			October, 2000	During the 9th Five-Year Plan
23	Qinglong Lake Scenic Spot	55.00	57.20	March, 1993		October, 2000	During the 9th Five-Year Plan
24	Huangshui Scenic Spot	504.00	117.50			October, 2000	During the 9th Five-Year Plan
25	Wushan Daning River Small Three Gorges Scenic Spot	370.00				October, 2000	During the 9th Five-Year Plan
26	Xiefeng Mountain Scenic Spot		100.50			December, 2004	During the 10th Five-Year Plan
27	Jiuchongshan Scenic Spot	47.10	105.50			January, 2006	During the 11th Five-Year Plan
28	Gujian Mountain Scenic Spot	109.90	109.90			January, 2006	During the 11th Five-Year Plan
29	Houping Tiankeng Scenic Spot	38.00	38.00			December, 2006	During the 11th Five-Year Plan

3) World Natural Heritage

There are mainly two karst landforms, one in the Jinfo Mountain, Nanchuan and the other one in Wulong. Wulong karst landform is located in Chongqing Wulong District. It is an organic part of karst landform in south China and an important representative of deep-seated canyon. It breeds three independent karst landform systems, namely Furong Cave System, Three Natural Bridges Karst System and Houping Erosion Tiankeng Karst System. It is developed and formed under the influence of large-scale crustal uplift in the Three Gorges area of the Yangtze River. Wulong Karst Landform consists of Furong Cave, Three Natural Bridges and Houping. It is a national AAAAA scenic spot. It was listed in the world natural heritage in 2007. The area of this nature reserve is about 135 square kilometres.

Picture 5-13 Wulong Karst Landform

2.Cultural Heritage

1) National Cultural Heritage

Chongqing is the second batch of national famous historical and cultural cities with profound cultural heritage and rich cultural relics resources. In 2016, the first national survey of movable cultural relics showed that there were 470,200 movable cultural relics (sets) registered in 165 state-owned cultural relics collection units in the city (the actual number was 1.4825 million pieces and volumes), including 42,200 precious cultural relics. There are 18 famous Chinese historical and cultural towns, 1 famous Chinese historical and cultural street, 1 famous Chinese historical and cultural village and 67 traditional Chinese villages. Dazu Stone Carvings are listed on the World Heritage List. In 2012, White Crane Ridge Inscription (白鹤梁题刻) in Fuling and Diaoyucheng in Hechuan were included in the Preliminary List of World Cultural Heritage. In 2018, Chongqing Municipal Bureau of Cultural Relics published *the List of Key National Cultural Relics Protection Units in Chongqing* (《重庆市全国重点文物保护单位名录》). There are 55 key national cultural relics protection units in the city, including 6 ancient sites, 2 ancient tombs, 9 ancient buildings, 8 grotto temples and stone carvings, 30 important modern historical sites and representative buildings.

Table 5-2 The List of Key National Culture Relics Protection Units in Chongqing

Name	Era	Location	Type
Longgupo Site	the Pleistocene	Miaoyu Town, Wushan County	Ancient Ruins
Diaoyucheng Ruins	Southern Song Dynasty, Yuan Dynasty	Fishing hill, Yucheng village, Diaoyucheng sub-district office, Hechuan District	Ancient Ruins
Gaojia Town Ruins	Paleolithic Age	Guihua Village, Gaojia Town, Fengdu County	Ancient Ruins
Tianshengcheng Site	From Southern Song Dynasty to Qing Dynasty	Liushui community, Zhoujiaba sub-district office, Wanzhou District	Ancient Ruins
Ruins of the Old Gulou Government Office	From Southern Song Dynasty to Qing Dynasty	Yamen area, Baxian County, Wanglongmen Street, Jiefang East Road, Yuzhong District	Ancient Ruins
Site Group of Zinc Smelting in Chongqing	From Ming Dynasty to Qing Dynasty	Qiyao mountain, Shizhu County; group 7, Langxi Village, Zhenjiang Town, Fengdu County	Ancient Ruins
Jingzhuba Rock Coffin Group	From the Warring States Period to Han Dynasty	Jingzhuba, Wuxi County	Ancient Tombs
Huinan Tombs	From Han Dynasty to Six Dynasties	Xinwan Village, Huinan Township, Fengdu County	Ancient Tombs
Dingfangque-Wumingque	Han Dynasty	No. 74 Renmin Road, Zhongzhou Town, Zhongxian County (Dingfangque); Youxi Village, Ganjing Town (Wumingque), Zhongxian County	Ancient Architecture
Zhang Fei Temple	Qing Dynasty	Jiangnan village, Shuimo Town, Yunyang County, moved to Long'an Village, Panshi Town in July 2003	Ancient Architecture

Continued

Name	Era	Location	Type
Shibaozhai Temple	Ming and Qing Dynasty	No. 17 Yinshan Street, Shibao Town, Zhongxian County	Ancient Architecture
Baidicheng	From Han Dynasty to Qing Dynasty	Baidi Village, Baidi Town, Caotang, Fengjie County	Ancient Architecture
Huguang Guild Hall	Qing Dynasty	No. 18, 19 and 22 Bajiao Garden, Yuzhong District; No. 4 Dongzheng Street; No. 7 Lane 1, Taihua Building; No. 19 and 44, Hongxue Lane	Ancient Architecture
The Main Hall of Dubai Temple	Yuan Dynasty	In Dubai primary school, Shanghe Town, Tongnan District	Ancient Architecture
Chongqing Ancient City Wall	Ming Dynasty	Zhongshan 1st Road, Qixinggang Street, Yuzhong District; No.1, Wanglongmen Dongzheng Street, Yuzhong District	Ancient Architecture
Peng's Ancestral Hall	Qing Dynasty	Liming Village, Lishi Town, Yunyang County	Ancient Architecture
Shuanggui Temple	Qing Dynasty	Jindai Town, Liangping District	Ancient Architecture
Beishan Cliff Statues	From Tang Dynasty to Song Dynasty	Longgang Village, Longgang Town, Dazu District (Beishan); Qunli village, Chengdong Town (Nanshan); Fohui Village, Shizhuo Town (Shizhuan Mountain)	Grottoes, Temples and Stone Carvings
Baoding Mountain Cliff Statues	Song and Ming Dynasties	Shanwang village, Baoding Town, Dazu District; Xiaofowan Village (Baoding Mountain); Xinsheng Village, Shima Town (Shimen Mountain)	Grottoes, Temples and Stone Carvings
White Crane Ridge Inscription	From Tang Dynasty to Qing Dynasty	Chongyi Office, Fuling District, Northwest of the Yangtze River	Grottoes, Temples and Stone Carvings
Cliff Statues of the Great Buddha Temple in Tongnan	From Sui Dynasty to Ming Dynasty	Shinian Village, Zitong Town, Tongnan District	Grottoes, Temples and Stone Carvings

Cliff Statues of the Second Buddha Temple in Laitan	Song Dynasty	Northeast of Erfo Village, Laitan Town, Hechuan District	Grottoes, Temples and Stone Carvings
Cliff Statues of Shimen Great Buddha Temple	From Song Dynasty to Yuan Dynasty	Liangting Group, Shimen Community, Shimen Town, Jiangjin District	Grottoes, Temples and Stone Carvings
Cliff Stone Carvings in Qutang Gorge	From Southern Song Dynasty to the Republic of China	Baidicheng Scenic Spot Management Committee, Fengjie County, Chongqing	Grottoes, Temples and Stone Carvings
Danzishi Cliff Statues	From Yuan Dynasty to Qing Dynasty	No.1, Jicui Village, Danzishi, Nan'an District	Grottoes, Temples and Stone Carvings
Former Site of Chongqing Office of the Eighth Route Army	From 1938 to 1946	No. 13, Hongyan Village, Yuzhong District; No. 50, Zengjiayan (Zhougongguan); No. 305, Zhongsan Road, Yuzhong District (former site of the CPC Delegation); No. 240, Minsheng Road (former site of *Xinhua Daily* Business Department)	Important Historical Records and Representative Buildings in Modern Times
Guiyuan	1945	Guiyuan (Zhang Zhizhong Residence), No. 117, Zhongsi Road, Yuzhong District	Important Historical Records and Representative Buildings in Modern Times
Former Site of "Sino-American Cooperative Organization" Concentration Camp	From 1943 to 1949	Martyr tomb area, Tongjiaqiao Street, Shapingba District	Important Historical Records and Representative Buildings in Modern Times
Former Residence of Zhao Shiyan	Qing Dynasty	No. 219, Zhaozhuang Road, Zhaozhuang Community, Longtan Town, Youyang Tujia and Miao Autonomous County	Important Historical Records and Representative Buildings in Modern Times
Yang's Residence	Qing Dynasty	Tianba Street, Shuangjiang Town, Tongnan District	Important Historical Records and Representative Buildings in Modern Times

Continued

Name	Era	Location	Type
West Chinese Academy of Sciences	From 1935 to 1949	No.42 Wenxingwan, Chaoyang Street, Beibei District	Important Historical Records and Representative Buildings in Modern Times
Former Site of Yucai School	From 1939 to 1945	Gusheng Village, Caojie sub-district office, Hechuan District	Important Historical Records and Representative Buildings in Modern Times
Former Residence of Liu Bocheng	1897	Zhoudu Village, Zhaojia Town, Kaizhou District	Important Historical Records and Representative Buildings in Modern Times
Former Residence of Nie Rongzhen	1899	Community 8, Langjia Village, Wutan Town, Jiangjin District	Important Historical Records and Representative Buildings in Modern Times
Former Site Group of Rural Construction in the Three Gorges of the Jialing River	The Republic of China	Beibei District	Important Historical Records and Representative Buildings in Modern Times
Teyuan	From 1931 to 1946	No. 37-49, Jialingqiao East Village, Yuzhong District	Important Historical Records and Representative Buildings in Modern Times
Former Site of Han and Tibetan Teaching Institute of World Buddhist Academy	1932	Beibei District	Important Historical Records and Representative Buildings in Modern Times

Former Site of the Third Army of the Chinese Red Army Headquarter in Nanyaojie	1934	Group 5, Nanyaojie Village, Nanyaojie Town, Youyang Tujia and Miao Autonomous County	Important Historical Records and Representative Buildings in Modern Times
Former Sites of Legislative Yuan, Judicial Yuan, Mongolian and Tibetan Committee of the National Government	From 1937 to 1946	Outpatient Department of Zhongshan Hospital, Yuzhong District	Important Historical Records and Representative Buildings in Modern Times
Former Site of the Political Department of the Military Commission of the National Government	From 1938 to 1945	Sanshenggong Village, Tuzhu Town, Shapingba District	Important Historical Records and Representative Buildings in Modern Times
Former Site of the Ministry of Foreign Affairs of the National Government	From 1938 to 1946	No.6 Collection Bureau, East Jiefang Road, Yuzhong District (No.3 People's Park)	Important Historical Records and Representative Buildings in Modern Times
Former Sites of Anti-Japanese War Financial Institutions in Chongqing	From 1938 to 1946	No. 41, Xinhua Road, Chaotianmen Street, Yuzhong District; No. 9, Daomenkou, Datong street, Yuzhong District; No. 14, Daomenkou, Datong Street, Chaotianmen Street, Yuzhong District; No. 74, Xinhua Road, Chaotianmen Street, Yuzhong District; No. 16, Datong Street, Chaotianmen Street, Yuzhong District; No. 112, Jiefang East Road, Wanglongmen Street, Yuzhong District	Important Historical Records and Representative Buildings in Modern Times
Former Site of the National Political Consultative Conference	From 1938 to 1946	No. 174 Zhonghua Road, Yuzhong District	Important Historical Records and Representative Buildings in Modern Times

Continued

Name	Era	Location	Type
Linyuan	From 1938 to 1946	No. A1, Linyuan; Shandong Street, Shapingba District	Important Historical Records and Representative Buildings in Modern Times
Former Site of the Third Office of the Political Department and the Cultural Affairs Commission of the Military Members of the National Government	From 1938 to 1946	Yuzhong District and Shapingba District; No. 8, Tianguanfu, Yuzhong District	Important Historical Records and Representative Buildings in Modern Times
Former Anti-Japanese War Sites in Huangshan, Chongqing	From 1938 to 1946	Nan'an District	Important Historical Records and Representative Buildings in Modern Times
Former Sites of Diplomatic Institutions of the Allied Countries in Chongqing	From 1938 to 1946	Nan'an District; No. 104 Pipashan Main Street, Lianglukou Street, Yuzhong District; No. 69 Cangbai Road, Lianglukou Street, Yuzhong District; former Public Security Bureau of Wusi Road, Jiefangbei Street, Yuzhong District; No. 35 Fenghuangtai Street, Nanjimen Street, Yuzhong District; No 176 e'ling Main Street, Lianglukou Street, Yuzhong District; No. 176 e'ling Main Street, Lianglukou Street, Yuzhong District	Important Historical Records and Representative Buildings in Modern Times
Former Anti-Japanese War Sites in Nanquan	From 1938 to 1946	Nanquan Town, Banan District	Important Historical Records and Representative Buildings in Modern Times
Former Site of the Executive Yuan of the National Government	From 1938 to 1947	No. 36 Zhongshan 4th Road, Yuzhong District	Important Historical Records and Representative Buildings in Modern Times

Former Sites of Anti-Japanese War Weapons Industry in Chongqing	From 1939 to 1945	Jiangbei Yanbi, Tongluoxia, Guojiatuo, Jiangbei District; Zhongshutuowachangzui Community, Qianwei Community in Dashiba Street, Jiangbei District; Shapingba District, Jiulongpo District, Dadukou District, the Former plant area of Chongqing Iron and Steel Co., Ltd., and Wansheng Economic Development Zone	Important Historical Records and Representative Buildings in Modern Times
Former Residence of the Chief of Staff of the Chinese Theater Headquarter of the Allied Countries	From 1942 to 1944	No. 63 Jialing New Road, Liziba, Yuzhong District	Important Historical Records and Representative Buildings in Modern Times
Former Headquarter of the League for the Defense of China	From 1942 to 1945	No.5, Xincun, Lianglukou, Yuzhong District	Important Historical Records and Representative Buildings in Modern Times
Former Sites of Chongqing Negotiation	1945	No. 64 Jialing New Road, Yuzhong District	Important Historical Records and Representative Buildings in Modern Times
Monument to the Victory of the Anti-Japanese War and the People's Liberation	1947	Jiefangbei CBD Pedestrian Plaza Center, Yuzhong District	Important Historical Records and Representative Buildings in Modern Times
Chongqing People's Auditorium	1954	No. 173 Renmin Road, Yuzhong District	Important Historical Records and Representative Buildings in Modern Times

Note: The statistics by December 2017.

Chongqing has built a database of 1.48 million movable cultural relics. It held a general survey exhibition of movable cultural relics and selected 354 treasures from the museum. 117 key projects for the protection of five major cultural relics were carried out, and the rescue and maintenance project of Dazu Stone Carvings — Thousand-hand Guanyin (千手观音) was rated as one of the top ten outstanding cultural relics maintenance projects in China, creating a precedent for the restoration of large-scale immovable cultural relics in China.

2) World Cultural Heritage

Dazu Stone Carvings are representative of the stone carving art in Bashu area, which are as famous as Mogao Grottoes in Dunhuang and are known as the bright pearl in the treasure house of Chinese grottoes art. Dazu stone carvings began in the early Tang Dynasty (in the middle of the 7th century) and went through the middle and late Tang Dynasty, the Five Dynasties (五代) and the Northern Song Dynasty (北宋). They flourished in the Southern Song Dynasty and continued to the Ming and Qing Dynasties. Buddhism is the main theme of stone carvings. There are more than 50,000 statues, represented by Baoding Mountain (宝顶山), Beishan Mountain (北山), Shizhuan Mountain (石篆山), Nanshan Mountain and Shimen Mountain (石门山) Cliff Statues, which show the significant development and changes of Chinese grotto art and religious belief in different aspects. They are the most magnificent representatives in the art history of Chinese grottoes from the 9th to the 13th century, and also the living examples of grotto art that represent the harmonious coexistence of "Buddhism, Taoism and Confucianism". In 1999, Dazu Stone Carvings were listed in the world Heritage List, which are the last monument in the history of the world grotto art. In recent years, Chongqing successively launched cultural heritage protection projects such as Baoding Mountain Dafo Bay water disaster control, Beishan Cliff Sculpture No.168 cave rescue protection, monitoring and early warning system construction, rescue and reinforcement. In 2017, *Regulations on the Protection of Dazu Stone Carvings in Chongqing* (《重庆市大足石刻保护条例》) were issued to further strengthen the protection of Dazu Stone Carvings and promote the scientific research on them.

Table 5-3 World Cultural Heritage—Dazu Stone Carvings

Name	Level	Area (m^2)	Era	Location	Description
Baoding Mountain Cliff Statues	Key National Cultural Relics Protection Unit	955,100	1174-1252 (from Chunxi to Chunyou in the Southern Song Dynasty)	Baoding Village, Dazu District, Chongqing	Including the statues of the Great Buddha Bay and the Small Buddha Bay with Shousi Temple as the center, built by Zhao Zhifeng, who was known as holding "the secret seal from the 6th generation of the founder". He spent more than 70 years to organize and build them. It is a large-scale Buddhist Tantric Taoism hall with nearly 10,000 statues.
Beishan Cliff Statues	Key National Cultural Relics Protection Unit	408,400	892-1162 (from Jingfu in Tang Dynasty to Shaoxing in the Southern Song Dynasty)	Longgang Street, Dazu District, Chongqing	Located at the top of the mountain (commonly known as Buddha Bay), the statue cliff is about 300 meters long and 7-10 meters high. The niches are as dense as beehives, divided into two sections, north and south. There are 264 niches and grottoes, including 1 Yin engraved picture and 8 scriptures. It is of great value to the study of historical geography, religious belief, the period of the grottoes, historical figures, etc.
Nanshan Cliff Statues	Key National Cultural Relics Protection Unit	375,000	1131-1162 (Shaoxing period of the Southern Song Dynasty)	Qunli Village, Tangxiang Sub-district Office, Dazu District, Chongqing	The cliff is 86 meters long and 3.5-10.2 meters high. Among them, there are five niches of statues, mainly including Sanqing Ancient Cave , the Virgin Shrine of Houtu, Longdong, Zhenwu Emperor Niches and other niches with Taoist themes. It is the most complete material reflecting the Taoist deities in Song Dynasty, with high religious, historical and artistic value.

Continued

Name	Level	Area (m^2)	Era	Location	Description
Shimen Mountain Cliff Statues	Key National Cultural Relics Protection Unit	57,600	1094-1151 (from Shaosheng period in the Northern Song Dynasty to the 21st year of Shaoxing in the Southern Song Dynasty)	Xinsheng Village, Shima Town, Dazu District, Chongqing	The carved cliff is 71.8 meters long and 3.4-5 meters high, including 12 niches. There are still 20 statues, 8 tablets and inscriptions, 8 cultivation records and the names of craftsmen such as Wen Weiyi, Wen Judao, Jian Zhongjin, etc.
Shizhuan Mountain Cliff Statues	Key National Cultural Relics Protection Unit	265,000	1082-1096 (from the 5th year of Yuanfeng to the 3rd year of Shaosheng in the Northern Song Dynasty)	Fohui Village, Sanqu Town, Dazu District, Chongqing	The cliff is 130 meters long and 3-8 meters high. It is a typical sculpture area combining Buddhism, Taoism and Confucianism, which is rarely seen in grottoes.

Picture 5-14 Dazu Baoding Stone Carving

3) Intangible Cultural Heritage

In 2010, the first general survey of Chongqing's intangible cultural heritage was basically completed, and 4,110 items in 10 categories, including folk literature, traditional music, traditional dance, traditional drama, quyi, traditional sports and acrobatics, traditional art, traditional techniques, traditional medicine and folk customs were found to be under protection. A large number of intangible cultural heritage projects with precious historical and cultural value and on the verge of loss, such as Chuanjiang Haozi (川江号子)[1], Nuo opera (傩戏), Dragon Dance (龙舞), Hand-waving Dance (摆手舞), Bayu Blowing (巴渝吹打), Folk Songs, Lantern Opera (灯戏), Lacquer Ware (漆器), Shu Embroidery (蜀绣), Root Carving, Stone Carving, Clay Sculpture, Paper Cutting, New Year Painting (年画), Bamboo Curtains, inkstone made of gorge stone (峡砚), all have been protected in time. Traditional music, traditional skills and folk literature are the most abundant resources, accounting for 20.5%, 18.3% and 17.9% of the

[1] working song on the Chuanjiang River

Picture 5-15 Wood Engraving New Year Painting *The Expedition*《出征》in Liangping

total census respectively; resources in ethnic minority areas in southeast Chongqing are relatively rich, accounting for 33.2% of the total census.

In 2016, with the approval of the State Council, 44 intangible cultural heritage projects in Chongqing were listed in national intangible cultural heritage projects in 4 batches. 40 representative inheritors were named by the Ministry of Culture as inheritors of national intangible cultural heritage projects in 4 batches. With the approval of the municipal government, 511 intangible cultural heritage projects municipal intangible cultural heritage projects in 5 batches were named, and 563 municipal intangible cultural heritage projects were named in 4 batches. One national level cultural and ecological protection experimental area, one national level productive protection demonstration base, 35 municipal level productive protection demonstration bases, 55 municipal level intangible cultural heritage inheritance and education bases, and 3 national level intangible cultural heritage project representative inheritors won Chinese Intangible Cultural Heritage Inheritance Award.

Table 5-4 List of National Intangible Cultural Heritage Projects in Chongqing

The First Batch (13 items in total)

Number	Serial number	Type	Item	Application area or unit
1	I-17	Folk Literature	Zouma Town Folktale	Jiulongpo District, Chongqing
2	II-15	Folk Music	Shizhu Tujia Luoer Tune	Shizhu Tujia Autonomous County, Chongqing
3	II-24	Folk Music	Chuanjiang Haozi	Chongqing Art Research Institute

Continued

<table>
<tr><th>Number</th><th>Serial number</th><th>Type</th><th colspan="2">Item</th><th>Application area or unit</th></tr>
<tr><td>4</td><td>II-25</td><td>Folk Music</td><td colspan="2">Nanxi Haozi</td><td>Qianjiang District, Chongqing</td></tr>
<tr><td>5</td><td>II-26</td><td>Folk Music</td><td colspan="2">Mudong Folk Song</td><td>Banan District, Chongqing</td></tr>
<tr><td rowspan="2">6-7</td><td rowspan="2">II-52</td><td>Folk Music</td><td rowspan="2">Blowing and Percussion</td><td>Jielong Blowing and Percussion</td><td>Banan District, Chongqing</td></tr>
<tr><td>Folk Music</td><td>Jinqiao Blowing and percussion</td><td>Wansheng Economic Development Zone, Chongqing</td></tr>
<tr><td>8</td><td>II-53</td><td>Folk Music</td><td colspan="2">Laizi Gongs and Drums in Liangping</td><td>Liangping County, Chongqing</td></tr>
<tr><td>9</td><td>III-4</td><td>Folk Dance</td><td colspan="2">Dragon Dance (Tongliang Dragon Dance)</td><td>Tongliang County, Chongqing</td></tr>
<tr><td>10</td><td>IV-12</td><td>Traditional Drama</td><td colspan="2">Sichuan Opera</td><td>Chongqing Sichuan Opera Theatre</td></tr>
<tr><td>11</td><td>IV-77</td><td>Traditional Drama</td><td colspan="2">Lantern Show (Liangshan Lantern Show)</td><td>Liangping County, Chongqing</td></tr>
<tr><td>12</td><td>VII-10</td><td>Folk Art</td><td colspan="2">Liangping Woodblock New Year Picture</td><td>Liangping County, Chongqing</td></tr>
<tr><td>13</td><td>X-51</td><td>Folk Custom</td><td colspan="2">Xiushan Lantern</td><td>Xiushan Tujia and Miao Autonomous County, Chongqing</td></tr>
</table>

The Second Batch (16 items in total)

Number	Serial number	Type	Item	Application area or unit
1	II-84	Traditional Music	Xiushan Folk Song	Xiushan Tujia and Miao Autonomous County, Chongqing
2	II-85	Traditional Music	Youyang Folk Song	Youyang Tujia and Miao Autonomous County, Chongqing
3	II-101	Traditional Music	Banyun Haozi (Liangping Tai Tune)	Liangping County, Chongqing
4	II-101	Traditional Music	Banyun Haozi (Longgupo Carrying Workers' Working Song)	Wushan County, Chongqing

Continued

Number	Serial number	Type	Item	Application area or unit
5	II-37	Traditional Music	Suona Art (Yongcheng Blowing)	Qijiang District, Chongqing
6	III-17	Traditional Dance	Tujia Waving Dance (Youyang Waving Dance)	Youyang Tujia and Miao Autonomous County, Chongqing
7	V-76	Quyi	Sichuan Bamboo Organ	Chongqing
8	V-88	Quyi	Chedeng	Chongqing
9	VII-21	Traditional Art	Shu Embroidery	Yuzhong District, Chongqing
10	VII-51	Traditional Art	Bamboo Weaving (Liangping Bamboo Curtain)	Liangping District, Chongqing
11	VIII-102	Traditional Skill	Production Technology of Grass Cloth (Rongchang Grass Cloth)	Rongchang District, Chongqing
12	VIII-127	Traditional Skill	Lacquer Painting Technique (Lacquer Painting Technique in Chongqing)	Chongqing Art Research Institute
13	VIII-156	Traditional Skill	Brewing Technique of Fermented Soya Bean (Yongchuan Douchi Brewing Technique)	Yongchuan District, Chongqing
14	VIII-159	Traditional Skill	Traditional Processing Technology of Pickled Mustard Tuber (Fuling Zhacai Production Technology)	Fuling District, Chongqing
15	VIII-81	Traditional Skill	Fan-making Technique (Rongchang Folding Fan)	Rongchang District, Chongqing
16	IX-5	Traditional Medicine	Acupuncture (Liu's Acupuncture Treatment)	Yuzhong District, Chongqing

The Third Batch (10 items in total)

Number	Serial number	Type	Item	Application area or unit
1	I-124	Folk Literature	Youyang Ancient Song	Youyang Tujia and Miao Autonomous County, Chongqing
2	II-123	Traditional Music	Gong and Drum Art (River Gong and Drum)	Yubei District, Chongqing

Continued

Number	Serial number	Type	Item	Application area or unit
3	III-5	Traditional Dance	Lion Dance (High Platform Lion Dance)	Pengshui Tujia and Miao Autonomous County, Chongqing
4	V-110	Folk Art	Sichuan Pingshu	Chongqing Quyi Troupe
5	V-75	Folk Art	Sichuan Dulcimer	Chongqing Quyi Troupe
6	V-77	Folk Art	Sichuan Ballad-singing	Chongqing Quyi Troupe
7	V-91	Folk Art	Singing with a allegro with coins in it	Wanzhou District, Chongqing
8	VIII-211	Traditional Skill	Tujia Stilted Building Construction Technique	Shizhu Tujia Autonomous County, Chongqing
9	VIII-98	Traditional Skill	Pottery Firing Technique (Rongchang Pottery-making Technique)	Rongchang District, Chongqing
10	IX-4	Traditional Medicine	Traditional Chinese medicine Preparation Method (Traditional pill-making Technique of Tongjunge)	Nan'an District, Chongqing

The Fourth Batch (5 items in total)

Number	Serial number	Type	Item	Application area or unit
1	I-149	Folk Literature	Folk Tales of Guangyang Town	Nan'an District, Chongqing
2	II-109	Traditional Music	Miao's Folk Songs	Pengshui Tujia and Miao Autonomous County, Chongqing
3	III-121	Traditional Dance	Dance with Cattle	Shizhu Tujia Autonomous County, Chongqing
4	X-84	Folk Custom	Temple Fair (Baodingjia Incense Temple Fair)	Dazu District, Chongqing
5	X-84	Folk Custom	Temple Fair (Fengdu Temple Fair)	Fengdu County, Chongqing

3.Scenic Spots

Chongqing is rich in tourism resources, including the beautiful Three Gorges of the Yangtze River, the exquisite Dazu Cliff Stone Carvings, the revered revolutionary memorial site, the site of the "war-time capital" during the War of Resistance Against Japanese Aggression, the South Hot Spring Park surrounded by Huaxi River and the North Hot Spring Park famous for its beautiful scenery. There are precious pandas, golden monkeys and other animals. Jinyun Mountain Scenic Spot is a national level scenic spot with a variety of subtropical plants. Diaoyucheng Ruins witnessed the fighting against the Mongolian army for 36 years. Nanshan Scenic Spot, Tongjing Scenic Spot, Simian Mountain Scenic Spot, Tomb of Bamanzi, Hanque (汉阙)[1] in Jiangbei and so on, attract tourists from home and abroad. By 2011, 34 hot spring scenic spots have been built and opened in Chongqing, which won the title of "Capital of Hot Springs in China" and the first "Capital of Hot Springs in the World" in 2012. In 2016, it ranked the seventh on the list of "The most popular domestic destinations in China". In 2017, there were 224 A level scenic spots in the city, including eight AAAAA scenic spots, such as Dazu Stone Carving Scenic Spot, Wushan Small Three Gorges, Wulong Karst Tourist Area [Tianshengsanqiao-Fairy Mountain-Furong Cave (天生三桥—仙女山—芙蓉洞)], Youyang Taohuayuan (Peach Garden) Scenic Spot, Wansheng Black Valley Scenic Spot (黑山谷景区), Nanchuan Jinfo Mountain Scenic Spot, Jiangjin Simian Mountain Scenic Spot and Yunyang Longgang Scenic Spot (龙缸景区). 12 demonstration counties and 23 demonstration sites for leisure agriculture and rural tourism, as well as 14 famous towns and 7 famous villages for landscape tourism with national characteristics were set up.

Ⅱ.Tourism Development

After the reform and opening-up, tourism industry in Chongqing started to develop. Domestic and foreign tourists increased year by year. A number of tourism

[1] Watchtower established in the Han Dynasty.

enterprises and professional tourism service teams specialized in tourism business emerged one after another, and the tourism service infrastructure and reception conditions were constantly improved. In recent years, with the theme of "Beautiful Chongqing, a city of mountains and rivers", Chongqing has built four quality trunk lines of tourism, namely, Chongqing City Tour with Mountains and Rivers, World Heritage Leisure and Vacation Tour in west Chongqing, Three Gorges Lake Scenery Tour Around the Yangtze River in northeast Chongqing, and Arcadia Ethnic Customs Tour in southeast Chongqing. There are more than 100 characteristic boutique tourist routes, including ancient town tourism, rural tourism, study tour, health and nutrition tour, cruise tour, hot spring tour, red tour, forest tour, ice and snow tour, etc.Ten tourism business cards have been formed, and they are City of Mountains and Rivers, Three Gorges of the Yangtze River, Cruise and Yacht, Hongyan Link (红岩联线), Hot Spring City, Yuxi Corridor (渝西走廊), Wujiang Gallery World Heritage, Bayu Ancient Town and Beautiful Countryside. According to the climate characteristics of Chongqing, the four seasons characteristic tourism routes are launched in different seasons, and the supply of tourism products is constantly rich. In 2017, Chongqing ranked first in the "2017 list of China's top 50 most popular tourism cities" released by ASKCI and the first in the "world's top 10 fastest-growing tourism cities" released by World Tourism and Travel Council (WTTC).

1.Tourist Reception

From 1978 to 1988, the city received 225,600 inbound tourists, with an average annual increase of 29.4% during the Sixth Five-Year Plan Period. In 1986, the city received 4.8364 million domestic tourists. In 1997, the city's total tourism revenue reached 7.34 billion yuan, of which the income of overseas tourists exceeded 200,000 yuan for the first time, reaching 261,200 overseas trips, and the foreign exchange income of international tourism reached 105 million dollars; it received 18.5 million domestic trips, and the revenue from domestic tourism was 6.47 billion yuan. In 2017, the city received about 542 million domestic and foreign trips, including 3.5835 million inbound tourists; the total tourism revenue was 330.804 billion yuan, of which 1.948 billion US dollars was earned from foreign exchange.

Table 5-5 Tourism Reception and Income of Chongqing in 2017

Name of index	Number	Year-on-year growth (%)
Reception of domestic and foreign tourists (10,000 trips)	54,230.21	20.3
Inbound tourists (10,000 trips)	358.35	13.2
Domestic tourists (10,000 trips)	53,871.86	20.3
Total tourism revenue (100 million yuan)	3,308.04	25.1
Foreign exchange revenue from tourism (100 million US dollar)	19.48	15.5
Domestic tourism revenue (100 million yuan)	3,176.55	25.4
Outbound tourists organized by outbound travel agencies (10,000 trips)	206.30	5.1

2.Tourist Facilities

After the reform and opening-up, in order to meet the increasing demand of tourism year by year, tourism facilities have been gradually improved and the tourism reception capacity has been enhanced. In terms of infrastructure, the construction of tourism infrastructure has been accelerated, and the construction of special roads for tourist attractions has been started, and the construction or renovation of tourist hotels has been started in succession, and a number of special tourist terminals have been built or newly established. In 1997, Fengjie Ancient Elephant Museum (奉节古象博物馆), Bayu Folk Culture Village in Yubei (渝北巴渝民俗文化村), Tongjing Hot Spring City, Fengdu Ghost King Stone Carvings (丰都鬼王石刻) and other influential new scenic spots were built. In 2000,

Chongqing Wildlife World was completed and opened. In 2006, Hongyadong Folk Custom Area was opened. In terms of tourist hotels, the People's Hotel is used as a hotel to receive foreign guests. The new Chongqing Yangzi Island Holiday Hotel was built. Six three-star tourist hotels, including Shaping Hotel and Southwest Hotel, have been built or expanded successively, and more than 40 one and two-star hotels and tourist designated hotels have been built. In 2016, Century Jinyuan Hotel, as the only hotel in the western region, was ranked among the top 20 five-star hotels in China. In 2017, there were 210 star-rated tourist hotels, including 28 five-star hotels and 61 green tourist hotels. In terms of travel agencies, in 1986, there were nearly 20 tourism businesses in the city. In 1998, there were 182 travel agencies and 1,920 tour guides in the city, with a total revenue of 639 million yuan. Travel agencies gradually developed from the traditional "small workshop" operation to the direction of collectivization and scale and marched forward to a new stage of large tourism, large market, large industry and large management. In 2017, there were 622 travel agencies in the city, including 95 overseas travel agencies (including 9 travel agencies to Taiwan too).

3. Tourist Commodities and Local Products

Chongqing has a wide range of local characteristic products, producing many precious Chinese herbal medicines, such as Shizhu Coptis, gastrodia tuber, Nanchuan Eucommia ulmoides, Wushan Temple ginseng (巫山庙参), etc. The geological and climatic conditions are suitable for fruit growth. Fengjie Navel Orange, Jiangjin Citrus, Cangxi Pear, Changshou Shatian Pomelo, Chengkou Mopan Persimmon have long-standing reputation. Chongqing is one of the main tea-producing areas in China.

Picture 5-16 Chengkou Bacon

Chongqing Tuo Tea (重庆沱茶), Cuiping Silver Needle Tea (翠坪银针茶) and Xinong Maojian Tea (西农毛尖) are all top-grade teas. Sichuan cuisine series, such as Baishiyi Dry-cured Duck (白市驿板鸭), Chengkou Bacon (城口老腊肉), Jinjiao Brand Spiced Beef Jerky (金角牌五香牛肉干), Fuling Pickled Mustard Tuber (涪陵榨菜), Hechuan Walnut Slices (合川桃片), Baoding Dongjian (宝顶冬尖), Jiangjin Crunchy Rice Candy (江津米花糖) etc. These products taste exquisite and are well-known at home and abroad. The folk handicrafts are famous all over the world. Shu embroidery, together with Su embroidery, Xiang embroidery and Yue embroidery, have been known as Four Famous Embroidery in China since the Southern Song Dynasty. Rongchang Folding Fan went out of China as early as the Qing Dynasty. There are also various kinds of bamboo weaving, Tujia brocade (土家织锦), Longshui hardware (龙水小五金), Three Gorges Inkstone, Qijiang Farmer Engraving (綦江农民版画), Beibei Glassware (北碚玻璃器具), Zhaofeng Ceramics (兆峰陶瓷) with great Bashu ethnic colors. In 2009, 108 new tourist commodities were developed in the city, mainly including brocade, ebony carving, embroidery, stone carving and so on, basically forming categories of tourist souvenirs, tourist handicrafts, tourist local products, tourist supplies, etc.

Picture 5-17　Rongchang Folding Fan

The city's first comprehensive commodity exhibition and sales market, Hongyadong tourist commodity exhibition and sales center, were built to organize and hold China International Tourism Commodity Exposition. In 2016, Chongqing won 1 silver medal and 2 bronze medals in the National Tourism Commodity Competition.

Chapter Six Development of Social Cause

Section One Education

Chongqing boasts a long history of education. In ancient times, an educational system with private schools, free schools and academies as the main body was formed. From the Yuan, Ming and Qing Dynasties to the Republic of China, the development of education was tortuous. After the founding of the People's Republic of China, new vitality was injected into the development of education.

Ancient academies in Chongqing were run by both government and private sectors. The official academies mainly included the Confucian Academy established in Hezhou (Hechuan nowadays) during the reign of Jingyou (景祐) (1034-1037). The Confucian Academy established in Kuizhou (夔州) (Fengjie nowadays) during the reign of Qingli (庆历) (1041-1048), and the county school established in Jiangjin in the 1st year of Zhiping (治平) (1064), and the county school established in Zhongzhou (Zhongxian nowadays) in the 3rd year of Shaosheng (绍圣) (1096). In the 1st year of Shaoxing (绍兴) (1131), the first Academy was established in Chongqing. The first two folk academies were both run by Jiangjin. Feng Zhong (冯忠), the county magistrate of Jiangjin County, founded Wuju Academy (五举书院) in the reign of Dazhong Xiangfu (大中祥符) (1008-1016), and Nanshan Academy in the reign of Kaitai (开泰) (1012-1020). Since then, Jinghui Academy, Lianfeng Academy, Zhulin Academy and Shaoling Academy in Kuizhou, Lianxi Academy in Hezhou, Beiyan Academy in Fuzhou (Fuling nowadays), Hongwen Academy in Zhongzhou, Longmen Academy in Tongliang, Fengshan Academy in Wuxi were established. Courses in academy included Classics, History (general knowledge and other books), Rhyme (poetry and rhyme), Calligraphy, etc. In the 15th year of Qianlong (1750), Jinyun Academy in the main city (near Daomenkou) was incorporated into Yuzhou Academy. In the 23rd year of Qianlong (1758), Yuzhou Academy was relocated and renamed Dongchuan Academy under the jurisdiction of Chuandongdao. It was the largest Academy in the main city of Chongqing (later was renamed as Chongqing Associated School and Chongqing No.7 Middle School).

In 1891, Chongqing officially opened port, and foreign churches began to set up schools. Dr. Spencer Lewis, a missionary of the American Christian Church, founded a private school called Qiujing School in Zengjiayan, and another private school called Qiming School in Daijiaxiang, Ba County. The British Christian Charity Church established Guangyi Academy in Duyou Street (都邮街), Ba County, which was later renamed as Guangyi Middle School. The French Church established French school in Ba County. By running schools, foreign missionaries objectively played a certain role in spreading western civilization and promoting the establishment of modern education system in China. Under the influence of western culture and education, some people of insight, imitating the models of Europe, America and Japan, actively advocated the establishment of new schools. In the 18th year of Guangxu (1892), Li Shuchang (黎庶昌), a representative who advocated Westernization Movement and an official of rectifying armed force in eastern Sichuan, founded Eastern Sichuan Westernization School in the urban area of Ba County, which was the beginning of the establishment of official schools in Sichuan. In this period, Danzishi School, Chinese and western schools, western schools and arithmetic schools were successively established. In the 30th year of Guangxu (1904), the Official Secondary School in Chongqing was formally established, and then the Official Secondary Schools in Baxian, Jiangjin, Hezhou, Yongchuan, Tongliang, Bishan and Jiangbei were successively established. In the 32nd year of Guangxu (1906), under the sponsorship of eastern Sichuan Daoyin

Zhang Duo (道尹张铎) and Du Chengzhang (杜成章), the gentry, Eastern Sichuan Normal School was established. It was the first formal normal school in Chongqing. Gao Zengjue (高增爵), the governor of Chongqing, founded Chongqing School of Public Law and Politics in Lailonggang of Ba County, which was the earliest school of higher education in Chongqing. Zeng Xianjie (曾先杰) founded a kindergarten in the urban area of Ba County, which was the beginning of early childhood education in Chongqing. In the 34th year of Guangxu (1908), there were 1,137 primary schools with 38,600 students in Chongqing, including 27 higher primary schools and more than 700 students, 65 lower primary schools, 24 half-day schools with more than 800 students. In the late Qing Dynasty, there were 14 middle schools, 26 vocational schools and 1 normal school in Chongqing. Chongqing modern education began to take shape. The establishment of schools and the new school system ended the feudal education system with the selection of scholars through imperial examinations as the purpose and The Four Books and The Five Classics as its main content. Modern scientific knowledge such as mathematics, Gezhi (格致) (physiological health, animals and plants), physics, chemistry and curriculum such as foreign language, physical education, music, fine art entered school and vocational education also developed rapidly. In 1912, Chongqing Xuetang (学堂) was renamed as schools, and all the supervisors (church leaders) were renamed as principals, and textbooks that did not conform to the spirit of the Republic were abolished. During the May 4th Movement in 1919, mass organizations such as "East Sichuan Students Salvation League" (川东学生救国团) and "East Sichuan Women's Salvation Federation" (川东女子救国联合会) were set up in succession to support the patriotic struggle of Beijing students, who demanded the return of Qingdao and the punishment of national thieves, and launched a massive campaign of promoting domestic goods and boycotting Japanese goods. Under the influence of the New Culture Movement, Chongqing educational circles were very active. In 1921, Chen Yusheng (陈愚生) came to

Chongqing to serve as Secretary General of the Yin Bureau of Chuandongdao and hired a group of young teachers with new ideas, working closely with the majority of students, abolished old education methods, adding new contents to courses such as Chinese language, ethics, self-cultivation, etc. The Sichuan Education Improvement Association (全川教育改进会) was set up, and the *New Journal of Education Improvement* (《教育改进新杂志》) was published monthly. It proposed to seek education improvement with a fair attitude, scientific methods and the spirit of experiment. The reform of the education sector affected the whole Sichuan.

In 1926, after Liu Xiang led the 21st army to Chongqing, the Military Department of the 21st army put forward the policy of developing education and carried out a comprehensive rectification of schools at all levels. In order to consolidate his rule, the patriotic movement in Chongqing was violently suppressed, resulting in the "March 31st Massacre" that shocked both China and abroad. The schools were under strict control, and many innocent students became victims.

In 1931, after the September 18th Incident, the patriotic enthusiasm of the students was high, and the student movements reached a climax. They took to the streets for many times to march and assemble and advocate for the necessity to resist against the Japanese aggression. In 1937, the War of Resistance Against Japanese Aggression broke out in an all-round way. In 1938, the national government moved its capital to Chongqing, and numerous government offices, factories and schools moved to Chongqing. The invasion of Japanese imperialists caused serious damage and disaster

Picture 6-1 Former Site of Fuling Beiyan Academy (涪陵北岩书院)

to education in China. Nearly 100 colleges, universities and secondary schools were forced to move to Chongqing, with more than 100,000 teachers, students and dependents. As a result of the relocation, the equipment, books and materials were severely damaged. During this period, Chongqing was the political, economic, cultural and educational center of the rear area, as well as the seat of the Southern Bureau of the CPC Central Committee. Anti-Japanese and national salvation movements were unprecedentedly high and education in Chongqing was unprecedentedly prosperous. In 1941, the nation began to promote national education, and the development of preschool education, secondary education and vocational education began to be emphasized. Private middle schools developed rapidly, famous schools with their own characteristics such as Private Nankai (南开) Middle School, Private Bashu (巴蜀) Middle School, Private Qiujing (求精) Middle School emerged. In 1945, there were 294 national schools with 93,000 students. 16,100 people and more than 3,000 teachers were enrolled in school. There were 42 vocational schools and 59 kindergartens (classes). From 1937 to 1944, more than 40 institutions of higher learning and colleges, such as Fudan University, moved to Chongqing successively, and there were more than 60 institutions of higher learning and colleges in Chongqing. With a large number of universities and scientific research institutions moving to Chongqing, famous experts and scholars all over the country gathered in Chongqing. They trained a large number of cultural and scientific talents for the country, and effectively promoted the progress of science and technology and the development of democratic

Picture 6-2 Former Site of Fudan University that moved to Xiaba, Beibei during the War of Resistance Against Japanese Aggression.

ideas in Chongqing. After the War of Resistance Against Japanese Aggression, the wartime education boom in Chongqing began to shrink.

Since the founding of the People's Republic of China in 1949, through taking over, adjustment and enrichment of schools at all levels, the cause of education has been developed. Chongqing began to reform the old education system, and to ban reactionary organizations, and to send cadres to schools to preside over or assist in the work, and to establish the leadership of the Communist Party of China in the school. Chongqing also exercised democratic management in schools and established Youth Leagues, Student Unions, Children's Teams, Education Unions and other mass organizations. From 1952 to 1956, according to the unified arrangement of the Ministry of Education, Chongqing institutions of higher learning adjusted their faculties and departments and initially addressed the problems of institutions of higher learning that were too small in scale, too numerous in departments, too insufficient in the number of teachers and too scattered in strength, etc. The talents and teachers cultivated basically met the needs of industrial construction in Chongqing and southwest China. Chongqing government at all levels adhered to the policy of opening schools for workers and peasants, and took effective measures such as recruiting workers and peasants' children first, reducing and exempting tuition and miscellaneous fees, so as to facilitate the enrolment of workers and peasants' children. The proportion of workers and peasants' children in the city's enrolment increased rapidly. At the same time, the education of workers and peasants, cadres and the democratic personages were also vigorously strengthened. By 1957, when the First Five-Year Plan was completed, there were 9 institutions of higher learning with 15,200 students and over 2,100 full-time teachers, 249 ordinary middle schools with 181,400 students and over 7,000 full-time teachers, and 16,200 primary schools with 1,539,800 students and 52,500 teachers. From 1958 to 1965, education in Chongqing went through "education revolution" and the educational cause was adjusted and enriched. The education system was further reformed; vocational and technical education, as well as adult education were developed, and literacy education was carried out; key schools were run well; political and ideological work were strengthened. The school order was more stable; the teaching quality was significantly improved, and great achievements were made in the development of education. From 1966 to 1976, the "Cultural Revolution" swept through schools in the city rapidly, and schools were forced to suspend classes. Institutions of higher learning stopped enrolling students, and numerous specialized talents were lost. Vocational and agricultural schools were all cut down; many secondary and technical schools were closed or merged; ordinary middle schools developed blindly, and education undertakings suffered serious damage.

Since the reform and opening-up, Chongqing earnestly implemented the policy of "Adjustment, reform, rectification and improvement", and it shifted the focus of school work by giving priority to teaching, gradually stabilized school teaching order and improved the teaching quality, and the school became an important base for the construction of socialist spiritual civilization. Schools at all levels attached great importance to physical and health education, and students' physique was significantly enhanced. Education in Chongqing was booming. Primary education was popularized in an all-round way; nine-year compulsory education was gradually implemented; the structure of secondary education became more reasonable; vocational and technical education developed rapidly; higher education improved and developed continuously in the process of adjustment; normal education was comprehensively reformed, and adult education developed in depth. After Chongqing became a municipality directly under the central government, the municipal Party Committee and the municipal government made the decision of "Invigorating Chongqing through Science and Education" (科教兴渝), and comprehensively promoted quality-oriented education, and it made the basic popularization of nine-year compulsory education and the basic elimination of illiteracy among young and middle-aged people [referred to as the "two bases" (两基)] as the top priority of Chongqing educational work, and it obviously strengthened the strategic position of education as the priority for development. In 1998, the *Regulations on the Implementation of Compulsory Education in Chongqing* (《重庆市义务教育实施条例》) was reviewed and adopted, and a series of normative documents were successively formulated and promulgated. The system of education laws and regulations has been continuously improved.

In recent years, the Municipal Party Committee and the Municipal Government adhered to the strategy of giving priority to the development of education, pushing forward the reform of the education system, creating a sound environment for the development of education. Historic progress has been made in various educational undertakings. The education highland in the western region and the education center in the upper reaches of the Yangtze River are taking shape. In 2017, there were 9,866 schools at all levels (excluding vocational and technical training schools) with 6.216 million students (excluding Chongqing Military Academy), 427,000 faculty members and 348,200 full-time teachers. The gross enrollment rate for 3-year preschool education, compulsory education, senior high school and higher education respectively reached 84.44%, 99%, 95.98% and 45.2% respectively. The educational reform took on a new look. An "overpass" was initially built for the growth of technical and skilled talents connecting secondary vocational school, higher vocational school and applied technical undergraduate and professional graduate students. The adjustment of the management system of primary and secondary schools directly under the Municipal Education Commission was completed, and the separation of education management, operation and evaluation was further promoted. New growth was achieved in the funding of education. During the 12th Five-Year Plan period, Chongqing financial investment in education reached 270.2 billion yuan. In 2017, a total of 94.835 billion yuan was invested in local education (excluding the central educational institutions stationed in Chongqing), and the proportion of education funds in general public budget reached 14.17%. Educational achievements expanded. 18 achievements of Chongqing won prizes in the First National Basic Education Teaching Achievement Award, and 17 achievements won prizes in the First National Vocational Education Teaching Achievement Award. Southwest University of Political Science and Law and Chongqing Medical University have joined the ministerial and municipal joint establishment. Chongqing University of Posts and Telecommunications and Chongqing Technology and Business University entered the Capacity Improvement Program for Universities in Central and Western China. The new drug innovation team of Chongqing University of Arts and Sciences won the champion of biomedical industry in China Innovation and Entrepreneurship Competition. Chongqing Automotive Collaborative Innovation Center led by Chongqing University passed the National Accreditation. New breakthroughs have been made in international cooperation and exchanges in education. At present, there are 44 Chinese-foreign cooperatively run schools and projects at or above the college level. There are Confucius Institutes (classrooms) in 13 countries, 11 experts from the "Thousand Talents Program for foreign experts", and platforms such as China-Australia Vocational Education Cooperation Alliance, China-Thailand Vocational Education Alliance, and "the Belt and Road" China-Poland University Alliance.

Table 6-1 The Number of Schools at All Levels in Major Years

Year	Institution of higher learning	Middle school	Primary school	Special education school	Kindergarten
1978	13	2,948	25,002		
1985	18	1,788	22,793	7	5,800
1997	22	1,606	16,261	37	5,741
2017	65	1,118	2,954	36	5,210

Table 6-2 The Number of Students in All Kinds of Schools in Main Years

Year	Institution of higher learning	Middle school	Primary school	Special education school	Kindergarten
1978	16,357	1,631,581	4,035,934		
1985	39,871	1,102,702	3,857,331	418	296,336
1997	83,764	1,002,915	2,854,307	1,706	590,464
2017	805,208	1,592,207	2,099,536	18,585	958,667

Section Two Science and Technology

Ⅰ. Development of Science and Technology

1. Agricultural Technology

In the 3rd year of Tongzhi in the Qing Dynasty (1864), Ba County sericulture bureau sent people to Japan to learn new methods of silkworm breeding and introduced new silkworm eggs. In 1874, Jiangjin County established the Agricultural Research Association to carry out agricultural technology research, which was the earliest scientific research organization in Chongqing. In the 1930s, the Institute of Biology, Agriculture and Forestry was set up by the Chinese Academy of Sciences in western China, and Sichuan Central Agricultural Experimental Field was successively established in Chongqing. During the War of Resistance Against Japanese Aggression, agricultural demonstration and popularization zones, popularization institutes, experimental farms and agricultural technical colleges were successively established, and agricultural resources investigation, cultivation of improved varieties, development and introduction of new varieties were carried out. Six scientific research institutions, including the Central Research Institute of the national government, moved to Chongqing successively. It enhanced the strength of Chongqing scientific research. In the 1950s and 1960s, the Municipal

Party Committee and the Municipal Government actively developed agricultural production, organizing farmers to strengthen the basic construction of farmland, sending scientific and technological personnel to the forefront of agriculture to improve farming and breeding techniques and to conduct hybrid rice experiments and to develop animal husbandry. In the 1970s and 1980s, scientific farming was carried out; cultivation techniques were improved; research on planting, management, conservation and harvest techniques of ratooning rice and low-yield fields was strengthened; agriculture was given priority and forestry; animal husbandry and fishery were developing in an all-round way. Grain production saw bumper harvest for several consecutive years, and vegetables, animal husbandry and fruits production increased year by year.

2.Light Industry Technology

Weaving, papermaking, printing and other manual technologies have long been in folk use. At the end of the 19th century, cable telegraph communication was introduced. At the beginning of the 20th century, telephone and radiotelegraphy were used. Since the 1930s, textile, papermaking, food processing and other industries began to use machines instead of manual operation. The chemical industry started, and the variety of light industrial products gradually increased. During the War of Resistance Against Japanese Aggression, dozens of light industry factories in east and central China moved to Chongqing, accelerating the development of Chongqing light industry. After the founding of the People's Republic of China, the technology of Chongqing light industry was improved rapidly, and a number of famous brand products were produced. The technology of silk product reached the advanced level in China. New equipment and technology were introduced into papermaking and printing. In the 1970s and 1980s, electronic and photoelectronic technology gradually became a new industry, and several new products of communication, broadcasting and audio-visual equipment were developed. The technology of inorganic chemical products reached international advanced level.

3.Heavy Industry Technology

In the middle of the Ming Dynasty, crude iron smelting and forging appeared in Chongqing. In 1905, Chongqing Tongyuan Bureau (铜元局), the first machinery factory in Chongqing, was built in Chongqing, introducing machinery and equipment from Britain, Germany and other countries to make copper and silver coins. In the 1930s, Xinxing Iron Works in Ba County set a precedent for coke iron making. Huaxing, Minsheng and other factories began to imitate the making of simple working machines such as turning, milling, drilling and planing. During the War of Resistance Against Japanese Aggression, several steel and machinery factories were relocated from east and central China. The steel and machinery industries began to become the major industries. With the rapid development of military industry, they were able to manufacture rifles, light and heavy machine guns, mortars, hill cannons, imitate the making of recoilless guns and other weapons. In 1949, there were 165 machinery factories in the city with an annual output of 7,400 tons of pig iron. In the 1950s and 1960s, Chongqing became the machinery industry center and steel production base in southwest China and developed a batch of new metallurgical and mechanical equipment. In the 1980s, induction furnace smelting technology was applied to produce 15 kinds of special steel, more than 800 steel grades and more than 800 kinds of fine alloy. The machinery industry became one of the pillar industries in Chongqing, with high reputation and better market for heavy-duty vehicles, minicars, motorcycles, etc.

4.Technology for Public Infrastructure Construction

Chongqing has a long history of energy, transportation, architecture, water conservancy and other infrastructure construction. In ancient times, Hechuan and

Bishan began to implement water diversion projects. In the 15th year of Jiaqing (1810), the coal in Longwang Cave was exported to Nanyang. In the middle of Qing Dynasty, folk architecture with Chongqing characteristics gradually took shape. In the 1920s and 1930s, Lu Zuofu founded Minsheng Company and opened the water transportation route from Chongqing to Hechuan. Vehicles and reinforced concrete buildings appeared. In 1939, the first natural gas well was drilled in Chongqing. During the War of Resistance Against Japanese Aggression, Euro-American structure and the combination of Chinese and Western style structure appeared in the urban and suburban areas in Chongqing, with more highrise buildings and a stereoscopic transportation system gradually taking shape. Several domestic and foreign air routes were opened up; water transportation and road transportation extended in all directions; new thermal and hydropower plants were built. After the founding of the People's Republic of China, Chongqing infrastructure construction has been increasingly strengthened. In the 1980s, the infrastructure of energy and environmental protection was further strengthened, and highrise buildings mushroomed, and water, land and air transport vehicles and facilities reached the modern level.

5.Medical Research

In the 1930s and 1940s, Chongqing established the Bacillus Calmette-Guerin (BCG) laboratory, which was the first to carry out the BCG trial in China. In the 1960s and 1970s, scientific research institutions and organizations were successively established by basic medical and health units in Chongqing and made significant scientific and technological achievements in the research of anorectal diseases, traditional Chinese medicine dosage form reform, burn treatment, birth control technology, etc. In 1978, after the National Science Conference, Chongqing medical research entered a new stage of development. In 1985, 6 medical scientific research institutions were established with 38 affiliated scientific research institutions, and each Chinese and western pharmaceutical factory was equipped with full-time scientific research personnel. Many famous scientific research talents emerged, and 37 national-level award-winning scientific research achievements and 779 provincials, municipal-level achievements were successively made.

6.Research on the Basic Theory of Natural Science

Chongqing mathematics, physics, chemistry and other basic theoretical research began in the 1930s. In 1930, Chongqing established West Chinese Academy of Sciences, with Institutes of Physics, Chemistry, Biology and Geology to carry out research work. In 1932, Chongqing University established the School of Science to carry out research on basic theories of natural science. During the War of Resistance Against Japanese Aggression, educational and scientific research institutions such as Central University, Fudan University, Institute of Physics and Institute of Geology of the Central Research Institute moved to Chongqing successively. As a result, the number of basic theoretical research institutions in Chongqing increased, and basic theoretical research was strengthened. In 1956, the Soil Research Office of the Chinese Academy of Sciences was established, and Southwest Agricultural College was entrusted as trustee. Colleges and universities carried out basic theoretical research, and they wrote and published academic articles.

Ⅱ.Scientific and Technological Achievements

After Chongqing became a municipality directly under the central government, the strategy of "Invigorating Chongqing through Science and Education and "Strengthening Chongqing by Talents" was put forward. Through system innovation, reform and mechanism establishment, breakthroughs were made in hybrid rice, hybrid corn, waxy wheat, vegetables, pigs, greenhouse breeding and film seedling raising in open field, vaccine and gene technology in the field of agriculture and forestry science and technology; key technologies such as TD-SCDMA third generation mobile communications, intelligent transportation systems, major Computer Numerical Control gear-making equipment, natural gas vehicles, motorcycle electronic fuel injection, magnesium alloy research, development and application in the field of engineering, development and application of a series of biological shock tubes, the pathological research of compound burn and burn blast injury in the field of medical science and technology, the research of silkworm genetic tissue and the working framework of Lepidoptera insect gene in the field of basic science and technology, all have been made breakthroughs. A number of major scientific research achievements have been made, including the emergence of self-owned brand enterprises such as BOE, CHANGAN AUTO, Chongqing Machinery and Electronics Holding (Group) CO. LTD., Zongshen Industrial Group Co., Ltd., Chongqing Pingwei Enterprise CO., LTD , Haifu Medical, and a number of innovative small and medium-sized enterprises such as Hengyiming, Zisun Technology, and Chongqing Graphene Technology Co., Ltd. In recent years, Chongqing scientific and technological work adhered to the principle of quality first and efficiency first, taking the supply-side structural reform as the main line, deepening the reform of the scientific and technological system, improving the innovation governance system, focusing on strengthening the three key supports of technology, capital and innovation ecology for regional innovation and

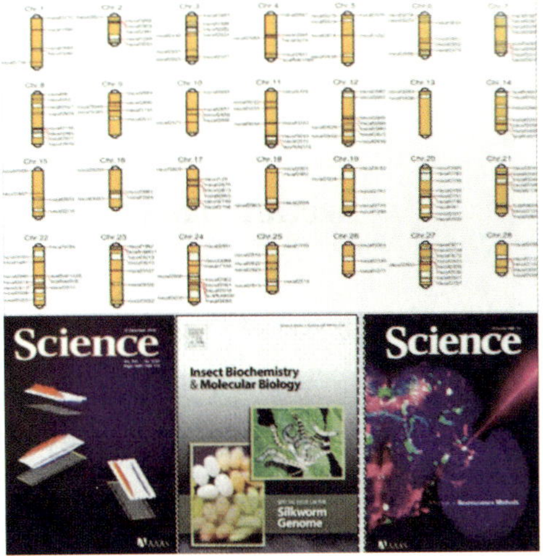

Picture 6-3 Genome frame diagram, fine diagram and genetic variation diagram of bombyx mori completed by Southwest University.

development, and firmly promoting the comprehensive innovation with scientific and technological innovation as the core. Chongqing strives to build itself into a scientific and technological innovation center in the upper reaches of the Yangtze River and a national innovation-driven demonstration city with high science and technology level and strong innovation capacity by 2020.

In 2017, the research and experimental development expenditure of Chongqing was 35 billion yuan, accounting for 1.79% of the city's GDP. There are 148 key laboratories at and above the municipal level, including 8 national key laboratories. There are 527 engineering technology research centers, including 10 national level centers. A total of 65,000 patent applications were accepted in the whole year, including 19,000 applications for invention patents. 35,000 patent authorizations were granted, including 6,138 invention patents, with an average of 7.25 invention patents per 10,000 people. Within the period of validity, there were 2,027 high-tech enterprises and 22,000 invention patents. In the whole year, 2,129 contracts were signed in the technology market with a transaction value of 12.17 billion yuan. Chongqing Comprehensive Science and Technology Innovation Index is 66.23%, and its urban innovation index is 60%, ranking the 10th in China Urban Innovation List in 2017.

Section Three Medical and Health Care

In the 18th year of Guangxu (1892), Chongqing Kuanren Hospital was founded in Linjiangmen, which is the first western medical hospital in Sichuan province. In the 2nd year of Xuantong (1910), there were only five hospitals and medical associations in Chongqing. In November 1927, Chongqing had a full-time health administration organization — the fourth section of the Public Security Department of Chongqing Municipal Hall that was in charge of health administration. In 1936, the number of medical institutions in urban areas increased to 19. In 1939, and there were 40 medical and health institutions in the city. By 1949, there had been 97 medical and health institutions in 9 districts and 4 counties of Chongqing. In the early days of the founding of the People's Republic of China, the city's medical and health services were in the recovery stage. Starting from the establishment of the public health system, the city concentrated on the implementation of the public health plan; it began to emphasize prevention and primary health care; it developed some labor intensive medical technology, and it formed a group of medical workers with low skills. In 1978, there were 4,789 medical and health institutions in the city, including 2,294 hospitals and health centers, 48,900 beds, 59,900 health technicians, and 12,900 medical practitioners.

In the 1980s, with the surging tide of reform and opening-up, the city's medical and health hardware facilities and medical conditions improved day by day. In 1985, the national medical reform was officially launched. The city's health service began to break the single national model of medical services, and it actively encouraged factories and mining enterprises to run hospitals, and it broke the framework of setting up medical institutions according to administrative divisions. The "large and comprehensive" medical system was transformed to a "small and specialized" one. Urban medical treatment strengthened the construction of specialized specialities such as hepatobiliary disease, respiratory diseases, burn, tumor, rehabilitation, occupational disease, geriatric disease and emergency medical treatment, and it basically completed the rural medical construction in four key health care counties, namely Qijiang, Dazu, Hechuan and Changshou. Chongqing adhered to the principle of attracting foreign investment and connecting with domestic investment, expanding foreign exchanges, introducing more than 10 foreign advanced technology and equipment projects in the form of low-interest loans, paying grants and technical cooperation. Chongqing Emergency Medical Center, jointly invested and built by China and Italy, introduced $4.5 million emergency medical equipment. 30 medical associations were set up, and a preventative health care system was to be established, and the construction of epidemic prevention outlets at all levels was strengthened, and a large number of modern medical equipment and instruments in large and medium-sized hospitals were added. Some health and epidemic prevention stations, maternal and child health centers (institutes) were established. The incidence rate of various acute infectious diseases, parasitic diseases and chronic diseases continued to decline. The new delivery methods were basically adopted, and the quality of medical treatment and service improved significantly. Most of the villages in the city set up different forms of medical stations, and many enterprises, public institutions and schools established staff hospitals and clinics (offices). The number of medical institutions and the number of advanced medical equipment increased significantly. In 1986, there were 5,075 medical and health institutions in the city, including 2,140 hospitals and health centres, 54,800 beds, 77,400 health technicians and 12,900 medical practitioners.

In 1992, the reform of the city's medical system was accelerated, and the proportion of local financial investment in medical services was reduced. Hospitals were encouraged to generate income and medicine mark-up was allowed. The planned immunization of the city's children meets the standard in an all-round way, and the incidence of infectious diseases declined year by year. The research and development of medicine and bioengineering had certain advantages, and new achievements were made in the revitalization of traditional Chinese medicine. Remarkable progress was made in patriotic health work. Drinking water and sanitation conditions have been improved in rural areas. 3 million people have access to tap water. Chongqing City of Sichuan Province won the title of "National Health City". Since 1993, the municipal Party Committee and the Municipal Government have established the objectives and tasks of the municipal health reform and development, adjusting the existing health resources, strengthening the health strength of the districts and counties, formulating many preferential policies in terms of the total cost of health, government investment, health service price, multi-channel financing and taxes. After Chongqing became a municipality directly under the central government, it further increased public health investment, and it initially established the emergency response mechanism for public health emergencies, accelerating the development of health services, completing the World Health Organization Project such as "Study on the Impact of Ecological Environment Changes on Disease Pattens and Countermeasures in the Three Gorges Reservoir Area" and "Establishment of Three-level Cancer Prevention and Treatment Network in the Three Gorges Inundated Area". Chongqing formulated the municipal health development plan and secondary health manpower training plan. Chongqing sent all kinds of scientific, technological and managerial personnel to the United States, Japan, the United Kingdom and Northern Ireland and other places for study and exchange, which strengthened the sustainable development of medical and health undertakings. At the same time, Chongqing carried out the urban primary health care, developing rural cooperative medical care, promoting the "three constructions" of rural health. Chongqing vigorously carried out the prevention and control of filariasis and other local diseases, establishing the health and epidemic prevention monitoring system of Chongqing reservoir area of the Three Gorges Project of the Yangtze River, formulating the *Implementation Measures of the Law on Maternal and Infant Health Care* (《母婴保健法实施办法》) and the *Regulations on Rural Primary Health Care* (《农村初级卫生保健条例》). These measures speeded up the pace of rural water reform and effectively improved the health level of urban and rural people.

In 2009, a new round of medical reform was launched in China, with the elimination of the practice of "subsidizing medical care with medicine" ("以药补医") as the key link. Chongqing was one of the first cities to push forward the medical and health reform. In 2010, Chongqing Jiangbei Public Hospital became the first pilot hospital. In 2011, Chongqing selected 15 public hospitals to carry out

10 reforms, including hospital group construction, personnel distribution system and clinical pathway management. In 2014, the city designated 20 districts and counties to carry out pilot comprehensive reform of public hospitals. In the same year, Chongqing was selected as one of the second batch of 17 national-contact pilot cities, of which Zhongxian County was included in the national pilot counties.

In 2017, Chongqing comprehensively launched the comprehensive reform of public hospitals. All public hospitals cancelled the drug mark-up and pharmaceutical service fee. The average medical expense of outpatients and inpatients were 196.3 yuan and 6014.2 yuan respectively. 439 medical service projects were adjusted, and supporting policies such as medical insurance reimbursement, financial subsidies, drug supply guarantee, hospital supervision, convenience for the people were further improved, and hierarchical diagnosis and treatment were further improved, ending the practice of subsidizing medical care with medicine. Chongqing also carried out hierarchical diagnosis and treatment, issuing implementation opinions on the construction of medical consortium, establishing four medical consortia modes, namely, pharmaceutical group, county medical community, regional specialized alliance and telemedicine cooperation network. Chongqing built 134 medical consortia and achieved 100% coverage in counties. 50 kinds of diseases were first diagnosed at the primary level, with remote diagnosis and treatment covering 70% of districts and counties, and the county-level medical treatment rate reached 90%. Chongqing implemented the "two-ticket system" (两票制) reform of drug procurement, establishing a mechanism

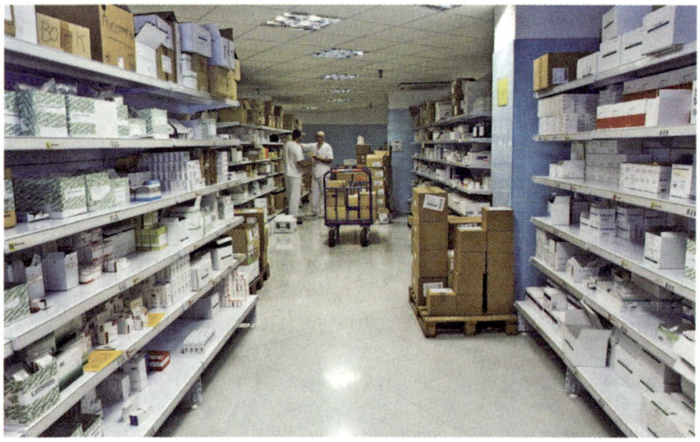

Picture 6-4 In 2017, Chongqing launched comprehensive reform in public hospitals and cancelled all drug mark-ups.

to guarantee the supply of drugs in short supply, building a provincial-level tracking system for pharmaceutical medical devices, namely, a public information platform for pharmaceutical intelligent logistics.

After many years of efforts, an overall progress was made in the city's health service and the service level has been significantly improved. The average life expectancy of the city's population increased to 77.3 years, and the natural population growth rate remained at 4 ‰, and the sex ratio of the birth population dropped to 107.83, and the maternal mortality rate and infant mortality rate dropped to 14.97/100,000 and 4.4 ‰ respectively. The medical service network has been gradually improved. There are 19,700 medical and health institutions in the city, including 749 hospitals and 18,700 primary-level medical, health and family planning institutions with 206,300 beds. The standardized construction rate of township hospitals and community health service centres reaches 100%, bridging the gap between urban and rural public health service facilities. There are 254,400 health workers in the city, including 190,500 health technicians. A total of 154 million people are diagnosed and treated in the city's medical and health institutions and 6.8375 million are discharged from those institutions each year, basically realizing the goals that never let difficult diseases be treated out of the city, serious diseases out of the county, and minor diseases out of the town (community). The public health service has been effectively improved. In 2017, the per capita subsidy for basic public health service in Chongqing was raised to 50 yuan, and the health literacy level of the residents reached 14.9%. The categories of public health services were gradually expanded, and the service items were expanded to 12 categories. The prevention and

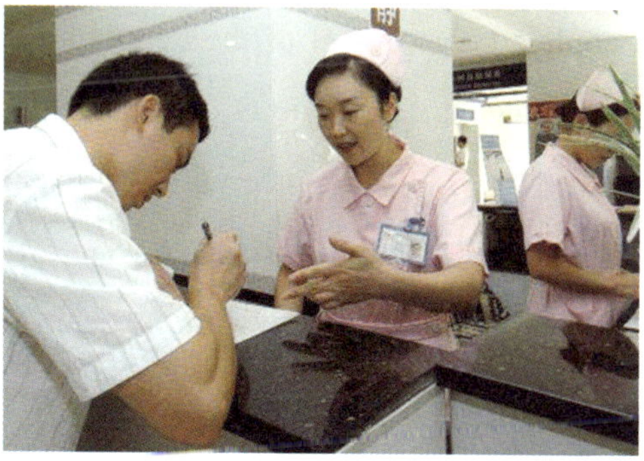
Picture 6-5 Service with a smile, building a harmonious doctor-patient relationship.

treatment of major infectious diseases made significant progress, and the success rate of tuberculosis diagnosis and treatment was over 90%. 27 national health districts and counties were successfully established. Medical and health services have been greatly improved. Projects such as the "National Health Insurance Project" (全民健康保障工程), the "Top Ten Public Health Construction Projects" (十大公共卫生建设工程), the standardized construction of community-level medical and health institutions were implemented. In 2017, the number of level-III hospitals in the city increased to 42, and the standardized construction of township hospitals and community health service centres was realized, and the four-level medical and health service network connecting the city, district, county, town and village was gradually improved.

Section Four　Social Security

In the early days of the founding of the People's Republic of China, the Communist Party of China and the state began to establish a social security system. In 1950, the Ministry of Labour of the Southwest Military and Political Commission issued *Detailed Rules on the Temporary Implementation of Labour Insurance Regulations for Workers in all Factories and Mines* (《各厂矿职工暂时施行劳动保险条例细则》). In 1951, the Administrative Council of the Central People's Government of the People's Republic of China promulgated Regulations of *the People's Republic of China on Labour Insurance* (《中华人民共和国劳动保险条例》). In accordance with a series of national policies and regulations, social security and material assistance were provided to the staff of government agencies and institutions in case of illness, death, disability and personal difficulties. During the "Cultural Revolution", organizations and organs at all levels in the city were abolished, and various systems were denied and abolished, and social security work could not be relied on, and the whole social security system was in disorder.

Since the reform and opening-up, various social security systems have been resumed. In 1986, the concept of social security was first put forward through the *Seventh Five-Year Plan for National Economic and Social Development* (《国民经济和社会发展第七个五年计划》).

Ⅰ.Social Insurance

Since the reform and opening-up, the construction of Chongqing social insurance system has started from scratch; the groups covered by this system has expanded from urban area to rural areas; the separated urban-rural system has integrated; the fund has been increased, and the level of insurance has been improved. In the early stage of reform and opening-up, the construction of the city's social insurance system regarded the city as the centre and the professional population as the priority. In 1986, Chongqing carried out the reform of the old-age insurance system for the employees of urban enterprises, starting from the establishment of pension fund pooling for enterprises owned by the whole people. At the same time, Chongqing began to establish the unemployment insurance system for employees. In 1993, the basic old-age insurance system for urban employees began to be implemented, regardless of ownership form, regardless of the status of workers and staff, and it managed by two lines of income and expenditure. In the early 1990s, some districts and counties began to try out work-related injury insurance, maternity insurance and rural social endowment insurance with low level of security. In 1996, the pilot reform of old-age insurance in government agencies and public institutions was carried out.

Picture 6-6 Social Security Card

Since Chongqing became a municipality directly under the central government, the city's social insurance industry has developed rapidly. The social insurance system has been continuously improved, and its coverage has been continuously expanded. A management system of overall planning and hierarchical management at the provincial level has been established. In 1999, Chongqing launched the reform of medical insurance system. In 2001, the basic medical insurance system for employees was formally established. In 2004, the city established a comprehensive work-related injury insurance system. In 2005, a comprehensive maternity insurance system was established. After the 17th National Congress of the Communist Party of China, the city actively explored the construction of a social insurance system for urban and rural residents, and the city further broke the household registration system, creating an integrated old-age insurance system for urban and rural residents and a cooperative medical insurance system for urban and rural residents, forming a relatively complete system of eight social insurance programs in five categories, achieving full coverage of social insurance system. Since 2013, Chongqing has fully implemented the serious illness insurance system for urban and rural residents and took the lead in launching the national insurance registration plan in 2013. In 2016, the old-age insurance of municipal government offices and public institutions was fully "integrated". There were no obstacles to the transfer of social insurance relations. The old-age insurance system for urban and rural residents was further improved. Steady progress was made in medical insurance reform, including the reform of the means of payment for medical insurance, the overall arrangement of medical insurance outpatient services for residents, and the online settlement of remote medical treatment. The management and service capacity of social insurance agencies was comprehensively improved. In 2018, 9.4581 million urban enterprise employees and 11.1963 million urban and rural residents participated in the basic old-age insurance scheme. The number of urban employees covered by basic medical insurance was 6.7831 million, and the number of urban and rural residents covered by basic medical insurance was 25.87 million. 5.7712 million people were covered by work-related injury insurance. 4.3949 million people participated in maternity insurance and 269,100 people enjoyed maternity insurance benefits. 4.9744 million people were covered by unemployment insurance. The number of people covered by insurance of all types in the city continued to increase, and the social security system gradually improved.

Ⅱ.Social Welfare

After 1979, the city's social welfare changed from "relief type" to "welfare type", from simple support to both support and rehabilitation, from the independent and closed management by the civil affairs department to the social and open-door management by social welfare service. In 1988, the city's social welfare services mainly adopted the elderly, orphans, the disabled and mental patients who had no support and no source of livelihood. The city's social welfare institutions actively created conditions to carry out self-financed adoption (treatment) business, and they gradually expanded the scope of adoption (treatment) as well as production and operation services. The pace of reform was further accelerated, and the institutions' (stations') president-responsibility system in welfare institutions was improved. In 1990, the *Nursing Work Rules for Urban Social Welfare Institutions in Chongqing* (《重庆市城市社会福利事业单位护理工作规则》) was issued, which proposed that graded nursing requirements should be implemented for the elderly, dementia personnel and disabled children in welfare institution. After the Fourteenth National Congress of the Communist Party of China, the city began to carry out rating evaluation on social welfare institutions, focusing on strengthening the internal safety management of social welfare institutions. With the support of the state, policy guidance and capital investment, the city gradually formed a social welfare system for children, so the elderly, the disabled and the rehabilitation of mental patients,

Picture 6-7 Activities of Chongqing Second Social Welfare Institute

and social welfare enterprises made great progress.

Since Chongqing became a municipality directly under the central government, it has strengthened the guidance of welfare institutions and social welfare work, and it has provided financial support and preferential policies to the welfare of the elderly, children and the disabled. Social welfare showed a trend of socialization; it formed a social welfare service network with different standards and levels; it faced the society and served the public. In 2001, the *Tenth Five-Year Plan for the Development of Social Welfare in Chongqing* (《重庆市社会福利事业发展“十五”计划》) was formulated to further accelerate the socialization process of social welfare. Chongqing actively explored a social welfare pattern with diversified investment subjects, public service recipients, market-oriented operation mechanism, diversified service methods, specialized service teams, and integration with volunteers as features. Chongqing also established a social welfare service system with state-run welfare institutions as the model, private welfare institutions as a supplement, urban and rural grass-roots welfare service networks as a support, and community welfare as a basis. In 2017, there were 745 social service agencies providing accommodation, with 89,100 beds. Among them, there were 688 service institutions for the elderly and the disabled with 82,000 beds and 44,400 adoptions. The construction of 200 urban community pension service centers (stations) and 1,000 rural happy homes was completed. There were 9 mental retardation and mental illness service institutions with 2,450 beds and 2,215 adoptions; there were 6 social service institutions providing accommodation for children with 2,579 beds and 938 adoptions.

Ⅲ.Social Assistance

Since the reform and opening-up, Chongqing has actively promoted various social assistance work. In 1996, the municipal government promulgated the *Interim Measures on the Minimum Living Allowance for Urban Residents in Chongqing* (《重庆市城市居民最低生活保障暂行办法》) and began to implement the minimum living allowance for urban residents for families in 11 eligible districts and counties including Yuzhong, Shapingba and Jiangbei. In 2003, Chongqing rural minimum living insurance system was piloted in Nan'an and Shuangqiao. In 2004, the rural medical assistance system was established to provide medical assistance for rural households enjoying "five guarantees"[1], rural households with minimum living insurance, members of families in extreme poverty and key rural special care groups. In 2005, the pilot programs of urban medical assistance were launched in 12 districts and counties, including Wanzhou, Qianjiang and Fuling. In the same year, the Municipal Government issued the *Opinions on Accelerating the Establishment of a New Social Assistance System* (《关于加快建立新型社会救助体系的意见》) to effectively guarantee the basic livelihood of people in need. In 2008, Chongqing took the lead in issuing the *Regulations of Chongqing Municipality on the Minimum Living Allowance for Urban and Rural Residents* (《重庆市城乡居民最低生活保障条例》), a local law that was to coordinate with the minimum living allowance for urban and rural residents. In 2009, the city comprehensively promoted the establishment of temporary assistance system. In 2011, Chongqing took the lead in establishing the social assistance foundation and gradually formed a temporary assistance work system in which the city, districts, counties (autonomous counties), towns and townships (subdistricts) shoulder different levels of responsibility and enjoy three-level linkage. In 2012, the city further improved the medical assistance

[1] "Five guarantees" mean that the aged, the infirm, old widows and orphans enjoy guarantees for food, clothing, medical care, housing and burial expense.

Picture 6-8 The 20th National “Ear Day”

system and gradually formed a medical assistance mode featuring “the connection between medical assistance and medical insurance, the combination of a variety of assistance methods, and the linkage between government assistance and social assistance”. In 2017, the city formulated the Guiding Opinions on Further Improving Temporary Relief Work, which effectively solved people’s sudden, urgent and temporary problems in basic life. In 2018, 311,400 people in the city enjoyed the minimum living allowance for urban residents and 580,900 people enjoyed the minimum living allowance for rural residents. 88,300 people who lived in extreme poverty in urban areas were assisted and supported by the government. 97,100 people who lived in extreme poverty in rural areas were assisted and supported by the government. 1,765,900 people in need were subsidized to participate in medical insurance.

Ⅳ.Social Special Care

Picture 6-9 2019 Chongqing Special Job Fair for Veterans ①

Since the reform and opening-up, the city’s social special care work has actively adapted to the needs of the state and the armed forces, developing through inheritance, advancing in reform and made major breakthroughs. First, the number of ex-servicemen who enjoyed special care and guarantee is constantly expanding. In 2004, junior non-commissioned officers were included in the scope of disability assessment, and the restriction that conscripts with mental illness and junior non-commissioned officers cannot be assessed as sick or disabled was abolished. In 2006, demobilized servicemen who returned home with sickness were included in the regular living allowances of the state. In 2007, demobilized military personnel who participated in wars and nuclear tests included in the scope of regular state pensions and subsidies. In 2011, retired rural soldiers over the age of 60, children of some elderly martyrs and retired uranium mining personnel were included in the scope of regular state pensions and subsidies. In 2017, the number of ex-servicemen who enjoyed special care and guarantee in the city was expanded to 9 categories, increasing to 245,500. Second, the city's special care security system has been gradually improved. In 2001, according to the city's average social wages, the standard of nursing fees for the special and first-class revolutionary disabled personnel was further adjusted. In 2002, the *Implementation Opinions on the Management of Medical Expenses of the Disabled Revolutionary*

Picture 6-10 2019 Chongqing Special Job Fair for Veterans ②

Soldiers above Class B in Chongqing (《重庆市二等乙级以上革命伤残军人医疗费管理实施意见》) was issued to establish and improve the medical expense guarantee mechanism for the disabled revolutionary soldiers. During the 12th Five-Year Plan period, the pension and subsidy standard increased by 90% to 147% respectively, and the pension preferential fund increased by 66%. In 2017, the city issued 2 billion yuan of pension and preferential treatment funds, and special care recipients enjoyed 360 million yuan of medical benefits. Third, steady progress has been made in the resettlement of ex-servicemen. In the resettlement of ex-servicemen, methods such as combining employment with self-employment, combining package arrangement with overall arrangement, and combining the planned arrangement with the market allocation were used. From 1986 to 2005, 370,800 demobilized veterans, over 2,200 retired military cadres and over 1,000 retired employees of the armed forces without military status were received. The military supply stations received more than 7,000 military trains with a total of over 1 million people. In 2017, more efforts were made to help retired soldiers find jobs. More than 6,400 retired soldiers were trained for conduct professional skills, and more than 4,000 self-employed retired soldiers were recommended to work in various enterprises.

Chapter Seven　Construction of Ecological Civilization

Section One　Environmental Conditions

Ⅰ.Atmosphere, Water and Acoustic Environment

1.Water Environment

In 2018, the overall water quality of Chongqing section of the Yangtze River mainstream was excellent. The water quality of 15 water monitoring sections was of class II. The overall water quality of the tributaries of the Yangtze River is good. Among the 96 monitoring sections of 114 rivers, the proportion of class I-III, class IV, class V and inferior class V water quality is 81.1%, 12.7%, 3.1% and 3.1% respectively, and the water quality in 86.7% of the sections meet the water function. Among the 72 sections of 36 primary tributaries in the reservoir area, the ratio of sections with eutrophic water quality was 25.0%.

In 2018, the water quality of centralized drinking water sources in Chongqing was good. The water quality of 66 centralized drinking water sources reached 100%.

Picture 7-1　The Three Gorges of the Yangtze River

2. Atmospheric Environment

Picture 7-2 Rail Transit Line 3

In 2018, Chongqing had 316 days of good air quality, 13 days more than that in 2017, including 96 days of excellent air quality, 220 days of good air quality, 49 days with air quality that exceeded the standard and no heavy pollution days. In 38 districts and counties (autonomous counties), Liangjiang New Area and Wansheng Economic and Technological Development Zone, 6 atmospheric pollutant concentration of 11 districts and counties, including Qianjiang District, Kaizhou District, Liangping District, Wulong District, Chengkou County, Yunyang County, Fengjie County, Wushan County, Shizhu County, Youyang County and Pengshui County, all reached the national secondary standard, taking the lead in meeting the urban air quality standard, accounting for 27.5% of the total evaluation units in Chongqing.

In 2018, the average annual dust collection in Chongqing was 4.43 tons/ km^2·month, which was 0.10 times higher than the reference standard (4.01 tons / km^2 ·month); the monthly average range was 4.10-4.81 tons / km^2· month.

In 2018, the acid rain frequency in Chongqing was 14.0%, and the pH value range of precipitation was 3.12 to 8.20, and the average annual pH value of precipitation was 5.49.

3. Acoustic Environment

In 2018, the average daytime equivalent sound level of environmental noise in Chongqing urban area was 54.4 decibels, and it upped 0.9 decibels year on year, and the average night equivalent sound level was 45.1 decibels. The average equivalent sound level of road traffic noise in the daytime was 66.1 decibels, it upped 0.1 decibels year on year. The average equivalent sound level at night was 55.1 decibels.

Ⅱ.Solid and Hazardous Waste

In 2017, Chongqing produced 19.432 million tons of general industrial solid waste, utilizing 13.7192 million tons (including 46,000 tons of storage in previous years), disposing 4.5691 million tons (including 55,900 tons of storage in previous years), storing 1.2374 million tons. The annual output of industrial hazardous waste was 604,900 tons, with the comprehensive utilization up to 300,800 tons (including 1,100 tons of storage in previous years), the disposal up to 236,900 tons (including 24,400 tons of storage in previous years), and the storage up to 92,700 tons. The utilization and disposal rate of industrial solid waste was 93.6%.

59 waste disposal sites (plants) have been built and have been put into operation with a total processing capacity of 20,290 tons per day. 5 waste treatment facilities (1 domestic waste sanitary landfill, 3 waste incineration power plants and 1 kitchen waste treatment plant) have been built in the main urban area, with a total designed capacity of 10,100 tons per day. 54 domestic waste treatment sites (plants) have been built outside the main urban area (including 50 domestic waste landfills, 3 domestic waste incineration power plants and 1 cement kiln collaborative disposal facility), with a designed treatment capacity of 10,190 tons per day. In 2018, 7.17 million tons of municipal solid waste were innocuously disposed. The rate of harmless disposal of municipal solid waste reached 100%.

The sludge harmless disposal capacity of Chongqing municipal sewage treatment plant reached 798,000 tons, and the comprehensive harmless disposal rate reached over 87%. Among them, the harmless disposal of sludge in the main urban area reached 423,000 tons, maintaining a 100% harmless disposal rate for four consecutive years. 29 districts and counties carried out the harmless disposal of sludge through self-built or purchased services, effectively reducing the harm of municipal sludge to the ecological environment.

Ⅲ.Landscaping

Picture 7-3 Chongqing People's Auditorium

Picture 7-4 Rope Bridge in E'ling Park

In 2018, the established green area of gardens were 59,430 hectares; the green area of parks were 27,852 hectares; the coverage area of landscaping were 63,601 hectares and there were 528 urban parks in Chongqing. The green coverage rate of the city's built-up areas was 40.43%; the green coverage rate was 37.78%, and the per capita park area was 16.34 square meters. In the main urban area, there were 28,430 hectares of established garden green space and 14,116 hectares of park green space, 30,111 hectares of garden green space and 212 urban parks. The green coverage rate of the built-up area of the main city was 39.57%; the green coverage rate was 37.36%, and the per capita park area was 17.80 square meters.

Ⅳ.Arable land, Forest and Grassland

By the end of 2017, Chongqing had a total cultivated area of 2,369,800 hectares, including 958,300 hectares of paddy field, 1,410,700 hectares of dry land and 800 hectares of irrigated land. The forest land area of the city was 67.91 million mu and the forest area was 59.64 million mu with a forest coverage rate of 48.3% and 221 million cubic meters of living trees.

According to the grassland resources inventory conducted by the Municipal Agricultural Department in 2018, the grassland resources area of the city was 5.03 million mu. The degraded grassland area in Chongqing was 1.3927 million mu, accounting for 27.7% of the total grassland area in Chongqing; the grassland was mainly of medium quality and high yield with an area of 3.116 million mu, accounting for 61.9% of the total area. The comprehensive vegetation coverage of grassland resources in the city was 85.4%.

Ⅴ.Ecological Conservation Area

Picture 7-5 Wuxi Hongchiba(巫溪红池坝) National Forest Park

In April 1979, Chongqing Municipal People's Government approved the establishment of Jinyun Mountain Nature Reserve in accordance with the Forestry Law of the People's Republic of China (Trial), which was the first nature reserve in Chongqing. Since 2000, Chongqing has taken the construction of nature reserves as an important part of the Western Development Strategy. Chongqing has strengthened the construction of ecological environment. Chongqing has accelerated the construction of natural reserves and has made great

Picture 7-6 Jinyun Mountain National Nature Reserve

strides in the construction of natural reserves.

By 2018, there were 58 nature reserves covering an area of 804,800 hectares in 30 districts and counties, accounting for 9.77% of the total area of the city. Among them, there are 7 national level nature reserves with an area of 254,000 hectares, 18 municipal-level nature reserves with an area of 242,000 hectares, and 33 nature reserves at the district and county level, covering an area of 309,000 hectares. Divided by types, there are 28 forest ecological types, covering an area of 431,000 hectares; there are 10 wildlife protection types, covering 130,000 hectares; there are 8 wild plant protection types, covering 136,000 hectares; there are 10 wetland ecological types, covering 67,000 hectares; there are 2 geological relics types, covering 41,000 hectares. There are 85 forest parks above the municipal level (including 2 ecological parks) with an area of about 2.8 million mu.

There are 36 scenic spots in Chongqing, which are distributed in 31 districts and counties (including 6 main urban areas), covering an area of 4,558.42 square kilometres, accounting for 5.53% of the city area. Among them, there are 7 national scenic spots with an area of 2,147.30 square kilometres, accounting for 2.60% of the city area; there are 29 municipal-level scenic spots with an area of 2,411.12 square kilometres, accounting for 2.93% of the city area. The core area of Wulong Karst World Natural Heritage Site is 60 square kilometres, and the buffer area is 320 square kilometres; the core area of Jinfo Mountain Karst World Natural Heritage Site is 67.44 square kilometres, and the buffer area is 106.75 square kilometres.

Picture 7-7 Xuebaoshan(雪宝山) National Nature Reserve

Table 7-1 List of Nature Reserves in Chongqing

Number	Name	Level	District/County
1	Chongqing Jinyun Mountain National Nature Reserve	National Level	Beibei District, Shapingba District, Bishan District
2	Chongqing Jinfo Mountain National Nature Reserve	National Level	Nanchuan District
3	Chongqing Dabashan National Nature Reserve	National Level	Chengkou County
4	Chongqing Xuebaoshan National Nature Reserve	National Level	Kaizhou District
5	Chongqing Yintiaoling National Nature Reserve	National Level	Wuxi County
6	Chongqing National Nature Reserve of Rare and Endemic Fish in the Upper Reaches of the Yangtze River	National Level	Jiangjin District, Jiulongpo District, Dadukou Distirct
7	Chongqing Wulipo National Nature Reserve	National Level	Wushan County
8	Chongqing Wangerbao Munici-pal Nature Reserve	Municipal Level	Wanzhou District
9	Chongqing Damushan Municipal Nature Reserve	Municipal Level	Fuling District
10	Chongqing Huaying Mountain Municipal Nature Reserve	Municipal Level	Yubei District
11	Chongqing Anlan Heron Municipal Nature Reserve	Municipal Level	Banan District
12	Chongqing Wuling Mountain Municipal Nature Reserve	Municipal Level	Qianjiang District

Continued

Number	Name	Level	District/County
13	Chongqing Xiaonanhai Municipal Nature Reserve	Municipal Level	Qianjiang District
14	Chongqing Simian Mountain Municipal Nature Reserve	Municipal Level	Jiangjin District
15	Chongqing Laoyingshan Municipal Nature Reserve	Municipal Level	Qijiang District
16	Chongqing Nantianhu Municipal Nature Reserve	Municipal Level	Fengdu County
17	Chongqing Baimashan Municipal Nature Reserve	Municipal Level	Wulong District
18	Chongqing Pengxi River Wetland Municipal Nature Reserve	Municipal Level	Kaizhou District
19	Chongqing Qiyao Mountain Municipal Nature Reserve	Municipal Level	Yunyang County
20	Chongqing Tiankeng Difeng Municipal Nature Reserve	Municipal Level	Fengjie County
21	Chongqing Jiangnan Municipal Nature Reserve	Municipal Level	Wushan County
22	Chongqing Dafengbao Municipal Nature Reserve	Municipal Level	Shizhu County
23	Chongqing Taiyangshan Municipal Nature Reserve	Municipal Level	Xiushan County
24	Chongqing Dabanying Municipal Nature Reserve	Municipal Level	Youyang County
25	Wujiang-Changxi River Fish Municipal Nature Reserve	Municipal Level	Pengshui County
26	Fuling Jiangdong Alsophila County Nature Reserve	County Level	Fuling District
27	Jiulongpo Baishiyi Egret County Nature Reserve	County Level	Jiulongpo District
28	Beibei District Jindaoxia County Nature Reserve	County Level	Beibei District
29	Beibei District Mao'an County Nature Reserve	County Level	Beibei District
30	Beibei District Small Three Gorges County Nature Reserve	County Level	Beibei District
31	Wansheng Heishan County Nature Reserve	County Level	Wansheng Economic Development Zone

Continued

Number	Name	Level	District/County
32	Banan District Shengdeng Mountain County Nature Reserve	County Level	Banan District
33	Qianjiang Xiaonanhai Wetland Nature Reserve	County Level	Qianjiang District
34	Jiangjin Gunziping Alsophila County Nature Reserve	County Level	Jiangjin District
35	Jiangjin Wetland County Nature Reserve	County Level	Jiangjin District
36	Jiangjin Zhongshan Heron County Nature Reserve	County Level	Jiangjin District
37	Hechuan Catfish County Nature Reserve	County Level	Hechuan District
38	Qijiang Wanlong County Nature Reserve	County Level	Qijiang District
39	Qijiang Changtian County Nature Reserve	County Level	Qijiang District
40	Dazu Xishan Alsophila County Nature Reserve	County Level	Dazu District
41	Bishan Huangling Heron County Nature Reserve	County Level	Bishan District
42	Chongqing Three Gorges Longhe Valley Wetland Nature Reserve	County Level	Fengdu County
43	Dianjiang Changshou Lake Wetland County Nature Reserve	County Level	Dianjiang County
44	Wulong Furong River Black Langur County Reserve	County Level	Wulong District
45	Yangshuihe Wetland County Level Nature Reserve in Chongqing Three Gorges Reservoir Area	County Level	Wulong District
46	Zhongxian Baying County Nature Reserve	County Level	Zhongxian County
47	Zhongxian Jinghua County Nature Reserve	County Level	Zhongxian County
48	Zhongxian Shizi County Nature Reserve	County Level	Zhongxian County

Continued

Number	Name	Level	District/County
49	Zhongxian Wetland County Nature Reserve in Chongqing Three Gorges Reservoir Area	County Level	Zhongxian County
50	Zhongxian Tianchi County Nature Reserve	County Level	Zhongxian County
51	Yunyang Three Gorges Xiaojiang Wetland County Nature Reserve	County Level	Yunyang County
52	Fengjie Swan Lake County Nature Reserve	County Level	Fengjie County
53	Wushan Liziping County nature reserve	County Level	Wushan County
54	Chongqing Three Gorges Wushan Wetland Nature Reserve	County Level	Wushan County
55	Shizhu Shuimoxi Wetland County Nature Reserve	County Level	Shizhu County
56	Youyang Sandaigou Giant Salamander County Nature Reserve	County Level	Youyang County
57	Pengshui Maoyunshan County Nature Reserve	County Level	Pengshui County
58	Pengshui Qiyueshan County Nature Reserve	County Level	Pengshui County

Section Two　Environmental Control Measures

Ecological civilization is the harmony between man and nature, a civilized realm and social form of harmonious development between man and nature, and an advanced state of human social civilization. The construction of ecological civilization is fundamental to the sustainable development of the Chinese nation. Since the 18th National Congress of the Communist Party of China, the CPC Central Committee with Comrade Xi Jinping as its core has made the construction of ecological civilization as an important part of the overall layout of the "fivesphere integrated"(五位一体) plan [1] and the coordinated implementation of the "four-pronged comprehensive" strategy (四个全面) [2], carring out a series of fundamental, long-term and pioneering work to promote historic, transforming and overall changes in the protection of the ecological environment.

Ⅰ.Improve Political Standing and Enhance the Understanding of the Construction of Ecological Civilization

As the only municipality directly under the central government and an important central city in the central and western regions, Chongqing shoulders the important responsibility of urban ecological environment construction and water resources protection in the Three Gorges Reservoir Area. Strengthening the construction of ecological civilization in Chongqing is not only related to the development and environmental improvement of Chongqing, but also to the ecological security of southwest China, and the long-term benefits of the Three Gorges Project and the sustainable development of the economic belt along the Yangtze River. The construction of ecological civilization is an arduous task and glorious mission that requires great responsibility. We should strive to build a beautiful Chongqing with economic development, beautiful environment and sound ecology in accordance with the requirements of building a beautiful China.

The construction of Chongqing ecological environment system is guided by Xi Jinping Thought on Socialism with Chinese Characteristics for a New Era. This construction fully implements the spirit of the 19th National Congress of the CPC and the Second and Third Plenary Sessions of the 19th CPC Central Committee, fully implements the goals of "Two-Points Positioning", "Two Lands" and "Two Highs" proposed by General Secretary of the CPC Central Committee Xi Jinping to

[1] This refers to promoting balanced economic, political, cultural, social and ecological progress.

[2] This refers to making comprehensive moves to build a moderately prosperous society in all respects, deepening reform, advancing the law-based governance of China, and strengthening Party self-governance.

Chongqing, and this construction implements the important directive requirements of "Three Roles" (三个作用) and the creation of a sound political environment. Chongqing is to study and use Xi Jinping Thought on Ecological Civilization deeply, putting the restoration of the ecological environment of the Yangtze River in an overwhelming position, working together to promote conservation, refrain from large-scale development, exploring a new path of high-quality development guided by ecological priority and green development. Chongqing should strengthen the "upstream awareness"(上游意识), and Chongqing should shoulder the "upstream responsibility"(" 上游责任 "), and Chongqing should make overall plans to fight the key battle of pollution prevention and control, and Chongqing should effectively build an important ecological barrier in the upper reaches of the Yangtze River. Chongqing will comprehensively implement the river chief system in the city's river reservoirs, building a river reservoir management and protection mechanism with clear responsibilities, orderly coordination, strict supervision and strong protection, and Chongqing will speed up the construction of a beautiful city with beautiful mountains and rivers. Chongqing held the Municipal Mobilization Conference for further promoting the Development of the Yangtze River Economic Belt and the Conference on Ecological and Environment Protection, issuing policy documents such as *Opinions on Further Promoting the Development of the Yangtze River Economic Belt and Accelerating the Construction of A Beautiful Land with Beautiful Mountains and Rivers* (《关于深入推动长江经济带发展加快建设山清水秀美丽之地的意见》), *Chongqing Action Plan for Ecological Priority Green Development* (2018-2020) (《重庆市实施生态优先绿色发展行动计划（2018—2020 年 ）》), *Implementation Plan of Chongqing Pollution Prevention and Control* (2018-2020) (《重庆市污染防治攻坚战实施方案（2018—2020 年）》), *Implementation Plan of Chongqing Land Greening Improvement Action* (2018-2020) (《重庆市国土绿化提升行动实施方案（2018—2020 年）》).

Chongqing Municipal People's Government has set up "Five Major

Environmental Protection Actions"(五大行动) (blue sky, clear water, tranquillity, green land and rural actions), issuing *The Implementation Plan of Chongqing Blue Sky Action* (《重庆市蓝天行动实施方案》), *The Implementation Plan of Chongqing Clear Water Action* (《重庆市碧水行动实施方案》), *The Implementation Plan of Chongqing Tranquillity Action* (《重庆市宁静行动实施方案》), *The Implementation Plan of Chongqing Green Land Action* (《重庆市绿地行动实施方案》) and *The Implementation Plan of Chongqing Rural Action* (《重庆市田园行动实施方案》). The implementation of blue sky, clear water, tranquility, green land and rural action is the key content of Chongqing environmental protection work, such as the implementation of the spirit of the 18th National Congress of the Communist Party of China, the implementation of the State Council's plan for the prevention and control of air pollution in key areas, the plan for the prevention and control of water pollution in key river basins, the plan for the follow-up work of the Three Gorges, and the vigorous promotion of ecological civilization construction. It is a major measure taken by the Municipal Party Committee and the Municipal Government to strengthen environmental protection, and it further improve urban and rural environment quality, and it accelerate the construction of a beautiful city with mountains and rivers; it is a concrete action to solve the prominent environmental problems such as air pollution, noise pollution, water pollution, soil pollution, to create a good working and living environment for the people and to further guarantee and improve people's livelihood.

Ⅱ.Construct an Important Ecological Barrier in the Upper Reaches of the Yangtze River

By implementing the policy of jointly promoting large-scale protection rather than large-scale development and giving top priority to the ecological restoration of the Yangtze River, issuing *The Red Line for Ecological Protection in Chongqing*

(《重庆市生态保护红线》), delimiting the red line for ecological protection and control area of 20,400 square kilometres (accounting for 24.82% of Chongqing land area), carrying out the pilot projects to demarcate red lines for ecological protection in districts and counties, the management and control of ecological space is strengthened. By strictly implementing the 1-kilometre and 5-kilometre industrial management and control policies for the main stream and main tributaries of the Yangtze River, the "three lines and one single list"(三线一单)[1] is basically established. Chongqing has successfully applied for the national pilot project of ecological protection and restoration of mountains, rivers, forests, fields, lakes and grasslands, and Wulong District has successfully established the second batch of national practice and innovation bases that "Clear water and green mountains are golden mountains and silver mountains". The compensation mechanism for horizontal ecological protection has been established for all 19 secondary rivers with a drainage area of more than 500 square kilometres and flowing through 2 districts and counties.

Ⅲ.Improve the Quality of Ecological Environment

To resolutely fight the tough battle against pollution, Chongqing established a commander-in-chief system in which "the chief executive is in charge, and the person in charge is responsible for its implementation", setting up six sub-headquarters of water pollution prevention and control, air pollution prevention and control, identified 12 systems for ensuring ecological progress, including ecological civilization system reform and environmental protection supervision, and comprehensively carring out the central government's environmental protection supervision, rectification and verification and other landmark actions. It further

[1] Three lines refer to ecological protection red line, environmental quality bottom line, resource utilization online. One list refers to ecological environment access list.

implemented the five major environmental protection actions, namely, "clear water, blue sky, green land, tranquility and rural actions" and promoted the renovation of key rivers such as the Linjiang River and the Longxi River. 14 new centralized sewage treatment facilities in the industrial clusters were built. 450 kilometres of urban sewage pipe networks and 2,380 kilometres of township sewage pipe networks were added. The water quality of Chongqing section of the mainstream of the Yangtze River was generally excellent, and the proportion of excellent water quality of 42 national examination sections was 90.5% (the national assessment target in 2018 was 88.1%). The standard-reaching rate of the water quality of urban centralized drinking water sources was 100%, and in 2017, Chongqing was evaluated as "excellent" in the *Action Plan for Water Pollution Prevention and Control* (《水污染防治行动计划》).

Ⅳ.Promote High-quality Economic Development

Chongqing deepened the reform of streamline administration and delegate power in the field of ecological environment, formulating *Ten Measures on Optimizing Business Environment for Promoting the Development of Private Economy* (《关于优化营商环境促进民营经济发展十条措施》), *Notice on Further Improving the Efficiency of Environmental Impact Assessment (EIA) and Promoting High-quality Development* (《关于进一步提高环境影响评价工作效率推动高质量发展的通知》), *Notice on Further Improving Environmental Law Enforcement to Serve the Economic Development* (《关于进一步做好环境执法工作服务经济发展的通知》), and Chongqing focused on key projects and the construction of key projects so as to create a favourable government environment for the development of enterprises. It issued the *Work Plan for Further Deepening the Reform of "Streamline Administration and Delegate Power" and Promoting high-quality Economic Development* (《进一步深化"放

管服"改革推动经济高质量发展工作方案》). In 2018, 41 specific measures in 10 categories were put forward to improve the development level and efficiency of service enterprises. It promoted the industrialization of ecology and the ecological development of industries. It implemented the "three links" among the approval of EIA for construction project with EIA plans, environmental management of existing projects and regional environmental quality, and it promoted the implementation of major infrastructure projects such as high-speed rail, rail transit, and water conservancy projects. The city examined 77 planned EIA projects such as industrial parks, approving 3,810 EIA projects involving a total investment of about 623.5 billion yuan, while 45 projects that did not meet the requirements of environmental quality improvement were not approved, involving a total investment of about 18.9 billion yuan, adding "green elements" to economic growth.

Ⅴ.Solve Prominent Environmental Problems

Chongqing continued to do a good job in rectifying the problems assigned by the Central Committee. In 2018, 35 of the 37 rectification measures and 103 of the 115 specific problems identified by the central environmental protection inspector were completed; 33 of the 38 rectification tasks identified in the second return visit of the Office of the CPC Central Committee have been completed; and 40 of the 44 rectification tasks specified by the inspection investigation of the Office of the CPC Central Committee have been completed, all meeting the requirements of the rectification progress. Problems found in special actions such as the protection of centralized drinking water sources at or above the county level and the special action of "Waste Removal 2018" were all rectified. The municipal-level centralized supervision of all districts and counties has been realized, and more than 7,400 environmental problems in people's lives have been solved, and more than 1,400 key environmental problems and 94 accountability problems have been reported, and the rectification work was carried out in an orderly manner. More than 10 environmental protection special inspections were carried out. Rectification of difficult problems such as the relocation of Jiulongpo bulky wharf, the abolition of 106 catering ships, and the withdrawal of 95 mining rights from the nature reserves were urged to be completed. Numerous environmental infrastructures such as urban and rural sewage pipe network and waste leachate disposal have been built.

Ⅵ.Improve Environmental Protection Support Capacity

Chongqing promoted the revision and formulation of *the Regulations on the Prevention and Control of Water Pollution in the Three Gorges Reservoir Area and River Basins of the Yangtze River* (《长江三峡水库库区及流域水污染防治条例》), and *the Measures for the Prevention and Control of Radiation Pollution of Chongqing Municipality* (《重庆市辐射污染防治办法》), and Chongqing constantly improved the system of laws and regulations. It issued *the Implementation Plan for Deepening Environmental Monitoring Reform and Improving the Quality of Environmental Monitoring Data in Chongqing* (《重庆市深化环境监测改革提高环境监测数据质量实施方案》) to crack down on the falsification of environmental monitoring data. It established big data monitoring platforms at the municipal, district and county levels for water and atmospheric environment management and improved the ecological environment monitoring network. It strengthened supervision of nuclear and radiation safety in accordance with the law and strictly prevented and controlled nuclear and radiation environmental safety risks. The second general survey of pollution sources was carried out. In 2018, more than 230,000 sources of pollution were investigated on site and 65,000 households were investigated. It continued to strengthen consultation and cooperation among Yunnan, Guizhou, Sichuan and Chongqing. It advanced *the Implementation of the Key Work Plan for Joint Prevention and*

Control of Ecological Environment in Four Provinces and Cities in the Upper Reaches of the Yangtze River (《长江上游四省市生态环境联防联控重点工作方案》), and it strengthened joint prevention and control of regional environmental governance.

Ⅶ.Guarantee the Safety of Ecological Environment

Chongqing implemented the requirements of "Protecting the ecological environment with the strictest system and the strictest rule of law", improving the linkage and coordination mechanism of the Municipal High Court, the Municipal Procuratorate, the Municipal Public Security Bureau and the Municipal Ecological Environment Bureau in information sharing, case transfer, consultation and supervision, and the work of "punishment and responsibility for pollution control" was constantly strengthened. Chongqing also carried out the special action of law enforcement with sharp sword. In 2018, the city issued 5,519 administrative penalty decisions and a fine of 366 million yuan, including 640 major cases of five categories, 195 seizure cases, 171 production restriction and production suspension orders. 192 administrative detention cases transferred to public security organs, 75 cases suspected of environmental pollution crimes, and it has maintained a high pressure to crack down on environmental violations.

Chapter Eight Three Gorges Migration

Section One Demonstration and Planning

The Yangtze River is the longest river in China, with a total length of more than 6,300 kilometres and a drainage area of 1.8 million square kilometres. It is the largest river with the richest water energy resources in the world and the mother river of the Chinese nation. The Three Gorges of the Yangtze River, from Baidicheng in Fengjie, Chongqing to Nanjinguan (南津关) in Yichang, Hubei Province, is a grand and magnificent canyon.

The Three Gorges Project is a key project for the comprehensive treatment and development of the Yangtze River. The key to success lies in migration. Chongqing undertakes 85% of the resettlement tasks of this project construction. Chongqing Reservoir Area is located in the east of Chongqing, covering an area of 46,309 square kilometres, involving 15 districts, counties (cities) and 7 districts of Chongqing main urban area. The population of 15 counties (districts) in the Reservoir Area is 12.93 million. There are various types of forest and fruit resources in Chongqing Reservoir Area. The planting area of citrus

Picture 8-1 In 1919, Dr. Sun Yat-sen (孙中山) first proposed the idea of building the Three Gorges Dam in his *International Development of China*《建国方略》).

is large. Some towns are famous villages of Coptis Chinensis and they are rich in precious Chinese herbal medicine. Tung trees and Sapium sebiferum are planted universally. Agricultural production is based on planting with citrus, flue-cured tobacco and mustard tuber playing the leading role. The mineral resources in the reservoir area are various and rich in reserves. The reserves of coal, natural gas, rock salt and limestone are large. The industrial production mainly includes food, textile, chemical industry, building materials, machinery, coal and so on. With a long history and culture, the Reservoir Area is the birthplace of Bachu culture (巴楚文化), including Fengdu Ghost City, White Crane Ridge in Fuling, Shibaozhai in Zhongxian, Yunyang Zhangfei Temple, Fengjie Baidicheng and Daning River Small Three Gorges.

Ⅰ.Demonstration on Migration

The demonstration and planning of the Three Gorges Project has gone through a long and tortuous historical process. In 1919, Dr. Sun Yat-sen discussed the need to develop the water conservancy of the Yangtze River in his book *The International Development of China*. In 1933, the Ministry of Industry and Commerce of the Government of the Republic of China put forward *the Survey Report on Hydropower Generation in the Yangtze River* (《扬子江水力发电勘测报告》). The plan of low dam construction at Gezhouba Dam (葛洲坝) and Huanglingmiao (黄陵庙) was chosen, with an installed capacity of 300,000 kilowatts. After the founding of the People's Republic of China, the Three Gorges Project was surveyed, studied, demonstrated and planned for many times from the perspectives of flood control, power generation and navigation. In 1953, Chairman Mao Zedong inspected the Yangtze River on the "Changjiang" warship and proposed the construction of the Three Gorges Project. In 1954, the Yangtze River Committee proposed Huanglingmiao as the dam site of the Three Gorges Project with a water level of 191.5 metres. In 1958, the CPC Central Committee held an enlarged meeting of the Political Bureau, pointing out that the Three Gorges Project was needed to be built and could be built, and that the normal high water level of the Three Gorges dam should be controlled within 200 metres. Since then, the relocation of the Reservoir Area, cities, key factories and mines was started, and the projects on the staged development have been studied. In January 1981, the river of Gezhouba Hydro-control Project was successfully closed. In July of the same year, unit 1 began to generate electricity.

In April 1984, the State Council approved in principle *the Feasibility Study Report of the Three Gorges Project of the Yangtze River* (《长江三峡工程可行性研究报告》), which was designed according to the normal water level of 150 meters and the dam crest elevation of 175 metres. In October, Chongqing Municipal Party Committee and Municipal Government put forward that the 150-metres plan would turn Chongqing port into a "dead port", believing that the 180-metres plan would basically solve the shipping problem along the Sichuan river and would increase flood control capacity and make full use of the Three Gorges resources. In 1985, 167 members of the National Committee of the Chinese people's Political Consultative Conference (CPPCC) jointly proposed that tributaries of the Yangtze River should be developed before the main stream, and that the construction of dams would endanger the golden waterway, possibly causing civil air defence and ecological problems. After repeated demonstration, in 1989, the feasibility study report of the Three Gorges Project was recompiled. The construction plan was "First-level development, one-time construction, staged water storage and continuous migration". The crest of the dam was 185 metres high, and the normal water level was 175 metres; its total installed capacity was 17.68 million kilowatts, generating 84 billion kwh electricity annually. The total storage capacity was 39.3 billion cubic metres; the flood control storage capacity was 22.15 billion cubic meters; the navigation was improved by 570-650 kilometres; the double track five-level ship lock was improved. The reservoir submerged 356,900 mu of cultivated land; the population of the flooded area (1985) was 725,500; the planned relocation population (2008) was 1.1313 million. The total investment (the price level in 1986) is 36.108 billion yuan, including 18.767 billion yuan for pivotal projects, 11.061 billion yuan for reservoir resettlement and 6.28 billion yuan for power transmission and transformation. The total construction period was 18 years, and the construction period of the first batch of units was 12 years.

Through the exploration and efforts of several generations, on April 3th, 1992, the Fifth Session of the Seventh National People's Congress deliberated and adopted *the Resolution on the Construction of the Three Gorges Project of the Yangtze River* (《关于兴建长江三峡工程的决议》). The Three Gorges Project entered the concrete implementation stage from scientific demonstration. From October 1991 to June 1992, the government completed the physical index survey of 175 metres' submergence of the normal water level of the Three Gorges Reservoir and the preparations for the resettlement plan.

From March 1985 to the end of 1992, pilot resettlement work began in the Three Gorges Reservoir area in Chongqing. The state invested 327.96 million yuan to explore the way of resettlement in the development of large-scale agriculture and carried out urban relocation, pilot relocation of industrial projects, equipment renewal, talent training, etc. At the same time, the site selection and demonstration of ecological environment protection was carried out. After comprehensive comparison, from 1992 to 1993, Wanxian City and Fuling City were selected.

Picture 8-2　Parts of the Three Gorges Dam After Completion

Seven counties, including Wushan County, Fengjie County, Yunyang County, Kaixian County, Zhongxian County, Fengdu County, Changshou County, and 101 towns were relocated to new sites.

Ⅱ.Migration Rules

1.Rural Resettlement Planning

Chongqing Three Gorges Reservoir area is to resettle 384,500 people who lost the basic means of production due to the flooding of the reservoir and needed to be redistributed or employed, including 260,900 people be resettled in the districts (autonomous counties and cities) involved in the inundation of the reservoir area and 123,600 people be resettled outside. The total population of the Three Gorges Chongqing Reservoir Area planned to be relocated was 371,600, of which 248,900 were to be resettled in the counties (autonomous counties and cities) and 122,700 were to be resettled outside.

2.Relocation Planning of Towns

According to the new regional political and economic relations, the overall planning for the relocation of urban towns in the Three Gorges Reservoir Area of Chongqing requires comprehensive study of the nature, development scale, spatial development pattern, main construction standards and quota indexes of urban towns, and overall arrangement of construction land, functional zoning and overall layout of each construction project. The plan reasonably allocated the infrastructure of the town, dealt with the relationship between long-term development and short-term construction and guided the reasonable and orderly development of the town. According to the planning of Chongqing Three Gorges Reservoir Area, the total population of relocation in the town was 709,400, covering an area of 5,069 square kilometres.

3.Relocation Planning of Industrial and Mining Enterprises

In Chongqing Three Gorges Reservoir Area, 1,217 industrial and mining enterprises were completely relocated; 40 protection enterprises were protected and disposed, and 121 enterprises were relocated locally or partially relocated. According to the way of relocation, 783 enterprises were relocated nearby and 595 enterprises were relocated in other places. According to the relationship with cities and towns, 1,211 enterprises were relocated along with the city and 167 enterprises were relocated outside the town.

4.Reconstruction (Reform) Planning of Professional Projects

In Chongqing Three Gorges Reservoir Area, it was planned to build 669.4 kilometres of restored roads and 338 large bridges with a total length of 32,800 linear meters. It was planned to rebuild 8 ports in cities and counties, 71 market terminals and 79 docking stops. It was planned to rebuild 2,887 kilometres of transmission lines, 9 substations with a capacity of 110 kilovolts and 31 substations with a capacity of 35 kilovolts. It was planned to build 3,270 kilometres of communication lines. It was planned to build 14 radio and television stations in districts and counties, 92 radio and television stations in towns, 2 microwave stations, and 3,505 kilometres of broadcast trunk lines. It was planned to rebuild 47.3 kilometres gas pipelines, 2 gas storage and distribution stations and 1.51 kilometres river pipeline.

5.Conservation Planning of Cultural Relics and Historic Sites

In Chongqing Three Gorges Reservoir Area, 787 cultural relic protection projects were in the inundated area and resettlement area, including 246 cultural relics on the ground (57 were protected in situ, and 91 were relocated and 98 were retained for data). 541 were underground cultural relics.

6.Environmental Protection Planning

This plan includes environmental protection planning for the development and utilization of land resources, environmental protection planning for the relocation of cities and towns, the pollution prevention and control planning for the relocation and construction of industrial and mining enterprises and the construction of new secondary and tertiary industries, the population health protection planning, ecological construction planning, ecological environment monitoring and management planning, etc.

7.Planning of Protection Works

Around Chongqing Three Gorges Reservoir Area, there were many areas in need of protection around the submerged shallow water area, except for the Xiaojiang River in Kaixian County. The other areas to be protected were not large. In the middle reaches of the Xiaojiang River in Kaixian county, the fertile farmland in the alluvial flat dam was contiguous, and the population was dense. In December 1996, the partial and local protection scheme was adopted.

8.Estimated Compensation Investment

The total budget of resettlement compensation investment in Chongqing Three Gorges Reservoir Area was 31.555 billion yuan, including 5.025 billion yuan for rural areas, 11.557 billion yuan for urban towns, 6.243 billion yuan for industrial and mining enterprises, 2.981 billion yuan for professional projects, 249 million yuan for environmental protection, 143 million yuan for adjustment, 508 million yuan for survey and design, 723 million yuan for farmland occupation tax, 846 million yuan for protection works and 3.28 billion yuan for others.

9.Resettlement Planning and Project Budget Adjustment

In May 2006, the Three Gorges Project Construction Committee of the State

Council decided to adjust the Three Gorges resettlement plan and project budget. In 2007, an additional 7.951 billion yuan (the price level in May 1993) was invested in adjusting the resettlement plan and project budget of the Three Gorges Reservoir Area, and an additional 5.683 billion yuan was invested in Chongqing.

Section Two Resettlement of Migrants

In 1993, the resettlement work in the Three Gorges Reservoir Area entered the formal implementation stage. According to the Three Gorges Project's construction plan of "First-level development, one-time construction, water storage by stages and continuous resettlement", the relocation and resettlement of the Three Gorges migrants would be completed in four phases. From 1993 to 1997, the river was cut off and the resettlement task at 90 metres water level of the Three Gorges Reservoir was completed. On March 14th, 1997, the Fifth Session of the Eighth National People's Congress passed the proposal of the State Council for the establishment of Chongqing Municipality directly under the central government, and Chongqing officially became a municipality directly under the central government. The Municipal Party Committee and the municipal government have always been taking the resettlement work as the foundation of the city, giving full play to the city's efforts to complete the task of resettlement and relocation in an all-round way, sticking to the overall plan to ensure the stability and prosperity of the migrants, the protection of the ecological environment, the prevention and control of geological disasters and the economic and social development. From 1998 to 2003, the first batch of units began to generate electricity and permanent ship locks were opened for navigation, and the resettlement task under the 135 metres initial water level of the Three Gorges Reservoir was completed. From 2004 to 2006, the dam crest elevation of the Three Gorges dam was 185 meters, and the resettlement task under the 156 metres water level of the Three Gorges Reservoir was completed. From 2007 to 2009, the all units could generate electricity, and all key projects were completed, and the resettlement task under the 175 metres water level of the Three Gorges Reservoir was completed. The resettlement of the Three Gorges Reservoir involved a wide range of area, a long period of resettlement and a complex situation. In May 2006, the Three Gorges Construction Committee of the State Council decided to adjust the review and planning of new rural migrants, the review and estimate of new houses for urban and rural migrants, the review of land area for urban towns and the budget estimate of infrastructure.

In terms of the main tasks of resettlement, the resettlement work of the Three Gorges was mainly carried out in four categories.

First one is rural resettlement. The resettlement of rural migrants in Chongqing Reservoir Area was mainly carried out by means of land development and transformation, local back-up resettlement, land adjustment within the village group, local resettlement and non-local resettlement, centralized resettlement and decentralized resettlement, government resettlement in combination with self-provided resettlement, to encourage rural migrants to move out. The township governments were in charge of where these migrants are located and were responsible for each group and each household. After resettlement, rural migrants would all build their own houses.

Picture 8-3 On August 13th, 2000, the first batch of large-scale emigrants from the Three Gorges Reservoir Area left Yunyang for Shanghai.

Second one is relocation of towns. The local government was responsible for the land acquisition and infrastructure supporting construction for the relocation of the town. In the relocation and construction of towns, most districts and counties set up new town construction management committees or headquarters to take charge of the preliminary work, "four systems" project, completion settlement, acceptance and handover, etc. All districts and counties put forward the slogan of "Resettling schools first" and gave special support to public facilities such as schools and hospitals. In 2007, Chongqing increased 35.19 million yuan compensation for 318 schools, 32.29 million yuan for 210 hospitals, and 88.07 million yuan for urban and rural public cultural undertakings. Schools, hospitals and public cultural facilities in the Reservoir Area have been improved to some extent.

Thirdly, relocation of Industrial and Mining Enterprises. Since 1992, the central government has called on the whole country to support the Three Gorges immigrants, the most important of which was to support the technical transformation of relocated enterprises. In 1998, the State Council proposed to close down enterprises with no market for products, serious losses or serious environmental pollution. There were 1,391 enterprises (excluding 6 central enterprises) involved in the inundation of Chongqing Reservoir Area. 484 of these enterprises were relocated and 129,000 employees were resettled. 11.765 billion yuan of fixed assets were acquired after relocation and 907 bankrupt enterprises (including 365 heavily polluted enterprises) were closed down. The relocation and structural adjustment of industrial and mining enterprises changed the distribution of productive forces in the Reservoir Area and enhanced the economic strength of the Reservoir Area.

Fourthly, reconstruction of Professional Facilities. The reconstruction of professional facilities in the Three Gorges Reservoir Area was undertaken by the industry departments or professional companies. The owner unit carried out the reconstruction in combination with the industry development plan. The reconstruction of professional facilities in the reservoir area was combined with technical progress and network optimization to achieve upgradation. The highway reconstruction project was implemented by the transportation department of the district and county where the project was located in accordance with the road network reconstruction plan; the port and wharf reconstruction project was implemented in accordance with the reconstruction plan approved by the Ministry of Communications. The reconstruction of power facilities was mainly organized and implemented by the power departments of each district and county. Telecommunications facilities were uniformly implemented by China Telecom Corporation Limited Chongqing Branch. The reconstruction of radio and television in the Reservoir Area was mainly carried out in combination with the development of the industry.

By the end of 2009, a total of 1,138 million urban and rural migrants (489,500 rural migrants, 98,400 town migrants and 550,100 from other areas) were relocated from Chongqing Reservoir Area, accounting for 100% of the planning tasks. 483,700 rural migrants were resettled for production, accounting for 100% of the planning tasks. 37,250,400 square meters of urban and rural housing were also built (including 12,650,900 square meters of rural housing, 5,511,500 square meters of town housing, 12,620,600 square meters of urban and county housing, 6,827,400 square meters of industrial and mining enterprises housing), basically completing the Three Gorges resettlement tasks. Under the strong leadership of the CPC Central Committee and the State Council, with the strong support of the people of the whole country, the governments at all levels in the Reservoir Area and the migrants, completed the migration task on schedule through working hard in 2009, and ensured that the experimental storage in 2010 reached a normal water level of 175 meters, providing the necessary conditions for the Three Gorges Project to bring into full play the comprehensive benefits of flood control, power generation, and navigation, etc.

Section Three Supporting Construction and Development

From 2004 to June 2006, the Ministry of Finance issued a total of 1,373 supporting projects with an investment subsidy of 398 million yuan to help solve the production and living problems of immigrants and promote the sustainable economic development of the Reservoir Area. In May 2006, the State Council included the post-funded support for rural migrants from the Three Gorges Project into the scope of post-funded support for large and medium-sized reservoir migrants in China, and clarified the policy indicators for rural migrants in the city, involving 35,200 people in 27 districts and counties, 375 townships and 6,726 communities. In October 2007, the Ministry of Finance explicitly allocated part of the funds for the Three Gorges Reservoir Area (including 253 million yuan for Chongqing municipality) to solve the remaining problems of migrants and implement the assistance for urban immigrants. The Chongqing municipal government provided assistance to migrants from 24 districts and counties and 186 towns and townships (subdistricts) by means of hardship subsidy, special relief, employment training and project support.

The implementation of the Three Gorges Resettlement Support Policy directly increased the income of the migrants, helped the poor migrants to get through the difficulties, and special relief were provided to the poor migrants affected by serious illness, disability and natural disasters. Some of the migrants obtained jobs through skill training and embarked on the road of getting wealthy through project support. Through the implementation of industrial support policies, the shortage of industrial support in the Reservoir Area has been alleviated, and the employment opportunity for migrants has been continuously increased. A number of infrastructure and public welfare facility projects were implemented to basically alleviate the practical difficulties in the Reservoir Area and the resettlement area, such as the lack of access to travel, drinking water, school, medical treatment and electricity, thus promoted social harmony and stability in the Reservoir Area. In 2017, the general public budget revenue for Chongqing Three Gorges Reservoir Area reached 48.01 billion yuan.

In recent years, Chongqing has thoroughly implemented the spirit of the 19th National Congress of the Communist Party of China and the important speech of General Secretary Xi Jinping at the Symposium on Promoting the Development of the Yangtze River Economic Belt. Guided by the principle of "Promoting conservation, refraining from large-scale development", with "Ecological priority and green development" as the lead, Chongqing firmly established and

Picture 8-4 Binjiang Road (滨江路), Wanzhou

Picture 8-5 Fuling New Town

implemented the new concept of development, and continued to implement the project in accordance with the overall requirements of ensuring safety, focusing on the development of people's livelihood, highlightening ecological progress and promoting poverty alleviation, so as to ensure the orderly progress of the follow-up work of the Three Gorges Project.

Chongqing insists on giving overwhelming priority to the restoration of the Yangtze River ecological environment, accelerating the construction of ecological barriers in the upper reaches of the Yangtze River, and strengthening the comprehensive treatment of the Three Gorges Reservoir. In 2018, pilot projects to restore 12,000 mu of degraded areas was launched, and 162.5 kilometres of reservoir banks in towns along the Yangtze River was comprehensively renovated, and 2.645 million mu of afforestation was completed in the ecological barrier construction area and important tributaries in the reservoir area. Ecological agriculture and eco-tourism were vigorously developed; green ecology and low-carbon environmental protection was highlighted; the support of the development of tourism industry and characteristic planting industry was given priority, and herbivorous animal husbandry and ecological fishery in a controlled way was developed. The agricultural structure of the reservoir area was further optimized, and the effect of the industrial development was obvious. The characteristic ecological agriculture, such as citrus, mustard tuber and traditional Chinese medicine, grew rapidly. The ecotourism industry in Fengjie, Wushan and other districts and counties developed rapidly. The advantages of ecological resources in the Reservoir Area were gradually turning into the advantages of industrial development. At the same time, all regions in the reservoir area adhered to the principle of market-oriented innovation and innovation-driven development, strengthening the "two-wheel drive" (两轮驱动) of technology and market, promoting the sustainable growth of industrial economy. Rapid progress was made in infrastructure construction. In 2018, nearly 300 targeted assistance projects for rural resettlement, such as housing safety, road transportation, drinking water for people and livestock, irrigation and water conservancy, public services, village renovation, were implemented. The carrying capacity and service capacity of infrastructure were significantly improved. Environmental improvement projects, such as one pool and three renovations (一池三改)[1], garbage and sewage treatment were carried out, and they further improved production efficiency and reduced pollution discharge. Through policies such as streamlining administration, delegating power and reducing the burden on enterprises, Chongqing will continue to seek impetus for reform and vitality for the market, and form a favourable social atmosphere characterized by "mass entrepreneurship and innovation". The tertiary industry, such as trade and service industry, new financial industry and real estate industry, developed rapidly in the Reservoir Area. Chongqing will regularly provide regular support and assistance to immigrants, and Chongqing will strengthen employment training in the Reservoir Area. Chongqing also will vigorously implement comprehensive assistance in urban immigrant communities and further enhance immigrants' sense of well-being and gain.

[1] This refers to rural biogas digester and three renovations made in animal houses, kitchens and lavatories.

Appendix 1

Brief List of Historical Events in Chongqing

Period	Time	Event
Prehistoric Times	About 2 million years ago	Homo erectus "Wushan Man" appeared.
	About 5,000-6,000 years ago	"Daxi Culture" extended to the Three Gorges Area.
The Shang Dynasty	1254 B.C.-1195 B.C.	The King Wuding of the Shang Dynasty conquered the Ba State. The ancestors of the Ba people migrated from the west of Hubei Province and Hanshui River basin to the Wujiang River and Jialing River Basin.
The Zhou Dynasty	1046 B.C.-4th century B.C.	The Ba people took part in the Zhou Dynasty's crusade against the Shang Dynasty. King Wu of Zhou granted the surname Ji to Ba people and called them Ba Zi.
	316 B.C.-314 B.C.	Sima Cuo in the Qin Dynasty annihilated the Ba State and established Ba Jun. Zhang Yi built Jiangzhou City.
The Western Han Dynasty	134 B.C. -133 B.C.	Emperor Wu of the Han Dynasty sent soldiers from Ba and Shu to build Nanyi Road.
The Eastern Han Dynasty	25-36	Gongsun Shu proclaimed himself emperor and conquered Jiangzhou. In 36, Gongsun Shu died.
	184	Zhang Xiu, a native of Ba County, spreaded Five Pecks of Rice Religion and launched an uprising to occupy Ba County.
	213	Zhang Fei occupied Jiangzhou and captured Yan Yan.
The Three Kingdoms Period	222	Liu Bei entrusted his son to Zhuge Liang in Baidicheng.
	226	Li Yan built Jiangzhou City, which is located in Yuzhong Peninsula today.
The Western Jin Dynasty	279	Wang Jun's Water Division attacked Wu through Ba County and unified the whole country.
The Eastern Jin Dynasty	346	Huan Wen attacked Shu via Jiangzhou.

Continued

Period	Time	Event
The Sui Dynasty	583	Chuzhou was renamed Yuzhou.
The Tang Dynasty	892	Wei JunJing, the governor of Changzhou, chiselled the first stone carvings in Dazu Beishan (North Mountain).
The Northern Song Dynasty	1102	Emperor Huizong of the Song Dynasty changed Yuzhou to Gongzhou.
The Southern Song Dynasty	1189	Zhao Dun, Emperor Guangzong of the Song Dynasty, promoted Gongzhou to Chongqing Fu.
	1239-1279	Battle in Diaoyucheng.
	1249	The construction of Dazu Baoding Mountain Stone Carving, which was first carved in 1179 and was presided over by the monk Zhao Fengzhi, was completed.
The Yuan Dynasty	1363	Ming Yuzhen proclaimed himself emperor, named his kingdom Daxia, and made Chongqing his capital.
The Ming Dynasty	1371	Zhu Yuanzhang sent Tang He and Fu Youde to attack Daxia, and Daxia perished.
	1371-1398	Dai Ding, Chongqing garrison commander, built Chongqing City.
The Qing Dynasty	1644	Zhang Xianzhong captured Chongqing Fu.
	1797-1798	The White Lotus army of Eastern Sichuan conquered Changshou City twice.
	1863	The First Chongqing Missionary Case.
	1886	The Second Chongqing Missionary Case.
	1890	Yu Dongchen Uprising broke out.
	1891	Chongqing Opened Port.
	1895	Japan obtained the right to open Chongqing Port and to exercise the Chuanjiang River.

Continued

Period	Time	Event
The Republic of China	1911	The Chongqing Branch of Tung Meng Hui announced Chongqing's independence and established the military government of Shu. 57 prefectures in southeast Sichuan successively became independent and accepted the leadership of the military government of Shu.
	1912	The military governments of Chengdu and Chongqing merged to form the capital of Sichuan Dudu Fu. Sichuan was unified.
	1922	Chongqing Local League of China Socialist Youth League was established.
	1926	The Chongqing Local Executive Committee of the Communist Party of China was established with the approval of the Central Committee of the CPC and was responsible for leading the work in Sichuan. Yang Angong was appointed secretary. "Wanxian Massacre" occurred in Wanxian County.
	1927	"March 31st Massacre"; Sichuan provisional Provincial Committee of the Communist Party of China was established in Chongqing.
	1929	Chongqing was formally established as a city. Pan Wenhua was appointed as mayor.
	1930	The CPC Sichuan Provincial Committee was destroyed, and officials in Chongqing formed atemporary provincial committee.
	1931	The municipal government took over the Wangjiatuo Concession.
	1932	Liu Xiang and Liu Wenhui, warlords of Sichuan, broke out the battle of "Two Lius".
	1933	The Red Army of Sichuan-Shaanxi revolutionary base occupied five counties, namely Yilong, Yingshan, Daxian, Xuanhan and Wanyuan, and established the countylevel Soviet regime in Chengkou. The Red Army led by He Long captured Qianjiang couty.
	1936	Sichuan suffered from the worst drought in 100 years.

Continued

Period	Time	Event
The Republic of China	1937	Kuomintang Central Army entered Chongqing; The East Route of Sichuan Anti-Japanese Army went out of Sichuan, took boats in Chongqing and other ports in the lower reaches of the Yangtze River to the East; The National Government moved to Chongqing.
	1938	The Eighth Route Army Office and *Xinhua Daily* headquarters moved into Chongqing; The "Chongqing Bombing" began, which lasted for 6 years.
	1939	The Southern Bureau of the CPC Central Committee was established. On May 3rd and May 4th, Japanese planes bombed Chongqing; Chongqing was designated as a special city by the National Government; Tao Xingzhi founded Yucai School in Hechuan.
	1940	The National Government designated Chongqing as the "War-time Capital".
	1941	China Democratic League was established in Chongqing. "June 5th" Tunnel Suffocating Tragedy.
	1945	Mao Zedong came to Chongqing for peace negotiation and signed the "Double Tenth Agreement".
	1946	Cangbaitang Incident; Jiaochangkou Incident; The South Bureau of the CPC Central Committee and the Eighth Route Army Office moved to Nanjing.
	1948	Armed Uprising of Fengdawu; *Tingjinbao* Event; Huaying Mountain Uprising.
The People's Republic of China	1949	"April 21st" Student Movement; "November 27th" Massacre; Chongqing Liberation; The Southwest Bureau of the CPC Central Committee entered Chongqing, established the Southwest Military and Political Commission, which was stationed in Chongqing.

Continued

Period	Time	Event
The People's Republic of China	1950	The Eastern Sichuan Administrative Office was established in Chongqing. Main guidelines for the construction of a new Chongqing was made. Chongqing was established as a municipality directly under the Southwest Military and Political Commission.
	1952	The Southwest Military and Political Committee was changed to the Southwest Administrative Committee, which was stationed in Chongqing. The Eastern Sichuan Administrative Office was cancelled and merged into Sichuan Province with the Southern Sichuan Administrative Office, the Northern Sichuan Administration Office and the West Sichuan Administrative Office. Beibei was incorporated into Chongqing The Chengdu-Chongqing Railway was opened to traffic.
	1953	Chongqing became a municipality directly under the central government.
	1954	The Southwest Bureau of the CPC Central Committee and the Southwest Administrative Committee were cancelled. Chongqing People's Auditorium was completed. Chongqing Municipality directly under the Central Government was cancelled and Chongqing became a city under the jurisdiction of Sichuan Province.
	1956	Chongqing basically completed the transformation of agriculture, handicraft industry and capitalist industry and commerce.
	1959	Ba County and Qijiang County in Jiangjin District and Changshou County in Fuling District were assigned to Chongqing.
	1961	*Hongyan* was published.
	1964	The Strategic Area Construction in National Defence started. Chongqing became the central city of this construction.
	1965	Sichuan-Guizhou Railway was opened to traffic.
	1976	Jiangbei County in Jiangjin District was assigned to Chongqing.

Continued

Period	Time	Event
The People's Republic of China	1979	Xiangfan-Chongqing Railway was opened to traffic.
	1980	The State Council approved Chongqing as a foreign trade port along the Yangtze River.
	1982	The Jialing River Cableway was completed.
	1983	Chongqing became a city under separate state planning and a pilot city for urban comprehensive system reform. Yongchuan area was incorporated into Chongqing.
	1990	Chongqing Jiangbei International Airport was completed and put into use.
	1992	Chongqing was opened up as an open city along the Yangtze River.
	1993	The migration of millions of people from the Three Gorges began.
	1996	Chongqing was in charge of Wanxian City, Fuling City and Qianjiang City of Sichuan Province. The Chengdu-Chongqing Expressway was opened to traffic.
	1997	Chongqing became a municipality directly under the central government. Wanxian City, Fuling City and Qianjiang City of Sichuan Province were incorporated into Chongqing.
	1999	"Rainbow Bridge" collapse accident was occurred in Qijiang. Dazu Stone Carvings were listed in World Cultural Heritage.
	2003	The construction of Chongqing University Town was approved. "December 23rd" natural gas blowout accident occurred in Kaixian County.
	2005	Chongqing Light Rail Line 2, the first urban rail transit in west China, was opened.
	2006	The Three Gorges Dam reached a height of 185 meters. The Three Gorges Project was completed.

Continued

Period	Time	Event
The People's Republic of China	2007	Chongqing was listed as the national pilot area for comprehensive urban and rural reform.
	2008	Chongqing Lianglu-Cuntan Bonded Port Area was opened to port and was officially put into use.
	2009	Chongqing was designated by the State Council as a "National Pilot Zone for Urban and Rural Coordinated Comprehensive Reform".
	2010	National New Area—Liangjiang New Area was established.
	2011	China-Europe Express (Chongqing) started full program operation.
	2012	The first Chongqing International Marathon was held in Nanbin Road and Babin Road, Chongqing.
	2013	The Venue of Chongqing International Expo Centre was officially put into operation.
	2014	The former site of Chongqing Office of the Eighth Route Army, the site of Chongqing Bombing and the Kurishenko Martyrs Cemetery were selected as the first batch of national Anti-Japanese War Memorial facilities and sites.
	2015	The Chinese government and the Singapore government signed *the Framework Agreement on the Construction of the China-Singapore (Chongqing) Strategic Connectivity Demonstration Project* and its supplementary agreement in Singapore, officially launched the third intergovernmental cooperation project with Chongqing in operation.
	2016	Xi Jinping, General Secretary of the CPC Central Committee, President of the People's Republic of China and Chairman of the Central Military Commission, visited Chongqing and put forward "Two Points" positioning, "Two Lands" goals and "Four Solid" requirements for Chongqing.
	2017	The State Council approved the establishment of China (Chongqing) Pilot Free Trade Zone. Chongqing Jiangbei International Airport T3A Terminal was completed and put into operation.

Continued

Period	Time	Event
The People's Republic of China	2018	Chongqing proposed a work plan to resolutely win "Three Key Battles" and implement the "Eight Action Plans". The First China International Intelligent Industry Expo was held in Chongqing.
	2019	Xi Jinping, General Secretary of the CPC Central Committee, President of the People's Republic of China and Chairman of the Central Military Commission, visited Chongqing and put forward important instructions on Chongqing's "Two Points" positioning, "Two Lands" and "Two Highs" goals, and on how to play "Three Roles" and how to create sound political ecology.

Appendix 2

List of Organizational System Evolution in Chongqing

Period	Organizational system	Time	Location of government	Belong to	Jurisdiction
The Shang and Zhou Dynasties (about 1600 B.C.-476 B.C.)	The Ba State				To Yufu in the east (now Fengjie, Wushan and West Hubei province), to Bodao in the west (now Yibin and Luzhou in Sichuan province), to Hanzhong in the north (now Hanzhong and Ankang in Shaanxi province), to Qianfu in the south (now Qianjiang, Fuling, northwest Hunan province, northeast and north Guizhou province).
Warring States period (475 B.C.-221 B.C.)	The Ba State				Starting from the Three Gorges and Xijiang River basins of the Yangtze River in the east, to current Chongqing central area in the west. The current central area of Chongqing was its activity center.
The Qin Dynasty (221B.C.-207 B.C.)	Ba Jun	The 11th year of King Huiwen of the Qin Dynasty (314 B.C.)	Jiangzhou		It has jurisdiction over 11 counties, including Jiangzhou, Dianjiang, Langzhong, Dangqu, Jiangyang, Fuxian, Zhixian, Quren, Yufu, Yelang and Pang.
The Western Han Dynasty (206 B.C. - 8 A.D.)	Ba Jun		Jiangzhou	Yizhou	It has jurisdiction over 11 counties including Jiangzhou, Dianjiang, Zhixian, Langzhong, Quren, Anhan, Dangqu, Chongguo, Yufu, Fuling and Linjiang.

The Eastern Han Dynasty (25-220)	Ba Jun		Jiangzhou	Yizhou	During the reign of emperor He of the Han Dynasty (89-105), Bajun governed 14 counties including Jiangzhou, Dangqu, Quren, Langzhong, Yufu, Linjiang, Zhixian, Fuling, Dianjiang, Anhan, Pingdu, Chongguo, Xuanhan and Hanchang.
The Three Kingdoms Period (221-265)	Ba Jun		Jiangzhou	Yizhou	During the reign of Liu Bei (221-223), the forefather of Shuhan, Ba Jun had seven counties, namely, Jiangzhou, Dianjiang, Linjiang, Zhixian, Pingdu, Lecheng and Changan.
The Western Jin Dynasty (265-316)	Ba Jun		Jiangzhou	Liangzhou	Jiangzhou County, Dianjiang County, Zhixian County, Linjiang County.
Chenghan Period (304-337)	Ba Jun		Jiangzhou	Jingzhou	Jiangzhou County, Dianjiang County, Zhixian County, Linjiang County.
The Eastern Jin Dynasty (317-420)	Ba Jun		Jiangzhou	Liangzhou	Jiangzhou County, Dianjiang County, Zhixian County, Linjiang County.

Continued

Period		Organizational system	Time	Location of government	Belong to	Jurisdiction
The Northern and Southern Dynasties (420-581)	Liusong Dynasty	Ba Jun		Jiangzhou County	Yizhou	Jiangzhou County, Dianjiang County, Zhixian County, Linjiang County.
	Southern Qi Dynasty	Ba Jun		Jiangzhou County	Yizhou; Bazhou (480)	Jiangzhou County, Dianjiang County, Zhixian County, Linjiang County.
	Liang Dynasty	Ba Jun		Dianjiang County(Now Yuzhong District)	Chuzhou	Dianjiang,Jiangzhou (now Shunjiang Town, Jiangjin District).
	Northern Wei Dynasty	Ba Jun		Dianjiang County	Bazhou	Dianjiang, Zhixian County, Hanping County.
	Northern Zhou Dynasty	Ba Jun		Baxian(Now Yuzhong District)	Chuzhou	Ba County, Fuling Town.
The Sui Dynasty (581-618)		Yuzhou	The 1st year of Kaihuang (581)	Ba County	Xinzhou Governor Office	Ba County, Jiangjin County, Fuling County.
		Ba Jun	The 3rd year of Daye (607)	Ba County		

The Tang Dynasty (618-907)	Yuzhou	The 1st year of Wude (618)	Ba County	Shan-nandao	Ba County, Jiangjin, Wanshou, Nanping, Bishan.
	Nanping	The 1st year of Tianbao (742)	Ba County	Shan-nandao	
	Yuzhou	The 1st year of Qianyuan (758)	Ba County	Jiannan-dao	
The Five Dynasties and Ten Kingdoms (907-965)	Yuzhou		Ba County		Ba County, Jiangjin, Wanshou, Nanping, Bishan.
The Song Dynasty (965-1279)	Yuzhou		Ba County	Kuizhou Lu	In the 5th year of Huangyou, Song Renzong of Song Dynasty (1053), it ruled over Ba , Jiangjin, Bishan and Nanchuan.
	Gongzhou	The 1st year of Chongning (1102)			
	Chongqing Fu	The 16th year of Chunxi (1189)			
The Yuan Dynasty (1271-1361)	Chongqing Lu		Ba County	Sichuan Province	1 Administration Office; 3 counties: Ba, Jiangjin, Nanchuan; 4 zhou: Hezhou, Fuzhou, Zhongzhou, Luzhou.
The Period of Daxia Regime under Ming Yuzhen (1361-1371)	Chongqing Lu		Ba County		4 counties:Ba, Jiangjin, Qijiang and Nanchuan; 5 zhou: Hezhou, Fuzhou, Zhongzhou, Luzhou and Zizhou.

Continued

Period	Organizational system	Time	Location of government	Belong to	Jurisdiction
The Ming Dynasty (1371-1644)	Chongqing Fu		Ba County	Sichuan Province; Sichuan Chengxuan Administration Department	In the 19th year of Chenghua , Xianzong of the Ming Dynasty(1483), it governed 11 counties and 3 zhou, including Ba, Jiangjin, Bishan, Yongchuan, Rongchang, Dazu, Anju, Qijiang, Changshou, Nanchuan and Qianjiang; Hezhou, Zhongzhou and Fuzhou.
The Qing Dynasty (1644-1911)	Chongqing Fu		Ba County	Sichuan Province	In the 20th year of Qianlong, Emperor Gaozong of the Qing Dynasty, it ruled over: Jiangbei Ting; Ba County, Jiangjin County, Changshou County, Qijiang County, Yongchuan County, Bishan County, Tongliang County, Dazu County, Rongchang County, Nanchuan County, Dingyuan County.

The Republic of China (1912-1949)	Ba	1914	Ba County	Dong-chuan Dao	Ba County
	Chongqing City	1929		Sichuan Province	
	Chongqing City (a municipality under the juris-diction of the Executive Yuan of the National Government)	1939			
	Chongqing City (War-time capital of the Republic of China)	1940			
The People's Republic of China	Chongqing City	1950	The 1st District	South-west Region	The 1st District, The 2nd District, The 3rd District, The 4th District, The 5th District, The 6th District, The 7th District, The 8th District
		1952			The 1st District, The 2nd District, The 3rd District, The 4th District, The 5th District, Ba County.

Continued

Period	Organizational system	Time	Location of government	Belong to	Jurisdiction
The People's Republic of China	Chongqing City	1953	The 1st Distric	Sichuan Province	The 1st District, The 2nd District, The 3rd District (Shaci District), The 4th District (Dadukou, Lijiatuo District), The 5th District (Jiangnan District), The 6th District (Beibei District).
		1954			The 1st District, The 2nd District, The 3rd District,The 4th District, The 5th District, and The 6th District.
		1955	Shizhong District		Shizhong District, Jiangbei District, Shapingba District, Jiulongpo District, Nan'an District, Beibei District and Nantong Mining District.
		1959			Shizhong District, Jiangbei District, Shapingba District, Jiulongpo District, Nan'an District, Beibei District, Nantong Mining District, Ba County, Qijiang County, Changshou County.
		1966			Shizhong District, Jiangbei District, Shapingba District, Jiulongpo District, Nan'an District, Beibei District, Nantong Mining District, Dadukou District, Ba County, Qijiang County, Changshou County.
		1978			Shizhong District, Jiangbei District, Shapingba District, Jiulongpo District, Nan'an District, Beibei District, Nantong Mining District, Dadukou District, Shuangqiao District, Ba County, Qijiang County, Changshou County, Jiangbei County.

The People's Republic of China	Chongqing City (a city under separate state planning)	1983	Shizhong District	Sichuan Province	Shizhong District, Jiangbei District, Shapingba District, Jiulongpo District, Nan'an District, Beibei District, Nantong Mining District, Dadukou District, Shuangqiao District, Baxian, Qijiang County, Changshou County, Jiangbei County, Yongchuan County, Jiangjin County, Hechuan County, Tongliang County, Bishan County, Dazu County, Rongchang County, Tongnan County.
		1995	Yuzhong District		Yuzhong District, Jiangbei District, Shapingba District, Jiulongpo District, Nan'an District, Beibei District, Nantong Mining District, Dadukou District, Bazhi District, Yubei District, Shuangqiao District; Yongchuan City, Jiangjin City, Hechuan City; Qijiang County, Changshou County, Tongliang County, Bishan County, Dazu County, Rongchang County, Tongnan County.

Continued

Period	Organizational system	Time	Location of government	Belong to	Jurisdiction
The People's Republic of China	Chongqing (municipality directly under the central government)	1997	Yuzhong District		Yuzhong District, Dadukou District, Jiangbei District, Shapingba District, Jiulongpo District, Nan'an District, Beibei District, Wansheng District, Shuangqiao District, Yubei District, Banan District, Longbao District, Tiancheng District, Wuqiao District, Zhicheng District, Lidu district; Jiangjin city, Hechuan City, Yongchuan City, Nanchuan City; Changshou County, Qijiang County, Tongnan County, Tongliang County, Dazu County, Rongchang County, Bishan County, Kaixian County, Zhongxian County, Liangping County, Yunyang County, Fengjie County, Wushan County, Wuxi County, Chengkou County, Dianjiang County, Wulong County, Fengdu County; Qianjiang Tujia and Miao Autonomous County, Shizhu Tujia Autonomous County, Pengshui Miao and Tujia Autonomous County, Youyang Tujia and Miao Autonomous County, Xiushan Tujia and Miao Autonomous County.

The People's Republic of China	Chongqing (municipality directly under the central government)	1998	Yuzhong District		Wanxian (Wanzhou) District, Fuling District, Yuzhong District, Dadukou District, Jiangbei District, Shapingba District, Jiulongpo District, Nan'an District, Beibei District, Wansheng District, Shuangqiao District, Yubei district and Banan District; Jiangjin city, Hechuan City, Yongchuan City and Nanchuan City; Changshou County, Qijiang County, Tongnan County, Tongliang County, Dazu County, Rongchang County, Bishan County, Kaixian County, Zhongxian County, Liangping County, Yunyang County, Fengjie County, Wushan County, Wuxi County, Chengkou County, Dianjiang County, Wulong County, Fengdu County; Qianjiang Tujia and Miao Autonomous County, Shizhu Tujia Autonomous County, Pengshui Miao and Tujia Autonomous County, Youyang Tujia and Miao Autonomous County, Xiushan Tujia and Miao Autonomous County.

Continued

Period	Organizational system	Time	Location of government	Belong to	Jurisdiction
The People's Republic of China	Chongqing (municipality directly under the central government)	2000	Yuzhong District		Wanzhou District, Fuling District, Yuzhong District, Dadukou District, Jiangbei District, Shapingba District, Jiulongpo District, Nan'an District, Beibei District, Wansheng District, Shuangqiao District, Yubei District, Banan District and Qianjiang district; Jiangjin City, Hechuan City, Yongchuan City and Nanchuan City; Changshou County, Qijiang County, Tongnan County, Tongliang County, Dazu County, Rongchang County, Bishan County, Kaixian County, Zhongxian County, Liangping County, Yunyang County, Fengjie County, Wushan County, Wuxi County, Chengkou County, Dianjiang County, Wulong County, Fengdu County; Qianjiang Tujia and Miao Autonomous County, Shizhu Tujia Autonomous County, Pengshui Tujia and Miao Autonomous County, Youyang Tujia and Miao Autonomous County, Xiushan Tujia and Miao Autonomous County.

The People's Republic of China	Chongqing (municipality directly under the central government)	2006			Wanzhou District, Fuling District, Yuzhong District, Dadukou District, Jiangbei District, Shapingba District, Jiulongpo District, Nan'an District, Beibei District, Wansheng District, Shuangqiao District, Yubei District, Banan District, Qianjiang District, Changshou District, Jiangjin District, Hechuan District, Yongchuan District, Nanchuan District; Qijiang County, Tongnan County, Tongliang County, Dazu County, Rongchang County, Bishan County, kaixian County, Zhongxian County, Liangping County, Yunyang County, Fengjie County, Wushan County, Wuxi County, Chengkou County, Dianjiang County, Wulong County, Fengdu County; Qianjiang Tujia and Miao Autonomous County, Shizhu Tujia Autonomous County, Pengshui Miao and Tujia Autonomous County, Youyang Tujia and Miao Autonomous County, Xiushan Tujia and Miao Autonomous County.

Continued

Period	Organizational system	Time	Location of government	Belong to	Jurisdiction
The People's Republic of China	Chongqing (municipality directly under the central government)	2017			Wanzhou District, Fuling District, Yuzhong District, Dadukou District, Jiangbei District, Shapingba District, Jiulongpo District, Nan'an District, Beibei District, Wansheng District, Shuangqiao District, Yubei District, Banan District, Qianjiang District, Changshou District, Jiangjin District, Hechuan District, Yongchuan District, Nanchuan District, Qijiang District, Tongnan District, Tongliang District, Dazu District, Rongchang District, Bishan District, Kaizhou District, Liangping District, Wulong district; Zhongxian County, Dianjiang County, Chengkou County, Wuxi County, Yunyang County, Fengjie County, Wushan County, Fengdu County; Qianjiang Tujia and Miao Autonomous County, Shizhu Tujia Autonomous County, Pengshui Miao and Tujia Autonomous County, Youyang Tujia and Miao Autonomous County, Xiushan. Tujia and Miao Autonomous County.

Reference

Chronicles

[1] 重庆市地方志编纂委员会总编辑室 . 重庆市志：第 1 卷 [M]. 成都：四川大学出版社，1992.

[2] 重庆市地方志编纂委员会 . 重庆市志：第 3 卷 [M]. 重庆：西南师范大学出版社，2004.

[3] 重庆市地方志编纂委员会 . 重庆市志：第 4 卷 [M]. 重庆：重庆出版社，1999.

[4] 重庆市地方志编纂委员会 . 重庆市志：第 5 卷 [M]. 成都：成都科技大学出版社，1994.

[5] 重庆市地方志编纂委员会 . 重庆市志：第 6 卷 [M]. 重庆：重庆出版社，1999.

[6] 重庆市地方志编纂委员会 . 重庆市志：第 9 卷 [M]. 重庆：西南师范大学出版社，2005.

[7] 重庆市地方志编纂委员会 . 重庆市志：第 10 卷 [M]. 重庆：西南师范大学出版社，2005.

[8] 重庆市地方志编纂委员会 . 重庆市志：第 11 卷 [M]. 重庆：重庆出版社，1999.

[9] 重庆三峡移民志编纂委员会 . 重庆三峡移民志：库区原貌 [M]. 北京：中国三峡出版社，2007.

[10] 重庆三峡移民志编纂委员会 . 重庆三峡移民志：论证与规划 [M]. 北京：中国三峡出版社，2008.

[11] 重庆市志・经济地理志课题组 . 重庆市志：经济地理志 [M]. 重庆：西南师范大学出版社，2008.

[12] 重庆市地方志办公室 . 重庆大事记：1949—2009 [M]. 重庆：西南师范大学出版社，2009.
[13] 重庆三峡移民志编纂委员会 . 重庆三峡移民志：移民实施 [M]. 北京：中国三峡出版社，2010.
[14] 重庆市教育委员会 . 重庆市志：教育志（1986—2005）[M]. 重庆：重庆出版社，2012.
[15] 重庆市交通委员会 . 重庆市志：交通志（1986—2005）[M]. 重庆：西南师范大学出版社，2014.
[16] 重庆市卫生和计划生育委员会 . 重庆市志：卫生志（1986—2005）[M]. 重庆：西南师范大学出版社，2016.
[17] 重庆市科学技术委员会 . 重庆市志：科学技术志（1986—2005）[M]. 重庆：西南师范大学出版社，2017.
[18] 重庆市民政局 . 重庆市志：民政志（1986—2005）[M]. 重庆：西南师范大学出版社，2017.
[19] 重庆市经济和信息化委员会 . 重庆市志：工业经济志（1981—2005）[M]. 重庆：西南师范大学出版社，2017.
[20] 重庆市园林事业管理局 . 重庆市志：风景园林志（1986—2005）[M]. 重庆：重庆出版社，2017.
[21] 重庆市人民政府办公厅 . 重庆年鉴：2018 [M]. 重庆 : 重庆年鉴社，2018.

Others

[1] 蓝勇 . 西南历史文化地理 [M]. 重庆：西南师范大学出版社，1997.
[2] 周勇 . 重庆通史：第 3 卷 [M]. 重庆：重庆出版社，2002.
[3] 俞荣根，张凤琦 . 当代重庆简史 [M]. 重庆：重庆出版社，2003.
[4] 周勇 . 重庆抗战史：1931—1945 [M]. 重庆：重庆出版社，2005.
[5] 重庆市教育科学研究院 . 重庆历史：上册 [M]. 重庆：西南师范大学出版社，2011.

[6] 重庆市教育科学研究院 . 重庆历史：下册 [M]. 重庆：西南师范大学出版社，2011.
[7] 重庆市规划局，重庆市勘测院 . 重庆历史地图集：第 2 卷 [M]. 西安：西安地图出版社，2017.
[8] 重庆市地方志办公室 . 重庆历史政德任务 [M]. 重庆：西南师范大学出版社，2018.

Data Source

The data of this book comes from Chongqing Statistical Information Network（重庆统计信息网）.